A Fatal Friendship

ashoka UNIVERSITY

HEDGEHOG AND FOX

HISTORY AND POLITICS SERIES

"The fox knows many things,
but the hedgehog knows one big thing"

General Editor

RUDRANGSHU MUKHERJEE

Related Series Titles

Francis Robinson THE 'ULAMA OF FARANGI MAHALL

Brijen Kumar Gupta SIRAJ-UD-DAULAH AND THE EAST INDIA COMPANY

Rudrangshu Mukherjee AWADH IN REVOLT

Sanjay Subrahmanyam EMPIRES BETWEEN ISLAM AND CHRISTIANITY

Jennifer Dubrow COSMOPOLITAN DREAMS

Partha Chatterjee THE BLACK HOLE OF EMPIRE

Muzaffar Alam THE MUGHALS AND THE SUFIS

SherAli Tareen PERILOUS INTIMACIES

Charu Gupta HINDI HINDU HISTORIES

Michael J. Fisher COUNTERFLOWS TO COLONIALISM

ROSIE LLEWELLYN-JONES

A Fatal Friendship

The Nawabs, the British, and the City of Lucknow

New Edition, 2026

With a Foreword by

RUDRANGSHU MUKHERJEE

permanent black and ASHOKA UNIVERSITY

Published by

PERMANENT BLACK

'Himalayana', Mall Road, Ranikhet Cantt,
Ranikhet 263645

perblack@gmail.com

and

ashoka
UNIVERSITY

Distributed by

ORIENT BLACKSWAN PRIVATE LTD

Bangalore Bhopal Bhubaneshwar Chandigarh Chennai
Ernakulam Guwahati Hyderabad Jaipur Kolkata
Lucknow Mumbai New Delhi Patna
www.orientblackswan.com

ISBN 978-81-7824-714-4

First Edition 1985

New Edition 2026

Typeset in Adobe Garamond Pro
by Guru Typograph Technology, Crossings Republic, Ghaziabad
Printed and bound by Manipal Technologies Limited, Manipal

MIX
Paper | Supporting responsible forestry
FSC™ C043100
FSC www.fsc.org

Foreword

RUDRANGSHU MUKHERJEE

THERE COULD be no better phrase to describe the relationship between Awadh and the British rulers of India than the title of this book by Rosie Llewellyn-Jones – "A Fatal Friendship". The Nawabs of Awadh – later given the more elevated title "King" by the British – considered the British to be their friends and the latter, in turn, posed as friends. In reality, it was an entirely one-sided relationship in which the traders-turned-invaders took from Awadh whatever they could – territory, money, resources, and even men since Awadh was the main recruiting ground for the sipahis of the Bengal Army. As the historian Peter Reeves noted, Awadh was important to the British after 1801 not for what it could do but for what it had to offer.[1] British governors-general were candid about this: they saw Awadh as something to be eaten. Lord Wellesley promised London "a supper of Oudh".[2] Lord Dalhousie described Awadh as "a cherry which will drop into our mouths some day. It has long been ripening."[3] It was this one-sided and exploitative nature of the relationship that made the friendship fatal.

In terms of history, the friendship started in defeat and submission. In October 1764, the then Nawab of Awadh, Shuja-ud-daula,

[1] Peter Reeves (ed.), *Sleeman in Oudh* (Cambridge: Cambridge University Press, 1971), Intro., p. 6.

[2] See C.H. Phillips, *The East India Company 1784–1834* (Oxford: Oxford University Press, 1961), p. 104.

[3] Dalhousie to G.C. Bart, 30 July 1851: J.G.A. Baird (ed.), *Private Letters of the Marquess of Dalhousie* (London: William Blackwood, 1910), p. 169.

was part of a tripartite alliance to resist the advance of the British in eastern India. The other two parties in the alliance were Mir Qasim (Nawab of Bengal and mastermind of the alliance) and the Mughal Emperor Shah Alam. This alliance was defeated by the British army commanded by Hector Munro in Baksar on the borders of subah Bangla and the territory of the Nawab of Awadh. The price that the victors extracted from Shuja-ud-daula was the opening up of Awadh to British trade, both the trade of the East India Company and the private trade of the Company's servants.

Over the next thirty years, and then into the nineteenth century, this trade expanded and included British private traders who were not employees of the Company. The latter also established a political and military presence in the capital of Awadh, Lucknow, by posting a Resident and troops there. Whenever the British needed money for their wars in India, they "borrowed" from the Nawab. They never had any intention of repaying these loans. What is even more important is that, at the beginning of the nineteenth century (1801–3), the British carved out a large part of the Nawab's realm and annexed it.[4] What remained under the Nawab was finally annexed in 1856. The independent kingdom of Awadh thus ceased to exist with Lord Dalhousie delivering the fatal blow and ending the show of friendship.

It is important to note this context even though the focus of the present book is Lucknow and its changing architecture. Lucknow emerged as an important centre of politics and culture from the second half of the eighteenth century, especially under the nawabi of Shuja-ud-daula and Asaf-ud-daula. It was during this phase that Lucknow saw, under the patronage of the Nawabs, the construction of some grand buildings along the architectural styles established by the Mughals. Some of the buildings still stand, most no-

[4] See Rudrangshu Mukherjee, "Trade and Empire in Awadh, 1765–1804", *Past and Present*, No. 94, February 1982. Also, Richard Barnett, *North India between Empires: Awadh, the Mughals and the British, 1720-1801* (London: University of California Press, 1980); and Thomas R. Metcalf, *Land, Landlords and the British Raj: Northern India in the Nineteenth Century* (London: University of California Press, 1979), pp. 17–43.

tably the Imambara. Some of these buildings were destroyed when Lucknow became the eye of the storm – the great rebellion of 1857–8. From the summer of 1857 to March 1858, the city became a battleground. The British counterinsurgency forces had to reclaim Lucknow almost street by street, lane by lane.[5]

In the first half of the nineteenth century, the British built the Residency which became the haven for the white population of Lucknow during 1857. It was surrounded on all sides and shelled by the rebels, severely damaged, and has deliberately been kept in that state as a site of history. The other major non-nawabi building was La Martinière, later a school, constructed by the endowment of the French mercenary Claude Martin. This building suffered damage at the hands of the rebels but was later restored.

This history, briefly outlined here, forms the backdrop for Llwellyn-Jones', book which is essentially about the architecture of Lucknow. Time was when Lucknow must have been an exquisite city. That phase in the city's history is memorable not only because it was aesthetically pleasing to the eye – as the buildings that remain and more importantly the depictions of those buildings in paintings, lithographs, and photographs show – but also because of the city's culture and the manners: the famous adab of the people of Lucknow became the identifying mark of the city. For those who love Lucknow, this book summons up an era long past and swiftly moving into oblivion.

Llewellyn-Jones' book is an act of retrieval based on detailed archival research as well as fieldwork. She has looked at Urdu and English sources, at maps and pictorial documentation. She has spoken to individuals who had memories of what Lucknow was like before the forces of modernisation and the pursuit of Mammon began the process of transforming a graceful city into an urban concrete jungle. It would not be an exaggeration to say that there has not been a book like this one on Lucknow.

[5] See Rudrangshu Mukherjee, *Awadh in Revolt, 1857–58: A Study of Popular Resistance* (Delhi: Oxford University Press, 1984; repr. Permanent Black & Ashoka University, 2001).

As someone who has worked on the rebellion of 1857 in Awadh and inevitably on Lucknow's part in those fateful events, I am very proud to be associated with a new edition of *A Fatal Friendship*. I am more than certain that so is my dear friend Rukun Advani, the Ranikhet publisher whose bookseller father, Ram Advani, embodied the spirit of the *ancien régime* of Lucknow.

15 June 2025

Contents

Illustrations

(between pages 136 and 137)

Preface to the New Edition, 2026

NOT MANY historians get the chance to revisit books they wrote nearly fifty years ago. In 1980 I was awarded a PhD from the School of Oriental and African Studies, London, for my thesis on the nawabi architecture of Lucknow. The examiners included the distinguished historian Dr P.J. Marshall. Research for the thesis had begun following a degree in Urdu, and the first visit to Lucknow took place in 1972.

This was a world that seems almost as distant now as nawabi Lucknow was to me in the 1970s. No internet, no Wikipedia, and no archive.org. Research was done in libraries, using pencil and paper, and notes were typed up in the evening on a manual typewriter. Field research meant asking people questions and writing down their answers in a notebook. Photographs for this book were done with a Gandolfi half-plate camera mounted on a tripod which took time to set up before the wooden frames holding the light-sensitive plates could be inserted and the trigger pulled.

Approaches to publishers in England about turning my thesis into a book were not encouraging. Some simply did not answer, others cited the poor economic climate, always a handy perennial excuse. Then a friend said, "It's an Indian subject, so why don't you try an Indian publisher?", and everything fell into place. The manuscript was entrusted to a friend, George Michell, who carefully carried it to India and handed it over to Rukun Advani, newly arrived as an editor at Oxford University Press (OUP) in Delhi. There was some discussion over the title: "a fatal friendship" so vividly described the relationship between the rulers of Awadh and the East India Company that I held out for this against the caution of OUP. First published in 1985, the book was subsequently reprinted, appeared in paperback, and in a trilogy on Lucknow.

During research in the 1970s a significant number of people in Lucknow were willing and able to help me and they are acknowledged in the book. Among them, by a happy coincidence was my editor's father Ram Advani, who ran his eponymous bookshop in Hazratganj. This was a place that attracted research scholars from all over the world and in fact is cited as one of the reasons that the history of the city, of Awadh, and of Uttar Pradesh has been particularly well documented. Fruitful exchanges of ideas took place here over cups of tea, connections were made, and difficulties over access to records were smoothed out through Ram's extensive net of contacts.

Turning now to this new edition there is very little I would want to correct or alter. What I thought then is what I think now. The wealthy nawabs were shamelessly exploited by the East India Company and by Europeans in Lucknow. At the same time they were wildly extravagant in a poor and corrupt country. But out of this emerged a unique culture which produced some extraordinary architecture that has only recently been properly appreciated (sadly, after much of it has gone).

Inevitably there have been many changes in the city during the last half century. (The illustrations in this new edition differ from those in the earlier edition: some are in colour, and the reproduction is much better. Paintings which were previously unknown, like those of Sita Ram, have added greatly to our knowledge of the nawabi city.)

The Begum Kothi in Hazratganj was demolished to make room for a shopping centre. The Farhad Baksh and Chattar Manzil stand empty and deserted today while their fate is endlessly discussed, although riverside excavations have uncovered the previously hidden basement façades of Claude Martin's town house. Part of the façade of the Chattar Manzil collapsed a few years ago. Other nawabi buildings have gone, remembered only in photographs taken during the winter of 1975–6, although those that remain are much better cared for today. The Sibtainabad Imambara in Hazratganj, for example, which was formerly used as a carpenter's workshop and a storehouse for government records, is now fully restored as a place of worship.

During the principalship of La Martinière College by Carlyle Mcfarland blocked-up areas in the main building were reopened to reveal huge water tanks, which confirmed my belief that the building was designed as a fortress to be self-sufficient during a siege. The mystery of its original name, Constantia, was solved when research established that the building was intended as a Freemason's Lodge with the masonic legend "Labore et Constantia". Claude Martin's buildings, described in this book, were the inspiration for further research into his polymathic life which led to a trilogy: his biography, his collected letters, and his lengthy Inventory which gave us a valuable picture of a wealthy European in eighteenth-century India. (See the Select List of Publications, below.)

The Uprising of 1857, earlier known as the Indian Mutiny, was particularly hard fought in Lucknow because its last ruler, Wajid Ali Shah, had been deposed by the East India Company. The impact on the buildings of Lucknow after the event was described only briefly in this book, deliberately so, in order that it would not overshadow what had gone before. Again, as with initial research on Claude Martin, this sparked off further investigation into what happened to the city during the revolt, leading to several books on the Uprising.

So the city of Lucknow, and that "fatal friendship" between its nawabi rulers and the East India Company, has generated a large amount of my subsequent studies of colonial history, which continue with a forthcoming biography of Begam Hazrat Mahal to be published in 2026. There is still much to be learnt about the city and its Indian and European inhabitants over the seventeenth to twentieth centuries. Luckily the baton is now being taken up by young Indian historians who are as interested in their own past as I have been.

ROSIE LLEWELLYN-JONES

London, May 2025

Select List of Publications by Rosie Llewellyn-Jones

A Very Ingenious Man: Claude Martin in Early Colonial India (Delhi: Oxford University Press, 1992)

Engaging Scoundrels: True Tales of Old Lucknow (Delhi: Oxford University Press, 2000)

A Man of the Enlightenment in Eighteenth-century India: The Letters of Claude Martin 1766–1800 (Delhi: Permanent Black, 2003)

Lucknow Then and Now (edited; Bombay: Marg Publishers, 2003)

Lucknow: City of Illusion (edited; Munich and London: Alkazi Collection of Photography / Prestel 2006)

Hazratganj: A Journey through the Times (edited; Lucknow: Bennett, Coleman & Co., 2011)

The Last King in India: Wajid Ali Shah 1822–1887 (London: Hurst & Co. Publishers, 2014)

The Estate of Major General Claude Martin at Lucknow: An Indian Inventory (edited; Newcastle upn Tyne: Cambridge Scholars Publishing, 2021)

Lucknow 1857 (Delhi: HarperCollins India, 2022)

Preface to the First Edition, 1985

In 1972 I visited Lucknow for a week during a degree course in Urdu at London University. Attracted there by reading Maulana Sharar's *Guzashta Laknau*, his romanticised picture made the nawabi city appeal to me as a place worth seeing for a few days. Little of the city he described so nostalgically remained, though the battered palaces and the ruined Residency site hinted at a town of more solid importance than he had drawn. Oddly, no serious guidebooks were available to the casual tourist and those found concentrated almost solely on the siege of the city in 1857, as though the town had only briefly sprung into existence and faded from the map during a single year. True, there was mention of earlier nawabi buildings like the Great Imambara and brief referencesto the extraordinary Indo-European palaces of the eccentric Frenchman Claude Martin, but nothing of real worth to satisfy the mind and explain the origins and demise of so many fine buildings in and around the city. Returning to London I sought out the guidebooks I could not find in India, only to realise that what I wanted did not exist. So curiosity impelled me to begin my own researches in 1974.

There was no lack of descriptions of the city by Western writers, beginning with the commentary of Joseph Tieffenthaler, a Jesuit priest, in 1766, but followed over the next two hundred years by such a torrent of criticism of the architecture and social mores of Lucknow (one nineteenth-century writer solemnly compared it to Sodom and Gomorrah) that at times it seemed impossible to reconcile the two Lucknows – the battered and melancholic old city that exists today and the glittering, wicked one lost forever after the British annexation of Awadh in 1856.

How could mere buildings excite such vituperation from writers, politicians, and architects? Why was such a dreadful revenge visited on speechless monuments of brick and stucco when the English East India Company marched in as victors in 1858? Gradually I perceived that the answer lay in the fact that Lucknow's buildings were the outward symbol of what the British imagined to be wrong with the city and what the nawabs believed to be right and beautiful. Simply stated, this premise became honed and refined during the course of research until I arrived at the term "political architecture" to describe urban buildings erected during the eighteenth and nineteenth centuries by both Indian rulers (the nawabs) and putative rulers (the Company).

Though only one town was examined, similar studies of Indian towns during this period would undoubtedly exhibit many of the same motives for the development of a colonial city. But by a happy chance Lucknow was an almost perfect microcosm of a city in transition during that period of British intervention. It was a flourishing medieval city. It received a tremendous impetus with the arrival from Iran of the nawabi family, which brought vigorous new ideas and culture at the exact time when they had enough political freedom and unlimited wealth to impose their values on the city. It also provided a prime example of British interference in such a city before total colonial control was assumed. A hundred years earlier and Lucknow would have been no more than a medieval curiosity like Jaunpur. A hundred years later the nawabi dynasty could not have existed. It is the interplay between the nawabs and the Company, each jostling to impose their own worldview on Lucknow, which continues to fascinate.

The British contribution itself was made up of three separate elements which are closely examined in this book – the need for a military base (at first nominally under the nawabs' command), a civic and administrative centre for the expanding activities of the British Resident (again originally under the nawabs' auspices), and the eclectic talents of the European adventurers who rightly judged Lucknow to be a richly exploitable city. The ascension and decline of all these elements (except that of British civic administration after 1856), which can be traced in the city's buildings over the last two hundred years, as well as the gradual usurpation of nawabi authority by the British and consequent slipping away of real power from the Indian rulers, demonstrated by the city's buildings, would have provided sufficient material for a book. But two other important facets emerged that are perhaps the most intriguing of all. Given the furious though ultimately unsuccessful attempts of the nawabs to slough off British interference in the city's affairs, why did they at the same time wish to flatter and impress the West with their own interpretations of "classical" European architecture, so that by the mid nineteenth century Lucknow often reminded Europeans of handsome Western cities like Oxford, Dresden, or Leningrad, albeit with an "Oriental" touch? In some cases, as will be shown, the nawabs had been blackmailed and coerced into creating such buildings, often to the direct advantage of the East India Company, who subsequently used them for their own purposes. But there were many other "classical" structures erected entirely spontaneously by the nawabs, who would co-opt Company engineers for their construction. The nawabs' motives are carefully considered in this book, but if one was to engage in the fruitless task of apportioning blame for the demise of the city as an indigenous organism one would have to indict the nawabs almost as much as the British for their vacillating, half-hearted attempt to keep the city purely Indian. It was as if the nawabs had said: "We can create our own vision of a nineteenth-century European city more splendid than the Company officials could imagine or execute."

And they did. Unhampered by spatial considerations or social concerns, they neglected the old medieval city of Lucknow to produce a series of handsome palaces, religious buildings, gardens, and broad streets along the banks of the river Gomti. But ironically their beautification of Lucknow (as they perceived it) attracted some of the bitterest criticism from European commentators and led ultimately to the semi-ruinous state of much of the southern Gomti bank today.

The nawabi exuberance of exploiting newly discovered "classical" European architecture to create an Indo-European style produced chiefly sneers from Western visitors who believed that the nawabs had simply tried to imitate European buildings and failed because they did not understand the rules of Palladian architecture. With little or no hindsight of the complicated network which had led to the production of such buildings, it seemed to the critics one further example of the nawabs' superficial "Westernization" and extravagance, adding another argument to the belief that the problem of Awadh could only be resolved by annexation and sensible management of the province by British rule.

It was an unhappy coincidence that one of the most protracted sieges of the 1857 uprising took place in Lucknow. With perfect justification the British were then able to demolish large tracts of building when they regained control in 1858 in order to make the city defensible for themselves, and to express their contempt for the creators of Lucknow – whom they unjustly blamed for the dreadful loss of British life during the uprising. It is surprising that a number of nawabi buildings still survive in Lucknow at all today. Only from a study of photographs and drawings made before the Company sappers moved in with gunpowder can an idea of nawabi Lucknow be gained. Much has also been lost or irretrievably altered since Independence. This book endeavours to rebuild the city before 1856, to people it with both the Indians and the Europeans who created it, to examine the motives and dreams of its builders, and to reflect on the political strategy that used architecture as its ammunition.

Acknowledgements of the First Edition, 1985

I WOULD LIKE TO acknowledge with thanks the help given to me in England by the staff of the India Office Library and Records, the British Library, the School of Oriental and African Studies, the National Army Museum, the Library of the Royal Institute of British Architecture, and the Royal Academy Library; in India to the staff of the National Archives, New Delhi, the library of Raj Bhavan, Lucknow, the Amir-ud-daulah Library, Lucknow, the library of the State Museum, Lucknow, and La Martinière College, Lucknow.

Among the people who have helped me I would particularly like to single out for thanks John Burton Page, John Harrison, Dr K.N. Chaudhuri, Professor Kenneth Ballhatchet, Joan Lancaster, Mildred Archer, Dr Monty Foyle for his constant encouragement and practical help, Mark Baijent who drew out the ground plans for me from my sketches, Andrew Green who took many of the photographs in India, Michael Fisher, and Professor Barney Cohn.

In India my thanks go to Suleiman, the Raja of Mahmudabad, for his unfailing hospitality, interest, and knowledge; Akilendra Singh, who spent much time accompanying me around Lucknow; Anwar Askari and his family for their interest and company in Lucknow; Charan Jit Singh Nanda and his family for their practical help and company; Mr Shaw, Headmaster of La Martinière, and his staff, especially Mr Frank d'Souza who always had time to talk to me; Mr Azeem, the superintendent of La Martinière, for practical help and time gladly given up; and those people of Lucknow who allowed me to wander round at will inside their homes, interview them, and photograph their houses.

1

The "Three" Cities of Lucknow

As the Mughal emperor Aurangzeb lay dying in 1707, a Persian nobleman from Naishapur arrived in India. His name was Saadat Khan, his official title Burhan-ul-Mulk, and he was to found the nawabi dynasty of Awadh (Oudh). Saadat Khan had come from a Shi'a family in Persia whose fortunes had declined, and when he learnt that Aurangzeb's successor to the Mughal throne was a Shi'a he decided to leave his native land and seek employment at the Delhi court.

Although quickly accepted at the court, Saadat Khan was slow to achieve promotion in the Mughal hierarchy and it was not until 1719 that he found himself *faujdar* (superintendent) of a district in Agra. But having achieved this position he quickly established a reputation for suppressing lawlessness and the ability to put down rebel zamindars or landholders who were reluctant to make revenue payments to the Mughal emperor. It was Saadat Khan's job to collect the revenue payments and so successful was he that three years later he was appointed Governor of the province of Awadh in north-eastern India. Awadh was described at this time as being full of "semi-independent feudal barons of varying degrees of strength and political importance,"[1] each "baron" having his own army and civil establishments as well as exercising judicial rights over his subjects, his authority only being limited by the presence of rivals. It was symptomatic of the barons' semi-autonomous rule that on

[1] Srivastava, A.L., *First Two Nawabs of Oudh* (Lucknow 1933), p. 32.

taking up his new position of Governor, Saadat Khan literally had to fight his way into the city of Lucknow, aided by a party of local noblemen who had come to his defence.

Once inside the city Saadat Khan established his headquarters, an important psychological move, for a governor with no base in his own province would not have impressed the many petty and warring chiefs from whom he had to collect the revenue to remit back to the Mughal emperor at Delhi. Saadat Khan's policy of firmness paid off, and not only was he able to collect the revenue due but he was able to leave a deputy in his place when summoned to the Delhi court, without fear that his governorship would be usurped in his absence.

Saadat Khan chose as his deputy his nephew, Safdar Jang, who had come from the family home in Persia at his uncle's request. Having arrived in Awadh, Safdar Jang consolidated his position by marrying Saadat Khan's daughter and this strengthened his claim as deputy and successor to Saadat Khan, although the post of Governor of a province in the Mughal empire had not previously been considered hereditary for the obvious reason that dynasties would spring up and splinter the central government.

Saadat Khan, however, made it his business to become virtually independent of the Mughal emperor and to establish his own dynasty in the province – an object he achieved without much difficulty or exertion. For a time he was involved in petty skirmishes with local chiefs and also undertook excursions for the Mughal emperor against the Marathas and the Jats, two semi-autonomous groups that took advantage of the decline in central government. But the break with Delhi is dated from 1728 when the Mughal emperor tried to transfer Saadat Khan to Agra, only to have his order disobeyed, and from that time on there was no further attempt made to dislodge the Governor from the province he had made his own.

After the death of Saadat Khan in 1739 Safdar Jang naturally assumed the position of Governor of Awadh and was able to attend the Delhi court safe in the knowledge that his position in the province was now unassailable. The relationship between the Governors of Awadh, or "nawabs", and the Delhi court, was a tenuous one. While the title "nawab" is derived from the Persian word for "deputy", implying recognition of the ultimate sovereignty of the Mughal emperors, in fact the Awadh nawabs only obeyed royal orders when it suited their convenience. On Safdar Jang's death in 1754 his son Shuja-ud-daula was confirmed by the Mughal emperor in all the posts held by his father, thus cementing the hereditary right of the family to the governorship of Awadh. By this time too the idea that revenues collected from Awadh should be submitted to the emperor had changed and the province of Awadh became wealthy at the expense of the Delhi court.

Shuja-ud-daula prospered and by 1761 he had become powerful enough to attract the attention of the British who were pushing into the heart of India from the bases where they had originally settled as traders of the East India Company. The Company, a commercial concern, combined business with territorial expansion and irresistible political manoeuvring. The first contact between Shuja-ud-daula and officials of the Company was made when the nawab asked for British aid "to settle the affairs of the Empire"[2] – an indication of the nawab's status in the political spectrum – and Henry Lushington, a Company official, was sent to the Awadh court to spy out the land. Also in Lucknow at this time was the shadowy figure of Father Wendell, a priest, but unofficially another spy. Not only did Shuja-ud-daula attract British attention, but he had become important enough for a considerable number of French mercenaries to join him. While these mercenaries had left the British army, they were not completely reconciled to the idea of the British gaining control in India. Neither was Shuja-ud-daula, and in a reversal of his earlier policy he issued an ultimatum to the British that they should either confine themselves to trade or be prepared to fight. The British chose the latter course and defeated Shuja-ud-daula, French mercenaries and all, at the battle of Buxar in 1764, thus consolidating their position in northern India.

[2] Srivastava, A.L., *Shuja-ud-daula* (Calcutta 1939), p. 125.

The defeated Shuja-ud-daula was then declared a rebel by the British, and to add to his humiliation the victors persuaded the Mughal emperor to dismiss the nawab as Governor of Awadh. To symbolize his fall the British marched detachments of their own troops into Lucknow and Faizabad (the city that had grown up around the camp of Saadat Khan, the first nawab). Shuja-ud-daula's flag was torn down, his *kotwal* (town officer) beaten up, and his palace occupied by Major Carnac, a Company official, who held his own durbars there. The unhappy Shuja-ud-daula attempted to rally sympathetic groups to fight, but was unsuccessful and reluctantly surrendered himself to the British and acknowledged them as his masters. The British, having won this acknowledgement, now became magnanimous towards the defeated nawab. They sensed that it would be more advantageous to reinstate the nawab in Awadh than to have him fomenting rebellions with other disaffected groups like the Marathas. The situation was still volatile enough in northern India for the British not to be completely certain which native rulers it was most expedient to have as friends and which as enemies. But in promoting Shuja-ud-daula they rightly calculated that the nawab, properly handled, would prove more profitable to them as Governor of Awadh than would a puppet governor of their own choosing. It should not be forgotten that the Company was, after all, in India to make profits, and although its commercial interests tend to be overshadowed by political exploits it never lost sight of its original objectives. The first treaty signed between the Company and Shuja-ud-daula was of enormous financial benefit to the British and was to become the basis for many further extortions during the eighty-one years of nawabi rule. Known as the Allahabad Treaty, it restored Awadh to the nawab, except for the areas of Kora and Allahabad which were given to the Mughal emperor, and ensured that the Company could carry on duty-free trade throughout the province; and it fined the nawab Rs 50,000 to meet the Company's expenses during their recent war with the nawab. In addition the latter agreed to pay the expenses of the Company's troops stationed in Awadh which were to assist in defensive wars he might undertake if his dominions were threatened.[3] Although this first treaty was not observed to the letter (for example trading did not become easier in Awadh until 1788),[4] it is vital for an understanding of the British presence in Awadh because it explains the three main elements of British infiltration into the province, namely the soldiers and military paraphernalia for the defence of the province, the presence of determined traders, and the beginning of the financial burden of the nawabs on the British.

In 1773 Shuja-ud-daula and the Company signed a further treaty in which Kora and Allahabad were sold back to the nawab for fifty lakhs (another financial burden), payment by the nawab for Company troops was increased, and the nawab agreed to receive a person of trust, nominated by Warren Hastings, to reside near him – the first British Resident to the Awadh court.[5] Two years after the signing of this treaty Shuja-ud-daula died and one of his many children, Asaf-ud-daula, succeeded to the *musnud* of Awadh.[6] Politically, relations between the new nawab and the Mughal court were effectively non-existent. The stability of emperors after Aurangzeb became increasingly more precarious, and the British manipulated them like puppets. The casual way in which they first bestowed the districts of Kora and Allahabad on the emperor, later taking back their "gift" and selling it to Shuja-ud-daula, typifies their treatment of the later Mughals. The nawabs too had abandoned any pretence of serving their former royal masters, although it was not until 1819 that they formally renounced their allegiance to the Delhi court, and then it was only in order to assume the title of "King" bestowed on them by the British (though all members of

[3] Aitchison, C.U., *A Collection of Treaties, Engagements and Sanads*, vol. 8 (Calcutta 1909), p. 124.

[4] Marshall, P.J., "Economic and Political Expansion: The Case of Oudh", *Modern Asian Studies*, 9, 4 (1975), p. 466. Hereafter P.J. Marshall.

[5] Home Misc. Series. No. 345, Origins of the Residency, pp. 329–48, I.O.L.

[6] Modave, Comte de, *Voyage en Inde du Comte de Modave 1773–1776*, texte établi et annoté par Jean Deloche, École Française d"extrème Orient (Paris 1971), p. 158. Hereafter Modave.

the new "royal" family continued to use the title "Mughal" in their names until annexation in 1856).[7]

It is not necessary to relate the many political manoeuvres that occurred between the beginning of Asaf-ud-daula's reign and the deposition by the British of the last nawab, Wajid Ali Shah, in 1856. Suffice it to say that I concur with the anonymous author who described relations between the British and the nawabs as "a fatal friendship". But, during this brief period of "friendship",[8] Lucknow flourished to an unique degree and was considered, without exaggeration, "the last example of the old pomp and refinement of Hindustan, and the memento of earlier times."[9]

What kind of a city was Lucknow? The traveller approaching it through the flat and monotonous landscape of Awadh (now within Uttar Pradesh), would not have found anything remarkable in its appearance. Straddling the river Gomti, the town offered only two small hills of note, both on the south bank, although the terrain within the city was uneven. The first settlers, who were Brahmins, chose one of these hills on which to build a shrine which remained until Aurangzeb's day, when it was replaced with a mosque at the emperor's command. To the south-west of this mosque runs the Chauk or main market place, the earliest street to be developed, and a pious traveller would doubtless have visited the tomb of Shah Mina near the Chauk. This celebrated Muslim mystic settled in Lucknow about 1450 and his tomb became a place of pilgrimage. Also near the Chauk were two family tombs of the Sheikzadas, the powerful land-owning families of medieval Awadh whom Shuja-ud-daula had been at such pains to subdue. The Sheikzadas owned the land east of the Chauk up to the Lakshman Tila, the site of Aurangzeb's mosque. In 1540, during the troubled reign of Humayun, the Mughal emperor is supposed to have camped near the Chauk,

[7] Bengal Pol. Con., 30 Oct. 1819, no. 26.

[8] Anon., *The Oude Catechism, or Answers to Questions Concerning Oude, its History and its Wrongs* (London 1857), p. 6. Hereafter *Oude Catechism.*

[9] Sharar, Maulana, *Guzashta Laknau* (Lucknow n.d.), p. 41. Hereafter Sharar.

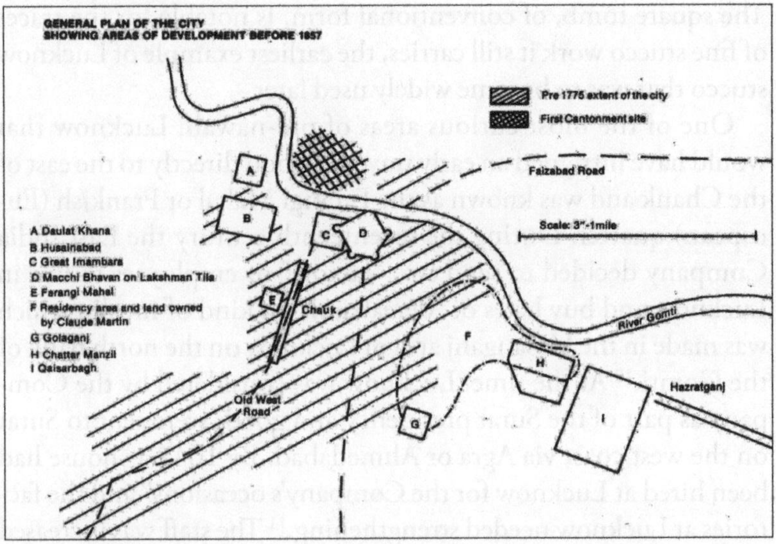

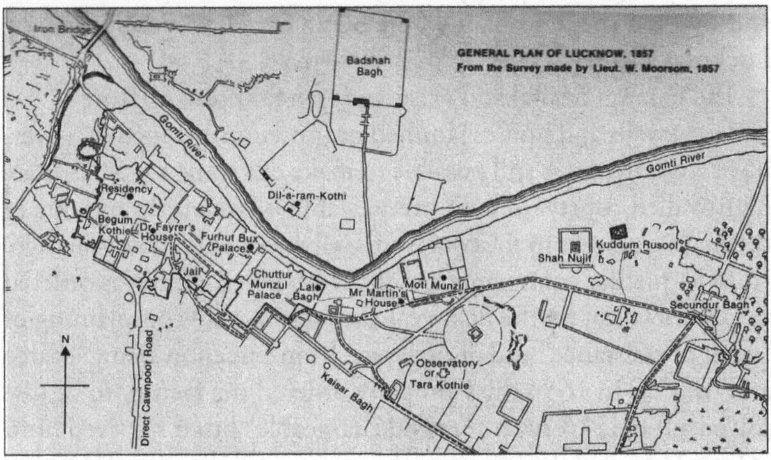

implying that the southern limits of the early city were bounded by the Akbari gate, which replaced an earlier gate. There is no evidence that the city was walled in medieval times.

To the west of the Chauk stands a fine Mughal tomb, that of Husain Ali, a commander in Akbar's army who died about 1600.

The square tomb, of conventional form, is notable for the traces of fine stucco work it still carries, the earliest example of Lucknow stucco that was to become widely used later.

One of the most curious areas of pre-nawabi Lucknow that would have intrigued an early traveller stood directly to the east of the Chauk and was known as the Farangi Mahal or Frankish (European) quarter. During the seventeenth century the East India Company decided to send two "factors" or employees to live in Lucknow and buy bales of "dereabauds", a kind of muslin which was made in the Hasanganj area of Lucknow on the north bank of the Gomti.[10] At the time, Lucknow was considered by the Company as part of the Surat presidency and goods were sent to Surat on the west coast via Agra or Ahmedabad. By 1647 a "house had been hired at Lucknow for the Company's occasions" and the factories at Lucknow needed strengthening.[11] The staff was increased and in 1650 Rs 70,000 were sent to the factors there to buy goods. Bales of indigo and "plenty of sugar" were also being sent to Surat and by then the dereabauds were being cured or bleached in the Lucknow factory.

The Farangi Mahal still exists today, a fantastic mixture of old and new walls and houses jammed promiscuously together, covering a large area. It is still possible to make out some kind of square high-walled courtyard with pre-nawabi houses inside and one of the main gateways to the courtyards fell down only a few years ago. In 1651 further enlargement of the cloth investment was ordered at Lucknow but by the next year the factors were complaining of "want of assistance" and of transport from Lucknow being "scarce and dear".[12] In 1653 the Company ordered the factory to be dissolved as being "very remote and chargeable" but it survived until at least 1655 and the Company house was still there too.[13] During

[10] Foster, William, *The English Factories in India*, vol. 1637–1641 (Oxford 1912), p. 278.

[11] Ibid., vol. 1646–1650, pp. 140 and 122.

[12] Ibid., vol. 1651–1654, p. 114.

[13] Ibid., p. 148.

Aurangzeb's reign the Farangi Mahal was given by him to a religious leader, the mullah Nazam Aladin Sahalvi, and there is no further mention of the British or their trade during the remainder of the seventeenth century.[14] Curiously enough the Company officials who began making contact with the nawabs a hundred years later seemed completely unaware of the early British traders of Lucknow and there was no attempt to set up a further British factory in the Farangi Mahal area nor, as far as I can tell, any more trade in dereabauds – though from the large sum of money invested in 1650 it was a factory of some good size and employing a number of local people.

When Saadat Khan forced entry into Lucknow he established his headquarters in the Panch Mahalla, a series of buildings belonging to the Sheikzadas of Lucknow, and sharing the Lakshman Tila with Aurangzeb's mosque. At first Saadat Khan rented the Panch Mahalla at a monthly cost of Rs 565, but he soon came to regard the buildings as his own and carried out alterations and improvements.[15] The "five palaces" which gave the site its name appear to have been merged together at an early date, so that from the north bank of the Gomti it seemed that one large building stood on the hill, "like a chateau, surrounded by walls and with high towers". Approaching the building itself the traveller would arrive first at a "great doorway and a vast forecourt in front of a tall battlemented wall supported by arcades, where the tambour players would sound the drums. Shuja-ud-daula had had much of the battlements and the apartments demolished and rebuilt in an even grander style."[16] Saadat Khan also developed various *ganjes* on both sides of the Chauk, a feature common to most northern Indian towns but one which has not previously been closely examined. A typical ganj is described by an eighteenth-century traveller to Awadh as

[14] Sharar, p. 59.

[15] *Gazetteer of the Province of Oude vol. ii* (Allahabad 1877), p. 366. Hereafter Gazetteer.

[16] Tieffenthaler, Joseph, *Description Historique et géographique de l'Inde*, vol. i (Berlin 1786–8), p. 256. Hereafter Tieffenthaler.

> the particular name to distinguish an enclosure, be it of masonry, of earth, or simple wooden planks, in which one finds housing and the stalls in which are sold the necessities for travellers, their steeds and their beasts of burden. It is just like a caravanserai. They are constructed either from a charitable idea, or from interest, for one hires or leases them out, for security is the greatest in these nooks, than in an encampment totally exposed, not only [do] the travellers prefer to sleep there, but many families have established themselves there. I have seen them full of people, and those that would pass for large towns.[17]

It adds a lot to the understanding of pre-industrial towns if a series of such ganjes can be visualized, clustered together and forming the nucleus of the town. In Lucknow these ganjes were developed off the Chauk, the backbone of Lucknow, and struck out at right angles. A Lucknow writer, P.C. Mookherji, described the town ganj as a square built round a crossroads, with two main gates and two smaller ones at the end of each road. There are often bazaar shops with lines of verandahs fronting the main road and private houses at the rear. The walls are pierced on all four sides and there are bastions at the four corners. There is often a tank nearby.[18] Mookherji also thought that the *nullahs* or stream beds running through the old part of Lucknow formed natural divisions between the ganjes, which are now raised quite considerably above street level. Many early visitors to Lucknow have commented on the irregular nature of the town, "the ground is so uneven that one cannot walk about in this city except by detours, climbing up here, going down there,"[19] and to the west of the Chauk even today buildings stand on small clumps of land divided during the monsoon by streams running down the nullahs between them.

The majority of Lucknow's ganjes were let out to families and shopkeepers, although in some cases shopkeepers would rent land from the nawabs or ministers who owned the ganjes and build small

[17] Modave, p. 142.

[18] Mookherji, P.C., *Pictorial Lucknow* (Lucknow 1883), p. 227. Hereafter Mookherji.

[19] Tieffenthaler, i, p. 256.

houses at their own expense. It was necessary, however, to obtain the approval of the owner of the ganj before building started.[20] Ganjes were often named after the owners or the occupations that were carried on in them, so that one finds in Lucknow Saadat Ganj founded by Saadat Khan, Tikait Ganj founded by Tikait Rai (Asaf-ud-daula's chief minister), Loha Ganj (the iron-workers' area) and Gola Ganj where an early arsenal was established.[21] Often the original pattern of the ganj has been broken down until all that remains is the name and the central crossroads. Encroachment and illegal building are the main reasons for the breakdown, and there is a story still current in Lucknow (though sadly unproven) that Asaf-ud-daula, conscious of this, would march forth every day with a band of workers armed with picks and shovels and wherever he found a building out of line, would have it demolished. If a court official who acted as a "town inspector" and made regular tours of the city is substituted for the nawab then the story is not so far-fetched as would at first appear.

By 1765 Lucknow was a town of considerable size and was described by a resident Jesuit priest thus:

> the length of this town from Recabganj in the south to Isaganj in the north is a mile and a half [this was all on the south bank of the Gomti], the breadth from Chodaganj in the east to the west is a mile or more. The town is not walled like Adjudea [Ayodhya] and Bangla [Faizabad). There are a great number of brick houses, but the majority are of lime or mortar, covered with tiles, standing on little mounds of barren land, here and there. The greatest part of the town extends towards the east, and covers an elevated place, the smallest part is in a gorge. The streets are narrow and stinking, because the inhabitants habitually throw all their refuse into the streets . . .[22]

Apart from the Panch Mahalla, the author (Tieffenthaler) continues, "you can also see buildings showing beautiful, even magnifi-

[20] Bengal Pol. Con., 19 March 1832, no. 54.

[21] *Gazetteer*, p. 368.

[22] Tieffenthaler, i, p. 256.

cent architecture, here and there in the town, but these are few in number. The market place [the Chauk] is narrow and has nothing remarkable about it. The houses of the merchants are of brick, tall and solidly built." He goes on to describe the Gomti which could be forded during the summer and notes that the north bank had "houses and other buildings along it". He also drew the earliest known map of the city, in which the huge gateway to the Panch Mahalla is shown, as is Aurangzeb's mosque on the Lakshman Tila.

Tieffenthaler was impressed by the large number of brick houses in Lucknow – which other early European visitors do not mention. The Comte de Modave, for example, wrote in February 1775, "Laknau is a large and nasty town . . . unremarkable except for one building the palace of the nabab on the river bank [the Panch Mahalla]. It is a great building composed of many different parts without any order, which do not correspond to each other. The mosques are small and have nothing splendid about them . . . Laknau after all does not merit consideration save by its commerce which is quite extensive."[23] Later in 1782 William Hodges, an English artist, was to come to similar conclusions: "The city is extensive but meanly built, the houses are chiefly mud and walls covered with thatch and many consist entirely of mats and bamboos, very few indeed, of the houses of the natives are built with brick, the streets are crooked, narrow and the worst I have seen in India."[24] The discrepancies in descriptions would seem to arise from the fact that both Hodges and Modave, who were only travelling through Lucknow, based their opinions on the area round the Panch Mahalla, the "official" quarters of Lucknow, rather than on the more prosperous and longer-established areas round the Chauk like the Farangi Mahal and the Ashrafabad Serai which housed the bullion market. All visitors are, however, unanimous on the dirt and squalor in the streets.

There are no population figures for Lucknow before 1775 when Asaf-ud-daula made the town his permanent capital, and there are

[23] Modave, p. 183.

[24] Hodges, William, *Travels in India during the Years 1780, 81, 82 and 83.* (London 1793), p. 100. Hereafter Hodges.

no reliable estimates until 1901, although several people volunteered guesses on the number of inhabitants. The earliest estimate of 1798, when Lucknow was said to contain half a million people (500,000), seems an unrealistically high figure.[25] The second figure, an estimated population of 300,000 in 1800, is probably more accurate and would have included people attracted to the splendid court of Lucknow during the twenty-five years earlier.[26] When the last nawab was deposed in 1856 the population fell quite drastically and stabilized at about 256,000 in 1901.[27] Assuming that roughly the same number of people who had been connected with the court left Lucknow after 1856 as had originally settled in the city, i.e. about 50,000, and given that the figure of 300,000 in 1800 is accurate, a pre-nawabi estimate of about 250,000 would make sense. Lucknow was considered a large town in the 1760s, with a stable population relatively unaffected by the later advent of the court, and it is not unreasonable to suggest that when the court was exiled in 1856 the population of the city would again settle down to approximately pre-nawabi figures. In the twentieth century the population rose to about 500,000 in 1951,[28] by which time the city had expanded considerably towards the east and north, which is why the 1798 figure of 500,000 is unreasonably high, since the town was physically much smaller at that time.

It would certainly be wrong to assume (as some writers have done) that Lucknow was merely a cluster of villages along the south bank of the Gomti which were welded together to form a corporate whole by Asaf-ud-daula and his successors.[29] By 1775, at the start of Asaf-ud-daula's rule, the city had a good record for exports of sugar, indigo and cloth to England and Afghanistan, a centre

[25] Tennant, Rev. William, *Indian Recreations* (London 1804), ii, p. 404. Hereafter Tennant.

[26] Hamilton, Walter, *The East Indian Gazetteer containing Particular Descriptions of Hindostan*, etc. (London 1828), ii, p. 131. Hereafter Hamilton.

[27] Mukerjee & Singh, *Social Profiles of a Metropolis*. Lucknow 1954–56 (Bombay 1961), p. 11.

[28] Ibid., p. 11.

[29] Hay, Sidney, *Historic Lucknow* (Lucknow 1939), p. 14.

for commerce with a bullion market, and a reputation for the working of copper, which was gilded, engraved and painted and formed one of the town's biggest industries. It would also be wrong to over-emphasize the impact of the nawabi court on the original city of Lucknow, despite the rise in population. Naturally the old town was affected by the arrival of the court in many ways, from the increase in prostitutes to the makers of silver and gold lace and the perfumiers. The nawabi fascination with European artifacts also filtered through to the old city, a good example being the introduction of lithographic presses which were quickly taken up by businessmen in and around the Chauk. In 1831, eighteen years after an Englishman, Mr Archer, had been employed on the King's lithographic press, there were at least seventeen presses in Lucknow which sent books all over India, and employed a considerable number of workers.[30]

But it would be a mistake to imagine that the old city underwent a complete change after 1775. Both the old city and the new areas that grew up round the court to the east of the Chauk had a high degree of independence. Neither was essential for the continuation of the other and the nawabi palaces and religious complexes could just as well have been constructed in another town like Faizabad or Cawnpore. Wherever the nawabi court settled it would have attracted the same crowd of adventurers and artists. Similarly the old city would doubtless have continued to thrive, though possibly at a slower pace, had the nawabi court not settled to the east. The town was self-sufficient before 1775 and there is no reason to believe that it would have declined during the nineteenth century. The rich and complex life of old Lucknow went on in much the same way, the *shroffs* (moneylenders) continued to flourish, the Mint which had been long established, continued to strike coins – albeit with the nawabs' titles instead of the Mughal emperors on them – stable industries like tobacco-growing, sugar-refining and spinning and weaving continued, social life revolved around the mosques, the

[30] Bengal Pol. Con., 6 Oct. 1849, no. 130.

madrassas and the bazaars. Perhaps most important evidence of all, the physical characteristics of the area remained the same, and to quote an Irish journalist, the native city was "an aggregate of houses perforated by tortuous paths, so that a plan of it would resemble a section of worm-eaten wood."[31] The tortuous paths continued to be peopled by beggars, both local and those who came in from the surrounding villages. Their wretched lives were hardly affected by the rich court in the "new" part of the city, except that when they became ill or near death on the streets they might be taken (if they were lucky) to the King's Hospital, supervised by European doctors, or to the Poor House (both in the old city). Those who were chosen for the Poor House then found they had to bribe the officials there to get bedding, food and sustenance which had been donated for them.[32]

Occasionally there would be minor upheavals in the old city when new groups of people moved in, either hoping for work at the court or because conditions in their own area had become bad. A report of 1828 mentions "Mewatties and different kinds of Sunnis, including Afghans, Uljas, Afreedees and Turkey Moghuls who are in the Service of the State", but these newcomers tended to settle on the outskirts of the old city where they set up their own colonies. The Mewatties, for example, lived on the south-western fringe of Lucknow near Talkatora.[33]

It was inevitable, however, that the "new" part of Lucknow to the east – the royal area with its palace complexes (rather than simple palaces) – would become the most celebrated part of the city. It was the most widely discussed, and the magnet that attracted poets, painters, writers, musicians, and artists from all over India and beyond. The fame of the Awadh court rapidly spread beyond the boundaries of the subcontinent, drawing to its centre a motley and curious crowd of foreigners, European and Middle-Eastern, all

[31] Russell, W.H., *My Diary in India in the Year 1858–9* (London, new edition, n.d.), p. 106.

[32] Bengal Pol. Con., 1 August 1856, no. 68.

[33] Bengal Pol. Con., 22 August 1828, no. 11.

of whom hoped to share in the new-found prosperity manifested in the brilliant, glittering city that was described in stark contrast to the old city of Lucknow. Ozias Humphry, a British artist, wrote in 1785, "I am assured by Mr Macpherson [the Governor General] that a residence of three or four months at Lucknow with Nabob Vizier [Asaf-ud-daula] will not fail to give me the fortune I came to seek in India, viz. 10,000 pounds – of this I am assured by those who are well acquainted with the state of affairs in these parts."[34] The fact that the artist received nothing like the amount he expected did nothing to deter others from seeking their fortune in Lucknow.

After Asaf-ud-daula's transfer from Faizabad to Lucknow the business of dealing with the revenue and tax collections from the province all centred on Lucknow. The main treasury was here, as were the main judicial courts, and important prisoners would be sent for trial to the capital. Similarly, the business of government took place here, the ambassadors and notables from foreign countries would be presented in Lucknow to the nawabs. The headquarters of the army was also here, the highest army officials living in the palace complexes. All these different functions, judicial, financial, governmental, military and diplomatic were centred on the palace complexes and there were different buildings within the complex allocated to them. In addition, each complex housed a great number of servants, not only domestics but also skilled craftspeople concerned with the upkeep of the royal buildings and gardens. There were servants who ministered to the panoply of state, the royal coachmen, the personal bodyguards, the people in charge of the royal tents and hunting equipment, the women of the zenana, and many others. Artists would also be housed in the complexes and some of the most famous religious buildings of the Shi'a faith in India were here, making this area a place of pilgrimage for the spiritual as well as the worldly.[35]

[34] Ozias Humphry Collection, Letter dated 29 December 1783, Royal Academy Library, London.

[35] Lucknow is still the centre of Shi'ism in India.

But whereas the court and the city functioned as two separate entities, the third factor that went to make up the city after 1775, the British Residency, depended entirely on the fact of the nawabi court being established in Lucknow. Although the officials of the East India Company were very much in a minority in the city compared with the free-booting European adventurers and mercenaries, the security of their position and the vast wealth to be gained legally or illegally ensured that the Resident and his staff lived in conditions that were luxurious compared with those of most other Europeans in Lucknow.

2

The Europeans of Lucknow

EUROPEANS who Lived in Lucknow between 1775 and 1856 can be divided into four categories – firstly the military men who were part of the East India Company's battalions stationed in and around Lucknow as a peace-keeping force paid for by the nawabs; secondly the civilian officials of the Company who included the Resident, his assistant, the Residency surgeon and chaplain, writers, and other staff; thirdly those Europeans who were employed by the nawabs in various capacities; and lastly Europeans who were classed as "Persons not in the Company's Service", i.e. freelancers who included soldiers, artists, traders, indigo planters, and shopkeepers. Occasionally a European changed categories by changing occupation, like John Munro Sinclair, who originally worked as a civil architect for the Company in the Western Provinces but who, in 1822, resigned from the Company in order to take up employment as civil engineer and "general mechanic" to the nawab,[1] or Felix Quieros who was working as a junior clerk in the Residency Office in 1855 but whose family had originally come to Lucknow from Calcutta to act as stewards and overseers for the estate of a rich European, Claude Martin. These last two categories of Europeans appear the most interesting since their presence in Lucknow was due mainly to their own efforts and initiative, unlike the military and officials of the Company who were posted there.

[1] Bengal Pol. Con., 16 March 1822, no. 40.

Why did such Europeans choose to settle in Lucknow and subject themselves to the often whimsical behaviour of the nawabs and frequent condemnation from the "official" British, and what did they do when they got there?

The earliest reference to Europeans in Lucknow (discounting the seventeenth-century traders who settled in the Farangi Mahal area) is to the soldiers of fortune who were attracted to the rising star of Shuja-ud-daula in the middle of the eighteenth century. René-Marie Madec and Jean Baptiste Joseph Gentil were among the mercenaries employed by the nawab to train his Indian troops in the new European manner, and there is a report of Monsieur Law's corps, consisting of 250 Frenchmen, who escaped from Chandernagore after its capture by Clive in 1756 and served under Shuja-ud-daula for a year, finally suffering defeat and capture by the Company's troops led by Major Carnac. Colonel Pédron, another Frenchman, served for some time under the nawab in a military capacity, and the notorious Somru – Walter Reinhardt – a European mercenary, served for four years, having trained battalions of infantry for the nawab.[2] Shuja-ud-daula's European mercenaries, however, were not notably successful in defending their new master against the Company's troops. Somru, for example, fled after his battalions were defeated in the battle of Buxar in 1764, and morale among the remaining mercenaries understandably ebbed. By 1774 when the Comte de Modave visited the nawab's court at Faizabad he found the French soldiers there so undisciplined as to be useless in any conflict – "This bizarre or rather, scandalous mixture would have spoilt the best arrangements in the world."[3]

M. Gentil, former mercenary, had stayed with Shuja-ud-daula after the defeat at Buxar in the capacity of "an advisor" and was responsible for introducing many French people to the court.[4] Gentil was "surrounded by French adventurers" more or less under his

[2] Compton, H., *A Particular Account of the Military Adventurers of Hindustan from 1784–1803* (London 1892), p. 378.

[3] Modave, p. 155.

[4] Modave, p. 156.

patronage, and his *Memoires sur l'Indoustan* published in 1822 is dedicated to "Choudja-a-ad-Doulah, constament l'ami et le protecteur des français." Also at the Faizabad court was Antoine-Louis Polier, another close friend of the nawab's, who had originally been the Company's chief engineer in Calcutta but was now appointed as "Architect to the Court of Shuja-ud-daula."[5] It seems likely that in this capacity Polier was the unnamed Frenchman who designed the fort at Faizabad, and since he later moved with the court to Lucknow he may well have influenced early European-style buildings in the city, though to what degree it is impossible to say unless further records come to light.

At the same time as these early mercenaries and courtiers were settling in Awadh, European traders were moving upcountry. One of the first was Monsieur Canonge who came from Mirzapore to Faizabad in 1768 with goods to sell, including broadcloths, the property of another Frenchman. M. Canonge intended to visit Gentil in Faizabad and his journey by boat up the Ganges is recorded because he needed two passes, a "*dastuck*" or "permission" from Mr Verelst, Governor of Bengal, and a "*perwanah*" (pass) from Shuja-ud-daula.[6]

But the most celebrated European in Lucknow, and the one to whom Europeanised building there probably owes its greatest debt, was Claude Martin, a Frenchman who combined the functions of trader, military adventurer, and architect. Martin enlisted in the French army and was fighting for his country in India at an early age. In 1760 he decided to change sides and joined the East India Company's troops, quickly working his way up to a position of trust in the Company, although he never gave up his French nationality. By 1766 he was promoted to Captain and was selected by Warren Hastings as a surveyor of roads in Bihar. After various military exploits for the Company he was appointed a surveyor in Awadh, and this was the start of his connection with Lucknow.[7] In 1776, at the beginning of Asaf-ud-daula's rule when the Company was bringing

[5] Bengal Pub. Con., 22 May 1780. No number given.

[6] The Orme Collection, No. 38, 6.5, I.O.L.

[7] Hill, S.C., *Claude Martin* (Calcutta 1901).

pressure to bear on the new nawab to put his affairs in order, the British Resident John Bristow recommended that the nawab "establish a grand Arsenal under Captain Martin because the Nawab's stores and ammunition are in so bad a state that he would find it extremely difficult to furnish any large Body of Troops going on Service. This measure would be a considerable saving to His Excellency because on the present footing his Arsenal is a great Expense and of little service."[8] Although Asaf-ud-daula was "hitherto entirely averse" to the idea, he was persuaded to accept Martin as Superintendent of the Arsenal, and Martin held this appointment until 1787. He was thus working both for the nawab, receiving his salary direct from him, and for the Company, rising to the position of Major General in 1796.[9] At the same time his relations with the nawab quickly changed from that of employee to one of confidant and advisor. He was accepted at court and became interested in all the intrigues and manoeuvring that went on there, without being directly involved. At the same time he retained close links with the Company in Calcutta and wrote on intimate terms to Warren Hastings.[10] He trod the delicate tightrope between the nawab's court and the Resident's office without ever seeming to lose the trust of either party, and at times was a link between the two – so much so that his views were solicited by both sides. In this role he, more than any other European, was responsible for directing the tastes of Asaf-ud-daula and his successor, Saadat Ali Khan, towards European architecture. He designed some of Lucknow's best buildings for them and made it his job to obtain furniture, ornaments, and trinkets from Europe.

Martin was not, of course, acting from altruistic motives in obtaining such goods – this is where he takes on the persona of trader, the least attractive of his many facets. He made a huge fortune at the expense of the nawab and other Indians and was roundly con-

[8] Secret & Military Con., 30 Dec. 1776. No number given.

[9] Some of this information is based on notes by Professor Theo Roy, author of the article entitled "Claude Martin – A Kindly Condottiere", *Bengal Past & Present*, vol. xcv, part 1, no. 180.

[10] Add. Mss. 29, 169 f. 425, B.M.

demned, even by his contemporaries, for exploiting the nawab at a time when it was considered perfectly acceptable for Europeans to go to India to make their fortunes. "His influence at the Court of Lucknow became very considerable, not only with the vizir [Asaf-ud-daula] but with his ministers: and that influence was the source of the immense fortune which he amassed," explained Viscount Valentia in *Voyages and Travels to India*, adding, "A more infamous or despicable character than the late General Martin never existed . . . The late Nawaub's [Asaf-ud-daula] idiotical propensities were another fruitful source of profit to him; he purchased different articles in Europe and sold them at 100 per cent, 200 per cent or 300 per cent, lending him at the same time to pay himself at 3 per cent per month."[11] At one time Asaf-ud-daula owed £250,000 to Martin.[12]

Not all of Martin's immense wealth came directly from the nawab's craze for European artifacts. He bought a great deal of land in and around Lucknow, including the site later known as the Residency complex, and here he either built or bought houses already standing which he rented out to other Europeans and Indians. On his death in 1800 his estate was valued at almost £40,000 in property and rent alone, and this was only in Lucknow: he also owned property and indigo farms throughout Awadh and Bengal. At least eight prominent citizens of Lucknow owed him sums of money, and nine other Europeans, including one of the acting British Residents, were written off as bad or doubtful debtors. The more one examines Martin's financial affairs, the more one is led to conclude that among the comparatively small and tight-knit group of Europeans in Lucknow, Martin was the central figure around which

[11] Valentia, Viscount George, *Voyages and Travels to India, Ceylon, the Red Sea, Abyssinia, and Egypt in the Years 1802–1806*, vol. i (London 1809), p. 164. Hereafter Valentia.

[12] Johnson, Daniel, *Sketches of field sports as followed by the natives of India* (London 1822), p. 163. Hereafter Daniel Johnson. Johnson wrote, "Whenever his Highness purchased any piece of mechanism, or other curiosity, Martin forthwith searched the world for something superior of the same kind, which he was certain of selling to him at an immense profit."

many of the financial, speculative, business, and political affairs of the European community revolved.

No other European matched Martin in his spectacular rise to riches and fame, although several others, in particular George Prendergast, Frederick Maitland Arnott, and the Orr family, did very well for themselves as merchants, landowners, and suppliers of European goods to the nawabs and other Indians in Lucknow. But it is necessary not to be dazzled by such brilliant entrepreneurs as Martin, Orr, etc. in order to gain a complete picture of European life in the city as lived by the less spectacular inhabitants there.

A list compiled mainly from the Bengal Directory (also known as the *Calcutta Annual Register*), first published in 1814, shows Europeans resident in the Upper Provinces, including Lucknow, and gives their occupations. A high proportion of Europeans were engaged in trade, although there is no evidence that Lucknow possessed a particular quarter given over to shops run by and for Europeans or Indians with European tastes. There were however several "Europe Shops", as they were called, run from the private houses of Europeans. The owners of such houses were referred to as merchants and traders as well as shopkeepers, since they usually bought goods for resale direct rather than through a middleman, and because they would sell goods on commission, and in some cases lend money too. The earliest shop noted in Lucknow belonged to a Jewish merchant called Charles Isaacs, and in 1790 an inventory of goods he sold included "7 or 8 chests of fine tea, 9 or 10 chests of Europe preserved fruits, Europe Pickles, Europe Cheeses and Brandy and other wines without number," and pieces of "White Cloth, Broad Cloth, silk and sweetmeats." There were also eight pieces of China velvet and three of embroidery which had been given to Isaacs to sell on commission.[13] It is not known where Isaacs' shop was situated but the remains of another house used as a shop still exist in the Residency area. This is the Begum Kothi, which served as a shop for at least twenty years, being sold to two merchants and

[13] Bengal Pub. Con., 14 May 1790. No number given.

European Occupations between 1775 and 1856	*Numbers employed*
ADC or bodyguard to the nawabs	6
Almoner of the Poor House	1
Armament maker	3
Astronomer or Observatory Assistant	4
Baker	1
Barber and *valet de chambre* to the nawabs	2
Boot, shoe and harness maker	1
Botanist	1
Builders, engineers, and architects	13
Chamberlain to the nawabs	1
Coach makers	2
Coachmen to the nawabs	4
Coffin maker	1
Cook	1
Court librarians	2
Court painters	5
Courtiers to the nawabs	4
Craftsmen	1
Doctors, surgeons, and apothecaries	18
Dog keeper	1
English teacher to the nawabs	1
Factory owner	1
Farrier	1
Female relatives (wives, daughters, sisters, mistresses)	35
Fire workers	2
Gardener	1
Indigo or cloth trade workers	7
Interpreter in the nawabs' service	1
Ironsmith	1
Jewellers, goldsmiths	2
Jockey	1

Contd.

Contd.

European Occupations between 1775 and 1856	*Numbers employed*
Juggler	1
Livery stable keepers or grooms	6
Mechanic to the nawabs	1
Musicians and piano tuners	15
Nawabs military forces	35
Nawabs' service, in an unspecified position	30
Painters (not at court)	3
Pensioners of the nawabs	11
People with several jobs	9
Postilion	1
Roman Catholic priests and "church superintendents'	3
Schoolteachers	16
Servants or assistants to other Europeans	9
Steward to Claude Martin's estate	2
Stewards for the nawabs	2
Superintendent of Boats	1
Superintendent of Canal	1
Superintendent of the City Hospital	4
Superintendent of the nawabs' Litho Press	1
Superintendent of the nawabs' stud	2
Traders, shopkeepers, merchants	39
Unknown occupation	50
Watchmaker	1
Writer in the nawabs' service	1
Young children	6

inherited by a third. The convenience of a Europe shop in the middle of the Residency area can well be imagined, and ownership of the property was hotly disputed at one point.

European shopkeepers in Lucknow obtained their stock normally from goods imported into Calcutta, which were then sent upriver to Cawnpore. From there the goods were originally sent in hackeries (covered carriages), although one shopkeeper in 1817 found this method "expensive and inconvenient" and sought permission to bring goods in boats up the Gomti.[14] Such goods had often been especially requested by customers, so shopkeepers were in effect acting as agents, and printed catalogues with prices from which customers could make their choice were circulated upcountry. Lists of goods available by this method were extremely comprehensive, including such indispensables as milk chocolate in 1793, cucumber-slicers, mousetraps, guns, and naturally the latest European fashions.[15] At the start of the nineteenth century regular companies were set up, often in Calcutta, to promote this "mail order" business and one of the last shopkeepers in Lucknow before 1857 was a Mr Dias who had set up business in 1840 as the agent for the Inland Transit Company. He estimated that he earned between Rs 180–200 a month in commission as an agent, plus the profits from the straightforward buying and selling of goods in the city.[16] Shopkeepers would also buy goods without specific customers in mind, usually from auctions of the property of deceased Europeans. Goods which had been obtained originally from Europe like furniture, silver, crockery, linen, wines and spirits, and even hair powder in one case, found a ready market on the death of owners who frequently died intestate, insolvent, and without recognised heirs – such was the precariousness of life among the early Europeans.

A number of doctors, surgeons, and apothecaries lived in the city and were employed both by the Company and by the nawabs. They were not expected to live in court and pursued their own profession for the Company while being "on call" for the nawabs. Dr William Stevenson, who in 1828 was requested by the nawab Nasir-ud-din Haider "to attend the Sick poor" of Lucknow, was at that time Junior Surgeon to the 14th Regiment of the Company's troops, stationed

[14] Foreign Pol. Con., 11 Jan. 1817, nos 137 and 138.

[15] Seton-Kerr, W.S., *Selections from Calcutta Gazettes 1789–1797* (Calcutta 1865), ii, p. 559. Hereafter Seton-Kerr.

[16] India Pol. Con., 9 April 1858, no. 25.

in the Mariaon Cantonment.[17] Dr Stevenson's name had been suggested to the nawab by Dr George Baillie, surgeon to Nasir-ud-din Haider and brother to a former British Resident at the court, John Baillie. In 1831 Stevenson was on the nawab's payroll as Assistant Surgeon, earning Rs 1500 per month, and a year later was in charge of the City Hospital at the same salary. Four years later Dr Stevenson requested an assistant to help him "in the general duties of the Residency, but especially in the diffusion of vaccination while the season is favourable,"[18] and he is last mentioned in 1840 when he wrote one of the half-yearly reports issued from the City Hospital. In addition to the Rs 1500 per month which Stevenson received from the nawab, he got an additional allowance of Rs 500 per month for a dispensary which he superintended in Lucknow, and Rs 740 per month from the Residency treasury, Rs 680 of which was for the vaccine establishment in his charge.[19]

Another source of employment for Europeans was in the nawabs' military service. Although by the treaty of 1801 Saadat Ali Khan had been made to cut his army drastically, he was still able to maintain a small force, a token perhaps of the early Europeans who had worked as mercenaries for his father, Shuja-ud-daula. A number of these Europeans or Anglo-Indians served successive nawabs for a considerable amount of time (for forty-three years in one case), although in 1856 the nawabs' regiments were transferred to the East India Company with, one is told, "an anxious desire to serve their new masters with alacrity and fidelity," true mercenaries in fact.[20] Those Europeans who retired in the nawabs' service and chose to remain in Lucknow received pensions from the court. One such person was William Bird who had taken service with Saadat Ali Khan in 1812 and worked for successive nawabs as a huntsman. He later became a livery stable-keeper and was pensioned off in 1832. He survived until 1848, receiving a regular pension, and his

[17] Bengal Pol. Con., 11 April 1828, no. 29.
[18] India Pol. Con., 5 March 1835, no. 93.
[19] Bengal Pol. Con., 22 Jan. 1830, no. 11.
[20] India Pol. Con., 13 June 1856, no. 321.

second wife also got a pension which she supplemented by earnings from a small shop in the city.

A particular European enterprise was the manufacture of small arms and the supplying of military equipment in Lucknow. Although the Company had forbidden the selling of arms by Britons to native powers, Frederick Maitland Arnott had a thriving business which he claimed "was known in the Alleys and Bazars (of Lucknow) and no one prevented it."[21] On his precipitous flight from Lucknow when finally challenged by the Resident, a list of his possessions was found to include a large brass gun, bags of scarlet cloths, "32 Kummer Bunds, grape shot and tent pieces." Arnott claimed that Asaf-ud-daula had commissioned weapons and uniforms, and the Resident, George Cherry, admitted in 1795 that "it had been much the practice prior to my arrival here for the Europeans Residing here to make Arms and Military Stores, which were sold to the Vizier and wherever purchasers could be found . . . the late Mr Pott left many Iron shot."[22] Another European, George Sangster, employed a number of Indians in his foundry which was in the compound or yard of his house, and on his death in 1792 "the tools and books of his Trade" were bequeathed to his son, who wanted to carry on "the business of the Foundry for his Excellency the Vizier."[23] Arnott's flight and the Resident's enforcement of the Company's prohibition put an end to this lucrative and extensive trade among the European community.[24]

The small number of women and children recorded cannot properly reflect the number that were present in Lucknow as dependants. Because women did not as a rule follow occupations, it was not considered necessary by the Company to record them and only two women, Mrs Lacy[25] and Mrs Pogoes Carapret,[26] are mentioned

[21] Bengal Pol. Con., 3 April 1795, no. 14.
[22] Bengal Pol. Con., 6 March 1794, no. 4.
[23] Bengal Pub. Con., 21 Dec. 1792. No number given.
[24] Bengal Pol. Con., 3 April 1795, no. 18.
[25] Bengal Pol. Con., 11 Oct. 1822, no. 50.
[26] Bengal Pol. Con., 30 Sept. 1831, no. 54.

with their husbands as being employed by the nawab Ghazi-ud-din-Haider in an unspecified position. Two women kept Europe shops in Lucknow: Mrs Bird, the widow of William Bird, and Mrs Whearty, also a widow, who employed two Hindus as her *munshi* (clerk) and *sircar* (superintendent).[27] A third woman, Mrs Sago, whose husband had been in the nawab's service, was headmistress of a small school in the Residency compound which had been set up by John Low, the British Resident, and Mrs Sago taught there for many years.[28] A very few women are recorded because they were the mistresses of Europeans or Indians, like Mukuderah Oolea Walters, Mrs Whearty's daughter. Mukuderah Oolea, born a Christian, converted to Islam when she became the mistress of the nawab Nasir-ud-din-Haider, and her mother, after the death of her second husband, became the mistress of Buksh Ali Khan, superintendent of one of the nawab's palaces.[29] By and large, however, women were not considered worthy of mention unless they acted in a troublesome or provocative manner, and Indian women who married British men and should therefore have been regarded as British citizens, were usually mentioned in disparaging terms.

The lack of information on European children in Lucknow is regrettable but by no means uncommon in similar pre-1857 studies. The infant mortality rate was distressingly high and children or babies were often only mentioned after particularly harrowing deaths. Annual returns of births, marriages, and deaths were only sent to Calcutta for one year (1828) and virtually all pre-1857 inscriptions have vanished from the Lucknow graveyards; and baptism and burial records were destroyed in the 1857 siege. In May 1857 the Company's priest, the Revd Polehampton, wanted to enlarge Mrs Sago's school for the "daughters and young sons of the poorer classes of Europeans in the City, who are now to be numbered by hundreds and who were mostly the children of uncovenanted servants of the Company." This figure had increased considerably after annexation,

[27] Bengal Pol. Con., 8 May 1812, no. 76.
[28] Bengal Pol. Con., 21 Aug. 1857, no. 171.
[29] India Pol. Con., 11 Jan 1841, no. 56.

when the Company brought in many officials to deal with the new administration of the city and province, and cannot be seen as representative of pre-annexation Lucknow.[30]

The most notable feature in the list of European names is that in several cases members of the same family are found working in Lucknow over quite a long period of time. The Braganca family was first recorded in 1805 when a Braganca seized by force the church and graveyard owned by Catholic priests in Lucknow.[31] Two members of the same family were subsequently recorded as piano-tuners and repairers of musical instruments, employed by successive nawabs between 1834 and 1855, while two other members received a court pension between 1837 and 1856. Similarly the Orr family had eight members variously employed in the city. James Orr arrived in 1779 and eight years later is recorded as working for the Company's accountant, John Wombwell, at a salary of Rs 2000 per month. At the same time James Orr also owned several cloth factories in Oudh and lived in a house in the Residency area. In 1795 James was joined by his brother Alexander;[32] in 1800 Robert and Alexander Orr are recorded as "merchants and traders" also working for the nawab, and there is a William Orr in an unspecified position at court. In 1836 John Orr was in one of the nawab's regiments and Patrick and Adolphus Orr held similar positions. Another family called Catania were recorded as having nine members present in Lucknow, three working briefly for the nawab about 1831, four more employed as musicians, merchants, and schoolmasters, and two more received pensions from the nawabs until annexation. The Quieros family, too, whose founder member Joseph Quieros Senior arrived from Calcutta in 1786, included members who worked in various capacities in the city and stayed on during the annexation and 1857. The last member to be buried in Lucknow was Edward Quieros, late of the Oudh Police, who died in 1900.

[30] Bengal Pol. Con., 21 Aug. 1857, no. 171.

[31] Bengal For. Con., 26 June 1805, no. 126.

[32] Bengal Pol. Con., 20 Feb. 1795. No number given.

Because the relationship between family members is seldom stated, it is not sufficiently clear how often brothers or other male relatives were invited to Lucknow to share the prosperity of the original adventurer, or whether the sons of European settlers found work in the city as they grew older. Certainly there was considerable stability and security for Europeans in the city, especially for those employed by the nawabs, as long as they remained in favour at court. Despite political uncertainties over the future of Awadh, the constant friction between the court and the Residency and the yearly riots in the town, Lucknow was still a very attractive place for Europeans who settled there and prospered. The average length of residence in Lucknow for Europeans was fourteen years, which argues for a good measure of stability in the city. There was a good deal of intermarriage between the European community, and in some cases orphaned European children were brought up by members of that community who were not related by blood ties but who, one supposes, did it out of kindness. The community could also be moved by a common cause, as in the case of James Walters who arrived in the city penniless in 1818 with eight young children. He had hoped to find employment, as his brother George had done before him, but was unable to do so. The European citizens clubbed together to set up a charitable fund for the children; this was administered by the Resident.[33]

The many interconnecting links between members of the European community are shown in a variety of ways, through bequests made to friends in wills, through marriage, through trade and money-lending, through association in crime and business (sometimes with a very thin dividing line between the two), and through property disputes, which were common. The widespread notion that most Europeans in Lucknow not in the Company's service were a group of "get-rich-quick" adventurers, was a powerful idea, despite many indications to the contrary. This idea was assiduously fostered by official complaints, usually from the Resident reporting to the Com-

[33] Bengal Pol. Con., 30 Jan. 1819, no. 62.

pany in Calcutta, from newspaper reports and magazines, and from the writings of travellers who seldom spent more than a few days in the city. One writer who spent no time at all in Lucknow nevertheless managed to produce a most damaging book which contained all the assumptions about the European community which readers in Britain had come to expect. The book was *The Private Life of an Eastern King* (1855), which is now assumed from internal evidence to have been dictated to the author, William Knighton, by Nawab Nasir-ud-din-Haider's English librarian, Mr Edward Cropley.

The book shows a weak and debauched ruler surrounded by European sycophants of the worst kind, constantly egging him on to bigger and better follies while they lined their own pockets at his expense. A contemporary newspaper account of 1837 relating the same story wrote, "The barber, Derusett, has retired from the service of the King [of Awadh] taking with him his Majesty's deep regret, and several lacs of rupees. The rest of the reptile tribe, the jeweller, the coachman etc. etc. will migrate when they have nothing left to consume."[34] Though Knighton's book was not published until 1855, the events it relates took place in 1837. The book enjoyed great notoriety and was praised by the *Calcutta Review* which added a strong plea for the annexation of Awadh (this took place the following year).[35] It is hardly coincidental that the publication of this book, so long delayed, should have occurred at this particular time, when the annexation question was being hotly discussed again. There are few less edifying spectacles than British writers condemning Europeans in the nawabs' service while failing to comment on the much greater political chicanery that went on between the British government and the Lucknow court. Of course there were Europeans who did exploit the nawabs, beginning with Claude Martin in the 1770s, but to believe that this constituted practically the sole occupation of non-official Europeans in Lucknow is simply not true. Most were too busy working to earn a living and bringing up

[34] *The Asiatic Journal*, New Series, vol. 22, part 2 (London 1837), p. 94.
[35] *Calcutta Review*, July–Dec. (Calcutta 1855), pp. 117–37.

their families to engage in dangerous games at court, even supposing they had been admitted through the barrier of pomp and protocol to the nawabi presence. A white face did not automatically mean a passport to the court any more than it was a guarantee of entry to the Residency. And those Europeans who were employed by the court often remained there for long periods, enjoying good salaries with pensions for themselves and their dependants, often more handsome than the Company could provide for its retired employees.

The Company's attitudes towards the non-official Europeans is worth examining in some detail since its uneasiness and at times downright hostility to them runs through the whole of the period. The official attitudes to "Persons not in the Company's Service" seem compounded of the familiar elements of nineteenth-century chauvinism, common in Britain and certainly not to be wondered at in India. A heading in the East India Parliamentary Papers for the 1840s reads succinctly, "*Foreigners* (Persons not being British Subjects) Removal of", and while the Company seldom went quite as far as to banish other Europeans, it often considered them a problem, especially if they had entered into alliances with Indian men or women. Britons who had formed such relationships were considered even more depraved, presumably on the grounds that they should have known better, and the more liberal days when it had been acceptable for British men to have one or two Indian wives were almost forgotten by the beginning of the nineteenth century – apart from a few rather embarrassing reminders like the court artist George Duncan Beechey, who with his three Indian wives lived until 1852 and became something of a tourist attraction in Lucknow.

The Company's objections to the non-British unofficial European residents of the city were not based on any logical grounds. Since the Company had "persuaded" Asaf-ud-daula to expel his French advisors from his court,[36] there had never been any hint that Europeans in Awadh might have political ambitions there. Any threats that

[36] Secret & Military Con., 3 April 1775. No number given.

there might have been to the stability of the nawabs' rule and the increasing British presence came from Indian sources, not European. Nevertheless, as the Company tightened its grip on Awadh, so did its chauvinistic attitudes to other Europeans increase, especially in a community like Lucknow where gossip appears to have been one of the chief pastimes. By the 1857 uprising the British were found expressing polite surprise at the bravery and courage of other Europeans trapped in the Residency area during the siege, as though these attributes were a peculiarly British characteristic.

The Company also objected to the unofficial Europeans on the curious grounds that many of them were of the "lower classes", i.e. shopkeepers, tradesmen, and small businessmen. The "poorer Europeans", as they were termed, were not expected to behave in a wholly rational manner: they were given to violent disputes, illicit relationships, large families which they could not always support, and petty bickerings in which they often expected the Resident to intervene. In short they were expected to behave in a scandalous way and while the majority of them led respectable, quiet, and hardworking lives, there were the exceptions who fulfilled all the Company's expectations. It is interesting to chart the lives of two such families, both for their picaresque details and for the official reactions to them, which are quite undisturbed by any feelings of understanding or responsibility other than financial.

The origin of the Walters family in India was quite in keeping with the prevailing mores of the end of the eighteenth century, before the long night of Victorian morality descended. Asaf-ud-daula had in 1776 requested that a Dr Hopkins Walters, a Company doctor, attend him in place of a previous British doctor.[37] Dr Walters did so, settled in Lucknow, and married an Indian woman. Two children were born, James and George Hopkins Walters, and in 1780 the doctor took them back to England while his wife remained in India. Unfortunately, the father died on the voyage and both boys were brought up by two friends of the late doc-

[37] *Calendar of Persian Correspondence*, iv, 21 (Calcutta 1911). Hereafter *Persian Correspondence*.

tor. George Walters returned to India after having served as a soldier in England, with the intention of setting up a Europe shop in Calcutta. A disastrous fire there destroyed all his goods and his bungalow, so he moved upcountry to Cawnpore and later borrowed money from an Indian banker to set up a shop in Lucknow.[38] After being granted permission to do so by the Company, albeit somewhat grudgingly, he (according to official reports by the Resident) seduced the eldest daughter of a British merchant, John Culloden, who had already been married to a Mr Wheарty and widowed at an early age. Her father had settled on her his shop in the Residency area, the Begum Kothi, and George Walters, after causing "a disgracefull affray" during the auction of Mr Whearty's goods after his death, married her and moved into her house and shop "to the detriment of the other Legatees," namely the rest of John Culloden's children.[39] It was unfortunate, wrote the Resident in 1812, that "a person of Mr Walters' character" was allowed to stay in Lucknow, but if he was compelled to leave his wife would then become destitute.[40] George Walters eventually solved the Resident's dilemma by dying when he was about forty years old, having run a successful business and avoided further clashes with the Company.

The other notorious family in Lucknow in the eyes of the officials was called, appropriately enough, Rotton. The founder member, Richard W. Rotton, had been a mercenary in the Maratha army, and on leaving in 1803 was granted a pension from the Company: the latter had arranged to recompense Britons on condition that they would no longer fight for a native power.[41] Richard Rotton had also been receiving Rs 2000 per month from Asaf-ud-daula for unspecified services, but Governor General Cornwallis had put a stop to that, telling Rotton that he could not receive such a sum and remain in Lucknow.[42] (It was a measure of the Company's power that they were able to intervene to such an extent in the

[38] India Pol. Con., 12 June 1812, no. 76.
[39] Foreign Pol. Index, 12 Oct. 1816, no. 30.
[40] Bengal Pol. Con., 12 June 1812, nos 72 & 74.
[41] Bengal Pol. Con., 2 April 1807, no. 79.
[42] Bengal Pol. Con., 29 Aug. 1794. No number given.

private arrangements between the nawab and one of his employees.) Richard Rotton chose to give up the nawabi salary and remained in Lucknow until his death in 1815.

His son, Felix Rotton, born about 1795, served in a military capacity under successive nawabs for twenty years, married several Indian women, and had about twenty-two children who were "complete natives in every sense of the word" according to official records. Felix Rotton was supposed to have converted to Islam and during the Uprising of 1857 fought for some months, with his sons, against the beleaguered British. The opprobrium heaped on him for this not unreasonable action can well be imagined, and the tone of pained surprise in official records still makes for rich reading after 125 years: "Mr. Rotton seems voluntarily to have remained with the Rebels till July last [i.e. July 1857], to be the father of rebels and to labour under the strongest presumption of disloyalty." He did nothing to help the British "although the descendant of a European himself, all his sons capable of bearing arms were hostile to us and he is answerable for the sons he begot."

Felix Rotton, on surrendering to the British forces in 1858, claimed he had meant to go into the Residency entrenchment but was asleep when Indian troops entered the city. The official investigators dismissed this claim as rubbish and took the trouble to establish that there was a "heavy cannonade" at the time when Felix Rotton said he was sleeping. The sons, despite the fact of their European descent, were seen during the siege of Lucknow with the rebels, together with some other "renegade Christians".[43] Possibly the sons' behaviour had been somewhat tempered by the memory of the scanty pension awarded to another branch of their family by the Company. Richard Rotton's brother, John, who served in the Company's forces stationed at Faizabad, was murdered by his son Edgar after he attempted to molest one of his daughters. The son fled to Lucknow where he was sympathetically received by the British Resident and awarded a pension of Rs 100 a month since he was a

[43] India Pol. Con., 29 Oct. 1858, no. 349.

dependant of a man who had served the Company. However, the Rs 100 was to be divided up between eleven members of the family and was "the sole means of their support,"[44] a figure which cannot compare very well with the Rs 2000 per month received by their uncle Richard Rotton from Asaf-ud-daula, until the Company put a stop to it.

Many more examples could be related of the official attitudes towards the "unofficial" Europeans in Lucknow, of pained indignation because the "lower classes" were unfortunately unable to act like gentlemen when suddenly called upon to do so, of the horror which mixed marriages provoked, and of the patronising attitudes towards the children of such marriages. But enough has been written to show that the European community in the city should not and cannot be seen as a corporate whole; they were, rather, many little factions crossing and recrossing each others' paths but with considerable gulfs of incomprehension between them.

From the measures that the Company adopted towards the unofficial Europeans in Lucknow it is a short step to examining the active steps that were employed to keep out such people, or if that failed, to restrict them as much as possible. The first attempt came early in 1775, shortly after Asaf-ud-daula's succession to the musnud, when the Resident John Bristow was told unequivocally by the Governor General, Warren Hastings, that the nawab "must make his Election between the French and the English as he cannot be in Amity with one of these Nations without bearing an Enmity to the other."[45] At this time it was estimated that there were about 150 non-official Europeans in Awadh and about thirty-five working for Asaf-ud-daula. When the nawab raised objections to the summary dismissal of a number of his employees he was threatened with the withdrawal of Company troops, leaving him undefended apart from his own undisciplined troops, who would have been led by the bizarre mixture of Frenchmen noted by the Comte de Modave a year earlier.

[44] Bengal Pol. Con., 12 Aug. 1831, no. 66.
[45] Secret & Military Con., 3 April 1775. No number given.

By 1786 a list made of Europeans in Lucknow numbered twenty-eight.[46] As well as official Europeans like the Resident, Colonel Harper, his accountant John Wombwell, and military officers stationed in the city, it also included two artists, the painters Johan Zoffany and Thomas Longcroft; the architect Colonel Polier and five men unconnected with the Company, one of whom, Louis Carvalho, was certainly pursuing his own business as a trader. Seven years later, in 1793, the Company again tried to limit the number of Europeans at the nawab's court, which seems to confirm that the measures of 1775 had not been successful. This time Asaf-ud-daula was allowed to employ craftsmen, carpenters, "and repairers of his Musical Clocks", but no "Gentlemen except Colonel Martin".[47] The next year the Governor General, in reply to a query from the Resident at Lucknow, said that no European was to reside in Oudh without Cornwallis' written permission, and that anyone who did so would not receive protection from the Company.[48] This meant in effect that unofficial Europeans residing without permission would be subject to Indian jurisdiction in case of trouble or civil disputes instead of coming under the judicial auspices of the Resident, as was normally the case.

Three years later the next Governor General, Sir John Shore, wrote to the Resident saying, "To whatever degree the Commercial Benefits of the Vizier's Country may be extended from the Trade carried on by Europeans in Oude, I cannot but be of the Opinion that they are more than Counterbalanced by the Political Evils resulting from the Establishment of Europeans there."[49] Lord Wellesley, who replaced Sir John Shore as Governor General, was similarly perturbed by the European presence in Awadh and wrote in 1798 that their presence was "a mischief which requires no comment. My resolution is fixed to dislodge every European, excepting the Com-

[46] Diary of Ozias Humphry dated 5 Feb. to 19 June 1786. Photostat of MS in Yale University. No pagination. I.O.L. Hereafter Diary of Ozias Humphry.

[47] Foreign Pol. Index, 12 April 1793. No number given.

[48] Add. Mss. 13, 523, f. 8, 30 March 1794.

[49] Add. Mss. 13, 522, f. 166, 29 Feb. 1796, Sir John Shore's letters.

pany's servants, from Oude."[50] But the Governor General was just as unsuccessful in pursuing his resolution as others had been before him, and many new names appear in the list of non-official residents by the end of the eighteenth century. The only tangible result of Wellesley's pronouncement was a treaty drawn up between the new nawab, Saadat Ali Khan, and the Company, which stated that the nawab "is bound to obtain the permission of the British Government previously to his entertaining Europeans of any description," but even this treaty proved unenforceable in practice.

By 1823 attempts to restrict Europeans appear to have been abandoned for good and shopkeepers, merchants, schoolteachers, and craftsmen could all apply to the Company for a pass which would allow them to reside in the city. The Company was still concerned, however, with Europeans employed directly by the nawab, and a note by the Governor General, Lord Hastings, that "no British Subject be permitted in future to enter into the Service of native Princes without the previous permission and Sanction of the British Government" was put to the nawab Ghazi-ud-din-Haider by the Resident in Lucknow.[51] This edict of Lord Hastings was meant to apply throughout India where the Company had a measure of power, and inspite of the nawab's arguments that he was an exceptional case he was, after 1823, obliged to seek written permission for Europeans he employed. The nawab did however win a concession from the Company in that he was to continue paying his European employees direct instead of their salaries being paid into the Residency treasury and then being passed on to them by the Resident. The nawab argued that such a move would "lower him in the Eyes of his Servants and Subjects" and would be "an encroachment on the internal management of his affairs", so the measure was quickly dropped.

From 1823, annual lists of Europeans working for the nawabs were compiled together with their monthly salaries, and in some

[50] Martin, Montgomery (ed.), *The Despatches, Minutes and Correspondence of the Marquess of Wellesley*, vol. i (London 1836), p. 388.

[51] Bengal Pol. Con., 18 July 1823, no. 13.

cases their occupations, and applications for Company passes for Europeans offered work by the nawabs, are also noted. Europeans who were offered such jobs had usually done a fair amount of soliciting for the coveted posts, and jobs were normally offered on the recommendation of someone already at court or someone in the Company. A list of 1837 names twelve Europeans employed by the nawab Nasir-ud-din-Haider, and in ten cases gives the name of the person who recommended them.[52] Four men: Carnegie – a silversmith and jeweller; Sago – the Chamberlain; Casanova – a painter; and Sinclair – a Civil Engineer, were recommended by the nawab's chief minister Hakim Mehndi, and on this minister's fall from grace in 1832 Carnegie and Sago were both dismissed, showing how closely some jobs were tied to the position of the patron who had solicited for them. Three men, including the notorious barber Derussett (the anti-hero of Knighton's book), had been recommended to the nawab by Residents in Lucknow; one man was recommended both by a well-known European merchant and the Governor General, Lord Bentinck, and the last, J.D. Lock, was the son of a painter employed by a former nawab whose mother had personally solicited Nasir-ud-din-Haider to give her son work on his father's death.

No mention was ever made of bribes or gifts to people at court in return for their patronage and recommendations but it would be naïve to suppose that money and goods did not change hands. A job at court could prove very lucrative as the salaries show (Rs 1000 per month for Casanova the painter, for example), as well as providing a pension in retirement, and of course the chance to promote other Europeans in turn. The disadvantages were that one's patron could fall out of favour, or that the nawab would find fault, justified or not, with an employee, which invariably led to instant dismissal and often the loss of earned salary since salaries were usually paid in arrears. Several sad cases are recorded of Europeans who had sold their houses and left good jobs (sometimes in Europe) to come to

[52] India Pol. Con., 27 Feb. 1837, no. 31.

Lucknow and work for the nawabs, only to be dismissed after a short while; or in the case of Seddon, the proposed principal of a college which was not set up, never to start work at all.[53]

Antoine de l'Etang, who had originally worked in the Royal Stables in Paris before the French Revolution, was offered a job at the Lucknow court by a "Gentleman of a most respectable Character" and gave up his job for the Company in Calcutta to take up the new position in Lucknow. He borrowed Rs 10,000 to pay the fares of his wife and four daughters from Europe to India and borrowed another Rs 3000 for furniture, house expenses, and servants, all on the strength of his wages of Rs 2000 per month from Saadat Ali Khan. (A house was provided for him by the nawab.) After just over a year in Lucknow a furious correspondence ensued between de l'Etang and the nawab over the former's alleged mistreatment of the nawab's horses. Recriminations and accusations flew between both parties. "Figure to yourself," wrote the nawab "how much vexation it must give to a man who is very fond of horses." The result was that de l'Etang was dismissed and only received his salary after prolonged correspondence. The Governor General interceded for him but could not obtain any money as compensation and de l'Etang, after many pleading letters, was finally offered a job in the Company, though not, one imagines, at Rs 2000 per month.

What restrictions did the nawabs themselves put on Europeans, other than outright expulsions as with de l'Etang? Asaf-ud-daula had appeared reluctant to place constraints on Europeans until forced to do so by the Company shortly after his succession in 1775. It has been shown that some Europeans did manage to slip through the Company's net and even to have dealings with Asaf-ud-daula, but it is not until 1788 that the first independent statement by the nawab was issued when he put out a notice through the Resident, E. Otto Ives, saying that he "does not think proper to consent to their [the Europeans] erecting houses or other buildings in his Dominions, and that they must therefore consider themselves as

[53] India Pol. Con., 16 Oct. 1837, no. 135.

prohibited from doing so."[54] The Governor General said in reply to this announcement (which was not of course adhered to) that had he known the nawab did not want Europeans to erect houses in Awadh he, the Governor, would not have granted their request "as it is a matter of perfect indifference to the interest of this Government." Two points emerge from this rather strange statement – the implication that the Governor General could grant Europeans permission to build houses in the nawab's dominions without apparently getting the nawab's consent, and secondly the deliberate lie that the presence of non-official Europeans was not a matter for concern to the Company when, as has been shown, they made prolonged attempts to restrict such people.

A year later in July 1789 Ives reported to the Governor General that the nawab "has declared it to be his determination not to allow in future of any European merchants coming to reside in his country, but to confine their commercial intercourse to the medium of *Gomastahs* [middlemen in trade]." The reasons for the nawabi statement, said Ives, was the "disgust he [the nawab] has conceived against those who are already here." The nawab also objected to the fact that European merchants could approach him through the Resident with their grievances, something which native merchants could not do.[55] The Governor General's reply to this announcement stated that it was the Company's intention to protect the nawab from "improper interference" by Europeans but that he, the Governor General, could not agree to a total prohibition on Europeans. The nawab, he wrote, could specify where he wanted Europeans to live but he must not prohibit them once they had a pass from the Governor General. They could however be recalled for "improper behaviour". But this seemingly categorical statement that it was for the Company to choose which Europeans entered Awadh, independent of the nawab's wishes, is contradicted by a report

[54] This prohibition did not of course refer to the Company bungalows that were being put up in the Residency area, nor to Company Cantonment buildings. Foreign Pol. Index, 20 June 1788. No number given.

[55] Bengal Pub. Con., 6 July 1789. No number given.

from Sir John Shore, the Governor General, who wrote in 1795: "The Rule for permitting Europeans to proceed to Lucknow renders it necessary that the Leave of the Vizier, communicated thro' the Resident should have been previously obtained."[56]

Whether Europeans wishing to settle in Lucknow took advantage of the confused pass system by playing off the Governor General's announcements against the nawab's is not clear. At one point the nawab was reported as having said he would not object to Europeans in Awadh "provided they confined their residence to Lucknow."[57] But this order proved as unworkable as those of the Company. All that emerges is the fact that in theory Europeans needed a Company pass and a nawabi pass in the eighteenth century, but in practice a number of Europeans arrived who were sanctioned by neither party. It was possible for them to evade surveillance and both enter and leave Awadh with comparative ease. There are few accounts in records examined of Europeans being deported once they had reached and settled in Lucknow, either by the nawabs or by the Company, though one cannot judge the amount of pressure which might have been applied to undesirable people in the city. In 1802 the new nawab, Saadat Ali Khan, again attempted to restrict non-official Europeans from settling in the city and evicted Louis Carvalho from a house which the latter had long occupied, as well as tried to prevent another old resident, Mr Paull, from re-establishing himself in the city. The Resident, Scott, wrote: "I believe his Excellency's [the nawab's] desire of totally eradicating from his dominions all European ascendancy, influence and inspection supersede every other consideration," and Scott suggested that the reasons for this not unnatural desire were simply that the nawab wished to engage in trade himself, or to give the monopoly of trade to his great friend Gore Ouseley and *his* friends.[58] Scott was not by any means an unbiased reporter, for there was tremendous

[56] Bengal Pub. Con., 26 Jan. 1795. No number given.

[57] Bengal Pol. Con., 29 July 1789. No number given.

[58] Add. MSS. 13,530, p. 31. Letters from the Residents at Lucknow, dated 22 Oct. 1802.

personal dislike between him and the nawab, and after many interventions by the latter Scott was replaced by Gore Ouseley who was Acting Resident for several years. No further attempts by the nawabs to restrict non-Company Europeans are noted, and the system of double passes was phased out early in the nineteenth century, Europeans who bothered to apply for passes now needing only one from the Company.

In retrospect, had the early nawabs' actions been consistent with their words and had Asaf-ud-daula and Saadat Ali Khan maintained a steadfast opposition to Europeans in Lucknow, if not Awadh, then the number of non-official Europeans would probably have been much smaller than it was. But these same rulers who voiced their objections through the Residents about Europeans in their city were at the same time not only actively encouraging some Europeans to settle in Lucknow but were giving them expensive houses as well – the nawab Asaf-ud-daula "gave me the House, Gardens, and Buildings formerly the Residence of Colonel Mordaunt at Lucknow," wrote Robert Beecher in 1814. It was "an House upon a large scale with Baths and every comfort – two large Bungalows and a Bowley [*baoli*, a kind of well] calculated to raise a great quantity of Water and an Extensive Garden planted with the choicest Trees. My idea of the value of the property is Rupees 50,000 [about £5000]."[59] Similarly there was Henry J. Clark's house which was erected on ground "purchased from General Martin's Executors by the late Vizier Saadat Ali Khan who immediately bestowed it in perpetuity on this Well-wisher" and gave him Rs 30,000 in addition towards the cost of the house.[60] But this same nawab was, according to Viscount Valentia, trying to buy back houses built by Europeans along the banks of the Gomti on land he had previously granted, in order to place some kind of restriction on land and houses owned by foreigners. "These [houses] were private property and were purchaseable by any person without his

[59] Foreign Pol. Con.. 9 Aug. 1814, no. 45.
[60] Foreign Pol. Con., 3 Feb. 1816, nos 22, 26 & 28.

Highness's consent. As the change of inhabitants is rapid, they have been on the market since his succession, and he has taken care to secure them all."[61]

It was this vacillating and half-hearted policy, giving with one hand and taking back with the other, that was the nawabs' ultimate undoing. They were not consistent in their policy on European traders in Awadh – while generally deprecating their activities they nonetheless continued to buy goods from them in excessive amounts, and though voicing disapproval of Europeans in Lucknow still continued to be the second largest employer (after the Company) for such people in the city. Had they firmly resisted the temptation of trading in European goods and of employing Europeans at court they might well have avoided some of the unwelcome attentions showered on them by the Company and might even have been allowed to muddle through until post-Mutiny days. But with hindsight it seems obvious that the half-hearted measures taken by the nawabs to limit the number of Europeans in Lucknow and Awadh were worse than useless – the real damage was not in the number, nor the quality, nor the professions of the Europeans, but in the fact that they were there at all.

[61] Valentia, i, p. 174.

3

European Dreams and Indian Fantasies

What kind of houses existed in Lucknow before European ideas on building began to change the city's face forever? It is necessary to consider this question thoroughly, for without an impression of the pre-European city it is neither easy to judge the enormous impact which Western architecture made nor to appreciate the considerable changes carried out in the city by Europeans and by Indians who became enamoured of the new style.

Although Lucknow had a larger Hindu than Muslim population during nawabi rule (as indeed it does today), Muslim influence became disproportionately greater in many of the arts, including architecture, and brick-built Hindu houses of the nawabi period closely resemble those of Muslims. Strictly speaking, there should have been a marked difference between Hindu and Muslim houses since the former neither required a purdah section for women nor a specific building for religious worship, as wealthy Muslim households did. But the overall plan of the well-to-do houses of both communities are so similar that a Muslim house may be taken as fairly representative of indigenous Lucknow building.

Such a house consists of two courtyards, side by side. The larger one, the *mardana* or men's quarter, opens on to the street through a narrow gateway, and the zenana or women's quarter can only be entered from the men's courtyard. Around each side of both courtyards are rooms, often with a small verandah that helps to shade the rooms from the sun and allows the inhabitants to enjoy the open air while being partially protected by the verandah roof. The rooms round the courtyard seldom have any windows in the far walls other than small high grilles for ventilation, and it is unusual to find interconnecting doors between the rooms except in the larger and grander houses. Of course there are variations depending upon the inclination and, more important, the purse of the owner, but the basic pattern remains remarkably consistent. P.C. Mookherji, who lived in Lucknow and wrote an outstanding book on the city, has an important chapter on domestic architecture in which he describes the house of a rich Muslim following the pattern mentioned above.[1] The gate opening on to the street will have a guard house, either on one side of the gate if it is one-storeyed, or in more elaborate buildings in a room over the main gateway. This can also house the *naubat khana*, a room with a balcony from which kettledrums and other musical instruments are sounded to mark the passing of the hours or the arrival of an important guest. Inside the first gateway may be a small courtyard around which are the servants' quarters, which in turn lead through another gateway directly opposite the first one into the mardana, a large and airy courtyard surrounded by cells or rooms. To one side but still flush with the line of rooms will be an *imambara*, a religious building connected with ceremonies of the Shi'a sect of Islam, or if the owner is a Sunni (as are the majority of Muslims) there will be a small *masjid* or mosque for the family's private worship. Near the imambara or masjid will be a large sitting room which is often like a hall divided by arches and columns, and usually facing the main gateway. To the side of this room will be the apartments of the divan, the manager of the house and the estate, since most owners of a house this size will undoubtedly have lands or a village outside the city. Further on will be the rooms of the *maulvi* who would instruct the boys of the family. The upper storey of the mardana would consist of more airy rooms and pavilions, used

[1] Mookherji, pp. 205–9.

during both winter and summer. In the hot season *tattis* or reed curtains made of *khus-khus* grass would be hung in the doors or archways. Water sprinkled frequently over these curtains, which give off a pleasant smell when wet, would help cool the room by evaporation. In the winter the tattis would be replaced by thick padded curtains, carpets spread on the floor, and small charcoal braziers or *sigris* used for heating. The steps to the upper storeys would, in the majority of cases, be on the outside of the building and would lead right up to the flat roof enclosed by a low parapet.

The zenana which leads off the men's quarters may have a wall directly in front of the gateway, or even two gateways linked by a passage to preclude any accidental sighting of the women from the men's quarters. Three sides of the zenana will consist of small living rooms while the fourth will house the kitchen and storerooms. There are no outside openings in the walls of the zenana, and even the roof will have a high solid parapet with small grilles let in at intervals. Traditionally the height of a zenana wall had to be such that a man standing on the back of an elephant could not see over the walls,[2] and in Lucknow at least no distinguished visitor, foreign or otherwise, was allowed to ascend a minaret or tower of a religious building without previous public notice having been given so that the women could conceal themselves.

Now consider a typically European-style house in the city, for example the Dilkusha which was built about 1800 by Gore Ouseley, friend of Saadat Ali Khan and one-time Acting British Resident. The immediate difference between the traditional house and the Dilkusha is that there are no interior courtyards and that one is presented with a solid block of masonry containing all the rooms with their different functions gathered together. Photographs of the Dilkusha show that the house expanded upwards rather than outwards and that the doors and windows were an essential element in the decoration of the façade. There is an imposing staircase lead-

[2] Parks, Fanny, *Wanderings of a Pilgrim in Search of the Picturesque*, vol. i (London 1850), 2 Sep. 1831, no. 9, p. 183. Hereafter Parks.

ing to the main door with its highly ornamental portico. There is no apparent shading from the sun other than the wooden venetian blinds at the glazed windows, and though it is not visible from photographs the very un-Indian towers at the corners of the building contain circular staircases, so it is not necessary to go outside the house in order to climb to the upper floors or the roof. All this is in such direct contrast with the traditional Indian house that it might seem at first that a synthesis between the two styles was impossible, and indeed many Lucknow buildings of nawabi times that sought to bridge the gap failed miserably by merely incorporating unimportant European decorations into an unchanged Indian house.

But a successful synthesis of styles was achieved in a surprisingly large number of houses in and around the city, and achieved with care, with wit, and occasionally with great dignity and splendour. Consider for example the Indo-European house of Barowen (also spelt Baronne) now known as Musa Bagh. Completed in 1803/4 for the nawab Saadat Ali Khan and probably based on plans by Claude Martin, it lies three miles due west of Lucknow. Traces of a nawabi brick road remain, leading in a line from the city palaces to Barowen but the usual method of approach was by river, the Gomti previously running nearer to the house than it does at present. As early as 1831 the road was considered "almost impassable" and it is this inaccessibility that has preserved so much of the building.[3] Only the villagers from the nearby village of Barowen who dig out chunks of masonry to dam their fields for irrigation purposes and a few half-hearted treasure seekers disturb the ruins of this magnificent building.[4] There is only one known drawing of Barowen from the river side, executed in 1814 by Robert Smith who accompanied

[3] Foreign Pol. Con., 2 Sept. 1821, nos 95–6.

[4] The house of Barowen was named after a neighbouring village, which was noted by Tieffenthaler in 1765 as being a large village lying about a quarter of a mile from the Gomti. The name Barowen applied to the house seems to have been discontinued about 1830 and it was not until I questioned local villagers on the names of surrounding villages that I was able to identify Musa Bagh as Barowen. The name Musa Bagh is supposed to be a corruption of Monsieur, meaning the

Lady Nugent on a tour of northern India. Barowen had then been standing for ten years and Smith's drawing shows the grandeur of the architect's concept, though it is not until one walks over the site that one appreciates the subtlety and understanding of the architect. The high wall in Smith's drawing that effectively divides the back and front of Barowen also marks the artificial hill which the architect utilised, for although the house is three storeys at the front and rises grandly from a flat plain, behind the wall there are only two storeys above ground and a large sunken courtyard which is reached by descending the spiral steps in the octagonal kiosks at the far corners of the building. The reason for the sunken courtyard was that the surrounding earth cooled the small rooms and the verandah here, while the front portion of the house made an impressive winter residence. The house is so constructed that it was possible to enter through the handsome semi-circular portico on the river side and to walk straight through the building into the sunken courtyard without descending any steps, as the courtyard floor is exactly level with the ground floor.

It is this perfect synthesis of a European house in the grand tradition with the practical Indian additions of a large open courtyard surrounded on three sides by small rooms – and the little airy pavilions on the roof – that make this one of the most satisfying buildings

---

Frenchman's Garden, but it seems more likely that *musa* is the Urdu word meaning "something that is bequeathed or willed, a legacy", or *mauza*, "a place, a plot of land, a village or a district". (Both meanings from Platt's *Urdu Dictionary*.) An old man who lived about a mile from Barowen recalled and translated a song he knew when young, supposedly relating to the treasure of Barowen. After instructions on how to reach the treasure, the song continues, "nine hundred bowls filled with gold and covered with silver plates are stored there. The chamber is decorated with diamonds, emeralds, rubies and pearls. You'll be dazzled on looking at the walls." The song is interesting, not because I believe there is any treasure in Barowen but because it illustrates the belief of local people in the vast wealth and riches of the nawabs. The immense sums of money which were spent on European furniture is here translated into something more easily recognisable as precious – i.e. rubies, emeralds, and pearls.

in Lucknow. No one who sees it, even in its ruined condition, could fail to speculate on the enrichment to architecture had this intelligent compromise been followed more often, but Barowen stands as an almost unique example of what might have been. A visitor in 1824 says that there "was a well-judged union of the comfort of the English with the splendour and magnificence of the Asiatic style throughout its numerous and extensive apartments,"[5] and an examination of the remaining ruins bears witness to the extremely high quality of the workmanship. There were delicate stucco friezes both on the interior and exterior walls, and a judicious use of sandstone for the brackets supporting the cornice round the two top floors and the plinths of the groups of columns. Two of the most interesting decorations are the stucco "sun-burst" designs inside the domes of the octagonal kiosks, where the "rays" spread down the domes and the face of the sun is the circular opening in the top of the dome; and the witty imitation of rolled up tatties or blinds over each arch in the courtyard, which are lovingly reproduced in stucco even to the string holding up the blind and the frill of material over each arch. Traces of red and white decoration still remain over some of these arches after more than a century of neglect.

Whatever the original motives behind their construction, these houses, and others like them, seem to have been little used except as places to which European visitors were taken during their conducted tours of Lucknow. It cannot be claimed that these country houses added much to the beautification of Lucknow as they were some way outside the city, nor were they designed for the edification of the population, because unlike Europeanised buildings inside Lucknow they were never accessible to the general public.

Now it is obvious that the change in style between these Indo-European houses and traditional buildings would lead to a reappraisal of the land surrounding them. The native house presents a rather forbidding and bleak appearance to a pedestrian in a typical

[5] Forrest, Lt. Col., *A Picturesque Tour Along the Ganges and Jumna* (London 1824), p. 164. Hereafter Forrest.

Indian street. Obviously the zenana portion of such a house is not built to look inviting, but then neither is the mardana. Often the only decoration at all on a street of Indian houses is over the gateway set in a high wall. There is no hint of what kind of building is behind the gate, and seldom any clue to the identity or status of the owner. It is still a very common experience in the older part of Lucknow to walk along narrow and filthy alleys where the sunlight never falls because of the proximity of high walls on either side, and then suddenly to enter an insignificant gateway into a large and splendid courtyard with highly decorated rooms, pleasant gardens and even fountains. The whole place is very clean because the sweepers sweep all the refuse out into the street – this is not regarded as belonging in any way to the owners of the house. In fact an Indian street seems to be regarded merely as the space between houses, a kind of no-man's land along which one walks gingerly, handkerchief held to one's nose, until the safety and cleanliness of a house is reached.

There is little reason to believe that Lucknow's old streets have changed drastically over the past two hundred years, from the time when Tieffenthaler and Hodges were complaining bitterly about their narrowness and filth. Now looking again at the Dilkusha, or any of the numerous European-style buildings of Lucknow, it is obvious that the architects designed these houses specifically to present a striking front to the passerby. Such houses must be seen in their entirety from the street, they cannot be appreciated from behind high walls. Every detail of their façades is intended to draw the eye and since one needs to be able to stand back some distance to admire these houses, they are not surrounded by narrow dark alleys, but by gardens, or at least wide streets. The houses become "public property", at least visually, and thereby the streets also are public streets, not merely spaces between houses. So the building of European-style houses meant not just a change in external decoration, nor the shifting of a few rooms and corridors, but in fact a reappraisal of the whole milieu in which the new houses were built. There is no doubt that the nawabs and their wealthy subjects who imitated them were making a conscious and deliberate decision when they asked Europeans in Lucknow to design such houses for them.

Asaf-ud-daula was particularly fond of the new-style houses and at the start of his reign in 1775 asked the British Resident at the Lucknow court to "procure him the plan of a house after the European taste." This was drawn up for him and subsequently executed by Captain Marsack who was in charge of one of the nawab's battalions stationed at Lucknow.[6] His successor Saadat Ali Khan, during whose time some of the greatest Lucknow houses were built, was responsible for making Hazratganj (in the newer, eastern part of the city), one of the most splendid streets. With its handsome European-style houses on each side of a broad road it led Bishop Heber to exclaim in 1825 that "Lucknow has more resemblance to some of the smaller European capitals (Dresden for instance), than anything which I have seen in India."[7] So the distinct change in the pattern of Lucknow's streets, away from the narrow nullahs and ganjes of the old city and towards the more "Europeanised" eastern part was, in no small way, attributable to the new taste of European-style housing.

Among the vernacular buildings those dwellings should be considered which were neither brick-built traditional Indian houses nor the Europeanised houses of the nawabs and rich Indians or Europeans – the bungalows. As the name implies, the idea of building small, single-storey houses, with thatched roofs and small verandahs formed from the overhanging thatch originated in Bengal. The advantages of bungalows in India are fairly obvious. They can be quickly erected using materials readily to hand – leaves and straw for the roof, sundried bricks or wattle and daub for the walls, with bamboo or wood supports for the eaves and the doors. The raised platform on which such bungalows usually stand can be

[6] Secret Index, 18 Sept. 1775. No number given. National Archives, New Delhi.

[7] Heber, Bishop Reginald, *Narrative of a Journey through the Upper Provinces of India from Calcutta to Bombay, 1824–1825* (London 1828), i, p. 383. Hereafter Heber.

made from beaten earth, with rubble for firmness, or planks. The peculiar shape of the roof, which has been frequently reproduced in Mughal buildings of stone, ensures good drainage during the monsoon.[8]

William Hodges' description of Lucknow houses in 1782 gave an impression of a poor town – "The city is extensive, but meanly built: the houses are chiefly mud walls, covered with thatch, and many consist entirely of mats and bamboos and are thatched with leaves of the cocoa nut, very few indeed of the houses of the natives are built with brick."[9] In fact Hodges was describing bungalows, and the hitherto odd statement that one of the nawabs lived in "his private mud-house" where the Qaisarbagh tombs now stand becomes more explicable.[10]

Living in a bungalow was not considered shameful or a sign of poverty, as Hodges had assumed; rather it was recognised as a simple and obvious expedient. Because of lack of time, lack of elaborate building materials or skilled craftspeople, one lived in bungalows as a temporary measure, or during certain seasons of the year, especially the campaigning season. Modave has a good description of a bungalow at Faizabad which grew up simply because it was the military base for operations by earlier nawabs, when it was called "Bangla" in recognition of this:

> It is a pavilion of bamboo covered with thatch or leaves from trees which one constructs in haste for some special occasion, like a marriage, a big fete, a meeting place during the hunt, or simply a meeting place. It is magnificently adorned with hangings, with beautiful chintzes and with mirrors or lustres etc. People dance and play and eat there. The *soubas* [subahs, or Governors] of Lucknow had one of these banglas put up

[8] The exhibition organised by Anthony King, University of Leicester, held at RIBA in January 1974, traced the development of the bungalow from its earliest indigenous form in Bengal to substantial British buildings in India in the late nineteenth century and eventually to twentieth-century adaptations in British seaside towns.

[9] Hodges, p. 100.

[10] Mookherji, p. 24.

> thirty years ago, in the place that is now Fezabad. The site on the banks of the river Gogra pleased them. It became a rendezvous for the Hunt, which gradually became a large town, something quite easy in the Indies where one does not build except of earth, and where five or six months can suffice to construct a town.[11]

Since a bungalow by its very nature is a rather ephemeral building, in its most basic form it tends to be neglected in descriptions of Indian towns. But it must not be forgotten that the majority of inhabitants of eighteenth-century Lucknow lived in bungalows rather than stuccoed houses.

One must now ask why the majority of Europeans chose to build in the European manner rather than to adapt or inhabit what already existed. Although there were perfectly good Indian houses, most early European settlers seem to have ignored indigenous building with the same perversity that kept them in clothes more suited to a chilly northern climate than the subcontinent. "When the English first visited India, they adopted a mode of building by no means consistent with common sense, and displaying a total ignorance of the most simple of nature's laws," wrote Captain Thomas Williamson in 1810. Houses built between 1750 and 1770 were constructed "more like ovens, than like the habitations of enlightened beings. The doors were very small, the windows still less, in proportion, while the roofs were carried up many feet above both,"[12] and in town houses in Calcutta during the middle of the century families passed uncomfortably hot days in rooms on the first floors until they realised that the ground floors which were being used as storage rooms, or even stables, were much cooler. Common sense prevailed to some degree and later town houses were built with taller ground floor apartments, with storage rooms on the smaller upper floors. But the point to be noted here is that these later, more sensible, modifications were made to "European"

[11] Modave, p. 439.

[12] Williamson, Capt. Thomas, *The East India Vade-Mecum*, vol. ii (London 1810), p. 6. Hereafter Williamson.

houses; there was no attempt to Indianise the houses at all. Why then were European-style houses, with all their faults, preferred?

The answer seems to be twofold – a feeling of superiority engendered by the possession of such houses, and the homesickness in an alien culture which could to some extent be ameliorated by the attempt to reproduce the familiar. Of course what might be considered familiar by some people was often a long way beyond the grasp of the ordinary European at home, but because of the cheapness of labour and materials in India even relatively humble Europeans could aspire to something much grander than was possible in their own country. All the evidence shows that it was considerably cheaper to build such houses in India, even when Indian workpeople had to be instructed in European methods. In India the average price for a large detached house in its own grounds at the end of the eighteenth century was about £4000, while a house of similar pretensions with the same amount of land in England was changing hands at the astronomical price of £85,000.[13] It was estimated that in 1778 an English house, Barrington Hall in Hertfordshire, not dissimilar in its ground plan to Claude Martin's town house, the Château de Lyon (later renamed Farhad Baksh), would cost £14,500 to build and was to consist of a brick core faced with stone dug locally.[14] The Château, also built with a brick core but faced with stucco was, on the other hand, sold in 1800 to Joseph Quieros, Martin's Spanish steward, for a mere £4000.[15] Even Beecher's "House upon a large scale" with its outbuildings and extensive garden was only valued at £5000 in 1814, and because this particular valuation was made in an effort to obtain compensation for the seizure of the estate, it was the highest value that Beecher thought he could put on the property. A single marble chimneypiece in an English country-house[16] cost more than the stables

[13] Hussey, Christopher, *English Country Houses*, vol. iii (London 1956), p. 27. Hereafter Hussey.

[14] Hussey, ii, p. 85.

[15] Valentia, i, p. 166.

[16] Hussey, iii, p. 54.

erected in Lucknow at about the same time (£98.8s. compared with £63).[17] A complete bungalow with glass windows, tiled roofs, and outbuildings could be built in India for only £500 in 1810,[18] while the Gothic church in the Lucknow Residency area cost only £540 in 1837, with a further £70 spent on the gates, the walls, the railings and the outbuildings.[19]

Why was it so cheap to build in India? Obviously wages for Indian workpeople were very low – a master mason received less than 6d. a day.[20] But the price of materials was also extremely cheap – as was the land: 100,000 nawabi bricks cost only £3.25.6d,[21] compared to £90 for the same quantity of purchased bricks in England.[22] Indian bricks were considered so cheap that they were used for road building. Stone, however, was expensive and difficult to obtain in Lucknow. Both marble and red sandstone had to be brought from Agra, Jaipur, or even further west and, in 1795, 3050 marble slabs of unspecified size were valued at £1000 in Lucknow, one-fourth of the price of a large house there.[23] This helps to explain why the art of imitating stone by using stucco was developed to such a very high degree. Where an elaborately carved marble fire-place would have been erected in a large English house, Indian builders achieved a similar effect with highly polished stucco built up over a brick core at a fraction of the price.

Although Europeans in India built themselves fine houses while marvelling at the small cost of materials and the low wages of the native builders, they never made any correlation between these wages and the wretchedness of the native workmen and women. The dirt and squalor of the old part of Lucknow was frequently

[17] Foreign Pol. Con., 19 June 1807, no. 66.

[18] Williamson, ii, p. 11.

[19] Foreign Pol. Con., 18 Sept. 1839, nos 94 and 95.

[20] *Gazetteer of the Province of Oude* (Allahabad 1877), ii, p. 393.

[21] Ibid.

[22] Hussey, ii, p. 98.

[23] The Cases of Ozias Humphry & James Paull. Hereafter Humphry & Paull. Add. MSS 13,532, F.9. B.L.

commented on but with no attempt at an analysis of why there should be so much visible poverty in a brilliant and splendid town such as this. No one thought fit to remark that a society in which Saadat Ali Khan paid his Scots engineer Captain Duncan MacLeod £150 per month in 1812,[24] while a master mason earned 15s. a month to construct the buildings that MacLeod designed, was not a particularly healthy society.

The Europeans were not always happy with the work that the native workers did so cheaply for them either. Thomas Williamson, writing about stucco decorations of rooms in the Upper Provinces in 1810, says: "These mouldings [*sic*] etc. are all done by means of trowels shaped for the purpose, and not by moulds, or stamps." The native workman will do them with "great ingenuity, consummate patience and often great delicacy; but, with respect to design, taste, composition, perspective, consistency, and harmony . . . he will prove himself to be completely ignoramus."[25] Almost forty years later Colesworthy Grant wrote quite seriously, "Home English readers may not be familiar with the fact of the almost non-existence of the fine arts in this country – engraving, for other than cards, name-plates and small maps, being unknown."[26]

While not denying that Indians possessed a range of skills, it was consistently denied that they had any taste and that therefore they had to be supervised by Europeans. A further manifestation of this devaluing of Indian work was the persistent idea that Claude Martin had imported Italian workmen to build his houses, particularly Constantia, to the south-east of Lucknow. Europeans found it difficult to believe that the beautiful stucco work inside the house and the statues on the parapets had been done by native craftsmen. In fact Constantia was only half-completed on Martin's death when he left his designs and plans to be executed by "my faithful servant Mutchoo" and his brother "Chutta Khaddir who both are very

[24] Foreign Pol. Con., 29 Feb. 1812, no. 19.

[25] Williamson, ii. p. 30.

[26] Grant, Colesworthy, *An Anglo-Indian Domestic Sketch* (Calcutta 1849), introduction, no pagination.

well acquainted how and in what mode I carry on these Buildings as well in buying material as in paying the workmen."[27] There is no evidence that Martin used European labour at all in any of his buildings; on the contrary there is every indication that local people worked under Martin's sole supervision and after his death under the direction of the two servants whom Martin had trained to read and interpret his plans. But it was part of the myth that anything out of the ordinary must have been done by Europeans, just as unfounded rumours today suggest that the Taj Mahal may have been built by Italians.

A very few commentators in Britain did remark on the scornful attitudes of their fellow countrymen towards India. The Hon. F.J. Shore wrote in 1835 – "First and foremost stands the fixed creed of the English, that everything of English origin, or appertaining to ourselves, must be superior to everything connected with the natives." Such an attitude, when carried to its perfectly logical conclusion, Shore complained, produced the syllogism – "Oude is a native government, – ergo, it is very inferior to the British rule."[28] Shore's protest went unheeded, for a decade later a writer in the *Calcutta Review* had to make the same point again: "It is too much the fashion to undervalue what is Indian. That which is noticeable in itself is not to be noticed because it is Indian."[29] Both are reasonable and just comments, but such attempts to hold the balance were quite swamped in the general belief that Indian things were automatically second rate. It is also of course a common human failing to undervalue what one obtains too cheaply.

The initial sense of wonder experienced by seventeenth-century Europeans in India quickly gave way to an innate sense of superiority often embodied in their large and pompous buildings. Consider for a moment the instructions issued by Lord Ongley to his architect

[27] Claude Martin's Will, dated 1 Jan. 1800. La Martinière copy, Lucknow. Hereafter Claude Martin's Will.

[28] Shore, Hon. F.J., *Notes on Indian Affairs* (London 1857), p. 269. Hereafter Shore.

[29] *Calcutta Review* (Calcutta 1844), Oct.–Dec., p. 381.

in 1770 – "I require a mansion worthy of the position I occupy with regard to my tenantry, and worthy of the landskip [*sic*] in which I have chosen to place it. First let it be convenient, next let it be elegant without ostentation, impressive without Italian or Gothick heaviness, desirable without exciting the envy of the covetous, yet calculated to impress the mean-spirited."[30] This was to be a house in England, but the sentiments when transposed to an Indian setting are entirely apt. Undoubtedly many Europeans in India saw the functions of their own buildings not only as places to live in, but as monuments designed to impress the humble native, his less humble Indian master, and other Europeans with less taste or money. Lord Wellesley, in attempting to justify the expense of the new government house in Calcutta, said that his English critics "ought to remember that India is a country of splendour, of extravagance and of outward appearances, that the Head of a mighty Empire ought to conform himself to the prejudices of the country he rules over, that the British, in particular, ought to emulate the splendid works of the Princes of the House of Timour."[31] In Lucknow too, this idea of educating by bricks and mortar is perfectly expressed in a description of the Château (Farhad Baksh), which not only "gave many proofs of his [Claude Martin's] own superior talents and ingenuity, to the great delight of the intelligent traveller and neighbouring natives," but also the building and its contents "have not a little contributed to impress the less informed of the natives of that remote part of the country with just ideas of the superiority of European taste and knowledge."[32]

It is no coincidence either that the style in which the majority of Europeans chose to build in India was the neo-Classical, Graeco-Roman revival which became increasingly popular in Europe in the last part of the eighteenth century. Many travellers in India during this

[30] Betjeman, John, *Ghastly Good Taste* (London 1933), p. 53.

[31] Bearce, George, *British Attitudes towards India* (London 1961), p. 47. Hereafter Bearce.

[32] "An Account of Colonel Martin's Villa, near Lucknow", *The European Magazine* (London 1790), vol. xvii, Jan-June, pp. 86–7.

period have declared that "European" towns and individual houses reminded them forcibly of Greece and Rome,[33] and the intention of the designers and builders of such houses was that the "intelligent traveller" would make the obvious correlation between those buildings which had once impressed barbaric races under Roman rule and similar buildings now used by the British who found themselves, as they imagined, masters of a pagan and unruly people. It is no exaggeration to say that European architecture was held to have a "civilising" effect on the "poor Indian, whose untutored mind Sees God in clouds or hears him in the wind."[34] Too many descriptions of "European" buildings in India have expressed this idea, either consciously or unconsciously, for it to be dismissed as a minor by-product of colonial thinking. By 1849 the idea of superiority in every sphere was so integral a part of European thinking that the following statement could pass not only uncriticized but be actively applauded – "The mission of the European to India was not to *find* a highly principled, educated and enlightened people, but to aid in *making* them so."[35] And how better to begin the task of carrying the white man's burden than by building a suitable house for him to reside in.

But the most potent factor that led Europeans to try to recreate a familiar world in an unfamiliar environment was that of homesickness. This intangible but powerful emotion should never be underrated in dealing with European attitudes in India. It seemed to affect everyone in some degree, from the rich and successful to the ordinary English soldier – who could hardly have led an easy life at home. Widespread among the British abroad was the feeling of being exiled from everything decent and good and the idea that time spent in India was an onerous duty that would be duly rewarded on one's home leave. The fact that quite often the "exiles"

[33] Nilsson, Sten, *European Architecture in India 1750–1850* (London 1968), p. 25. Hereafter Nilsson.

[34] Bearce, p. 11.

[35] Grant, Colesworthy, *Rural Life in Bengal* (London 1849), p. 47. Hereafter Grant.

returned with their health seriously impaired and were seldom able to afford the standard of living at home to which they had become accustomed while in India was usually glossed over in emotive but poignant passages like the following, written in 1845:

> We are wanderers, and not voluntary wanderers; and even the most fortunate – what is their sense of home? The merchant or the presidency civilian, or the staff-officer – the only fixtures of which Indian society can boast – may choose his own residence within a circle of half a dozen miles, but when he thinks of home, he sees the masts of the tall passenger ships, which make a forest of the Hoogly, or stud the ocean which washes the beaches of Madras or Bombay, and beyond this a snug English house, with its shrubbery and trim garden-walks, and its sunny fruit walls luscious with the ruddy peach and ruddier nectarine. An Indian home is but a lodging house, or way-side inn, in which the exile kills time, as best he can until it is permitted to him to proceed on the last stage of his journey homewards.[36]

The sense of impermanence was all the more strong since both civilian and military officers were usually transferred every three years on average, from one rented bungalow to another, so that they had little chance to put down roots in any one area of India, even had they wished to.

Even the European who had appeared to settle down in India (i.e. those outside the Company's service) and had bought or built a large house was not immune to similar emotions of homesickness. Claude Martin who died leaving an immense fortune and huge estates did not feel happy in Lucknow and longed for the intellectual stimulation of Europe where "a man of a Modest Independancy has a thousand Diversions if he Chuse to pursue arts, Sciences, phisicks or philosophy or visit Play Concert or Show." Though Martin had a large circle of European friends both in Lucknow and Calcutta he felt the hardest thing for the exiled European in India was "loosing [*sic*] a friend, constantly, as well as by the fatal strokes of Death, or Going home." His letters express well the feeling of insularity among Europeans, even those who spent long periods of time in India and

[36] *Calcutta Review* (Calcutta 1845), Jan.–June, p. 95.

who would have been expected to have had more contact with Indians than the Company's officials. Martin writes of his friends still remaining in India, but hastily qualifies this by explaining: "I don't mean among the Black peoples . . . sincerity, friendship, Gratitude are words not known in their Dictionary. You will say, how Could [I] live among such lot of Peoples? In reply I have lived very little among them really! Theirs Companys I alway avoided . . . I have been respected and that is all I wanted from the Natives."[37]

Such attitudes had many implications for both Indians and Europeans, but in the latters' case it tended to lead to petty and silly manifestations of homesickness and a denigration of all things Indian. One wonders at the assurance of a race which imported mouse-traps, not to mention cucumber-slicers, to India, "but such is the *perversity of human nature* that here nothing is fit to touch but what is British – but they go still further, and every thing must be made by some particular hand in London from a carriage to a farthing biscuit . . . in short everything is reckoned mere trash unless it comes from England."[38]

Visitors to the Lucknow Resident's "palace" in the cantonment to the north of the city were astonished but delighted at the sight of a herd of English cattle which Mordaunt Ricketts, the Resident, had had sent out about 1827.[39] These English cows reminded one traveller, Emma Roberts, of happy associations and "pastoral recollections" in English meads;[40] it had the same effect on another traveller, reminding him of "sweet home . . . but I looked in vain for the rosy-faced and elbowed dairy maids of Derbyshire, whose functions were ill-sustained by mustachioed and half-naked natives."[41]

[37] Ozias Humphry Collection. Claude Martin to Ozias Humphry, 11 March 1789. Royal Academy Library, London.

[38] Massie, W.H., "Eastern Sketches", MSS., 1826, f. 152, I.O.L.

[39] Mordaunt Rickett's wife had also received two English-bred calves as a new year present in 1824 from the nawab. Bengal Pol. Con., 14 Jan. 1825, no. 13.

[40] Roberts, Emma, *Scenes and Characteristics of Hindostan* (1837), i, p. 350.

[41] Mundy, Captain, *Pen & Pencil Sketches, Being the Journal of a Tour in India* (London 1832), i, p. 35.

Indian reality had a distressing way of intruding into the British way of life abroad. A further attempt to create a familiar atmosphere by building an "English village" near the Dilkusha, the large country house to the south-east of the city, was apparently a failure. A visitor in 1827 found only the ruins of some mud huts on the site and commented bitterly, "Heaven knows, the spire, the elms and hedgerows, and white-washed honeysuckled walls, were all left to the imagination; and even in the extreme of credulity, if such an idea could have existed, the furious hot winds would have parched it immediately."[42] Homesickness was felt and induced in every sphere, from the lack of intellectual stimulation, the bleakness of an Indian kitchen without the familiar dresser, stove and oven, and the absence of pleasant country walks where English children could pick wild flowers in safety without being leapt upon by "snakes, envenomed caterpillars, and ants half an inch in length."[43]

Many Europeans made no attempt to come to terms with their unfamiliar and, as they hoped, temporary surroundings, though long periods of service without leave often meant years abroad, if not death, in India. Others tried to rationalise or explain the exotic phenomena they saw by constant reference to more familiar things. Bishop Heber's writings on India are a particularly good example of this. He seemed unable to see Indian scenes without being constantly reminded of something nearer home. Calcutta reminded him of St Petersburg and Moscow, and when he got to Lucknow he described Hazratganj as "wider than the High Street at Oxford, but having some distant resemblance to it in the colour of its buildings and the general form and Gothic style of the greater part of them." The Rumi Darwaza and the Great Imambara on the other hand reminded him of Eaton, the Earl of Grosvenor's seat in Cheshire,[44] and his drawing of it (from memory) shows how Heber has completely changed the gateway in an attempt to make the exotic more

[42] Archer, Major, *Tours in Upper India* (London 1833), i, p. 23. Hereafter Archer.

[43] Grant, p. 89.

[44] Heber, i, p. 386.

explicable. The Indian towers on each side of the gateway now appear like European medieval towers with battlements along the top. The Indian arches have been narrowed and elongated to appear like arrow slits and the whole of the "cobra-head" design round the main arch has been lost, while the two small kiosks on columns become "look out" battlemented towers.

A European writer claimed as early as 1816 that Lucknow "will forcibly bring to the recollection of an Englishman those cities of his native land; the same streets, fine houses, and meadows fertilized by the Goomty."[45] Europeans, and especially the British, were desperately anxious to convince themselves that parts of India were like Britain: even a place as exotic as Lucknow could be familiarised (with a certain amount of licence) to resemble home, and later in the century when the British were able to build what *they* chose – as in Simla – they recreated areas which were practically indistinguishable from the real thing. Although it could be argued that Heber and others were trying to describe to those in Britain points of reference to help them understand India, this is disproved by other artists in the late eighteenth century like Thomas and William Daniell and William Hodges who made no attempt to patronise the spectators' intelligence, but presented what they saw in all its alien and sometimes inexplicable splendour. To sum up, it must be emphasised that whenever a "European" building was erected in Lucknow for any or all of the motives discussed above, it was another tangible reminder to the citizens that a strange and powerful race was settling in their city, influencing their rulers and introducing different ideas. And these new ideas, unfortunately, invariably seemed to lead to a denigration of Indian ways. "Englishmen . . . it is certain will find fault with every system of Government or politics which may not accord with the English model," wrote Nawab Wajid Ali Shah after his deposition by the British in 1856.[46] Had that realisation come to earlier nawabs there may well have been a total ban

[45] Anon., *Sketches of India* (London 1816), p. 151, B.L.

[46] Shah, Nawab Wajid Ali, *Reply to the Charges against the King of Oude* (Calcutta, no date, but post-1856), p. 38. Hereafter *Reply to Charges*.

on Europeans settling in Lucknow at all, apart perhaps from a segregated Residency area, and the history of Lucknow, architecturally as well as politically, might well have been very different.

But what were the motives of the nawabs who also chose to build in the European style? Apart from the political pressures I suggest there were four reasons that prompted them to build European-style houses for themselves – the prestige that such buildings brought them; a wish to imitate the elite of Europe; an immense curiosity with the artifacts produced by the West together with the financial means to gratify this interest; and lastly a yielding to the persuasions of Europeans in India who were anxious to sell things to the nawabs.

There was a considerable amount of Europeanisation at the courts of the early nawabs in Lucknow, exhibited in dress, in entertainments, in furnishings and trinkets, and especially in architecture though not, it seems, in the private and domestic lives of the nawabs and their noblemen. Because the descriptions of court life are all by Europeans it was natural that they would note the things which were most familiar, rather than incomprehensible rituals and customs – just as most writers describing the architecture of the city sought what they conceived to be familiar points of reference.

As early as 1786 Ozias Humphry, the artist, who was dining with Husain Reza Khan, Asaf-ud-daula's chief minister, remarked: "If I looked no further than the Tea table, I could persuade myself I was in London," to which the minister gallantly replied: "For some years their Interest had been so connected and Interwoven with the English that they endeavoured in all matters that they could with propriety to accommodate themselves to these Manners."[47] Asaf-ud-daula had in fact proved so accommodating towards the British that he lavished enormous sums of money on all kinds of knick-knacks that were brought to his notice, from mirrors and lustres costing two or three thousand pounds each to worthless little paintings and paper lanterns. Between 1787 and 1797 it was estimated that he had spent about one million pounds sterling on European ar-

[47] Diary of Ozias Humphry.

ticles, most of which he seems to have received duty free through various agencies in Calcutta or private individuals commissioned to buy goods for him.[48] Visitors who saw the Aina Khana where Asaf-ud-daula kept his treasures described it as a mixture of museum and lumber room, "full of European articles of every kind" with "clocks and watches by Cox & Co. of London and other persons" and "a valuable chronometer, or one which had been sold as such, [which] would be suspended next to a common watch of the most ordinary description, and which indeed, had possibly cost the Nabob as much as the chronometer."[49]

It was the price that Asaf-ud-daula paid for his treasures that alarmed many who, while criticising him for his extreme childishness and his wish to "procure every thing that was singular, or that he heard praised",[50] nevertheless blamed the Europeans in Lucknow for pandering to the nawab's eclectic tastes. Claude Martin was especially singled out for blame in obtaining goods for the nawab from Europe which he sold at a handsome profit, but he was certainly not alone in this. Several traders in Lucknow bought goods which they hoped to sell to the nawab or his wealthy noblemen, including James Paull who had "192 china toys and 62 tumbling boys" valued at £400 specially sent up from Calcutta,[51] and the artist Thomas Daniell brought with him some snuff boxes and knives which a friend had asked him to sell, and which the nawab bought.[52] Even the British Residents were not above selling curiosities to the nawabs at vastly inflated prices, a practice which though condemned continued for a considerable time. Whether Asaf-ud-daula saw himself as a serious collector and a patron of the arts in the grand European manner or whether he merely found it

[48] *Asiatic Annual Register* (London 1804), p. 11.

[49] Twining, Thomas, *Travels in India a Hundred Years Ago* (London 1893), p. 311. Hereafter Twining.

[50] Valentia, i, p. 155.

[51] Humphry & Paull, f. 9.

[52] Hardie M., and Clayton M., "Thomas Daniell & William Daniell", *Walker's Quarterly*, nos 35–6 (London 1932), p. 64. Hereafter Hardie & Clayton.

impossible to refuse European goods urged on him by greedy men is difficult to say. One suspects he intended the former, but generally became renowned for the latter. Certainly his court attracted an unusual number of British artists who expected the patronage of the nawab, even though they were frequently disappointed at the prices they eventually received for their paintings. William Hodges, Ozias Humphry, William and Thomas Daniell, Johan Zoffany, Thomas Longcroft, and Francesco Renaldi all passed through the court between 1775 and 1797 and Charles Smith, George Place, and George Duncan Beechey were resident painters in Lucknow.[53]

Saadat Ali Khan, Asaf-ud-daula's brother and successor, also had a strong predilection for European things, probably fostered by the early education bestowed on him with "much care" by Madame Galliez, a French lady from Chandernagore,[54] and by his "exile" spent in Calcutta after he was implicated in the murder of one of his brother's favourites in Lucknow. An Englishwoman who knew Saadat Ali Khan well said he was "certainly not a Mussulman [Muslim at heart, for I have frequently heard him ridicule their prejudices . . . he had unconsciously imbibed many English ideas . . . he understood the English language perfectly, and wrote it correctly but could not pronounce the words."[55] This nawab often wore European dress, including an English admiral's uniform, and two suits of "canonicals" which he had had made for him in Calcutta as well as "two Wiggs of every denomination according to the English fashion,"[56] and he enjoyed entertaining visitors in a Western way. "The dinner was French, with plenty of wine" in "an English apartment, a band in English regimentals, playing English tunes, a room lighted by magnificent girandoles [branched candle-brackets], English tables, chairs, and looking glasses, an English service of

[53] Archer, Mildred, *India and British Portraiture 1770–1825* (London 1979).

[54] Modave, p. 439.

[55] Deane, Ann, *A Tour through the Upper Provinces of Hindostan* (London 1823), p. 103.

[56] *Calcutta Review* (Calcutta 1845), Jan.–June, p. 78.

plate, English knives, forks, spoons, wine glasses, decanters and cut glass vases – how could these convey any idea that we were seated in the court of an Asiatic prince?"[57] asked Viscount Valentia, who was obviously impressed. Outside the court Saadat Ali Khan pursued his English addictions, even sending for an English huntsman from Calcutta and appearing in English riding dress. Valentia noticed that the nawab was "highly gratified by any comparison between himself and the Prince of Wales" (later George IV), and the father of a close friend of the nawab's, Pelegrine Treves, was an acquaintance of the English prince.

Ghazi-ud-din Haider, the next nawab, continued this partiality for "collecting European and especially English commodities of all sorts and descriptions,"[58] including an English coach rather like the Lord Mayor's coach with a Muslim coachman "in a livery of the latest London fashion"[59] and this nawab's minister, Hakim Mehndi, had a house at Fatehgarh which was "magnificently furnished in the European style with a profusion of pier-glasses, mirrors, French organs and fancy clocks of the most costly description" as well as "coo-coo clocks, musical boxes etc. for which the natives entertain a great passion."[60] There was little change during the next nawab's time: Nasir-ud-din Haider, the subject of Knighton's book, also appeared in the garb of an English curate and had an English mistress too. Even now (1835) Europeans were still playing on the nawab's weakness for European trinkets, and the Honorable Francis Shore was present when the British Resident induced the nawab to "buy a French toy at a most exorbitant price. The Resident himself exhibited the toy," reported Shore in disgust, and "recommended the purchase".[61] But the death of Nasir-ud-din Haider in 1837 marked a distinct change in the nawabs' attitudes towards European goods. Though the last three nawabs before annexation continued to build

[57] Valentia, i, p. 144.

[58] *Bengal Past and Present* (Calcutta 1922), Jan.-Dec., vol. 24, pp. 95–102.

[59] Mundy, i, p. 30.

[60] Mundy, ii, p. 29.

[61] Shore, p. 83.

in a style that was heavily influenced by the West, there are far fewer accounts of purchases of European articles and far less entertaining of visitors in the European manner. Both the next two nawabs, Muhammad Ali Shah who was an old and sick man when he became ruler in 1837, and his successor Amjad Ali Shah, showed a marked preference for indigenous rather than foreign articles; and the last nawab, Wajid Ali Shah, made no attempt to revive former festivities and was seldom seen by Europeans, preferring to remain in his Qaisarbagh palace (although two Indian paintings show that his rooms were furnished with English chaise-longues and European chandeliers and curtains).[62]

It is clear that there was at first a distinct bias towards the West and it is not surprising to find a considerable number of "European" buildings erected by the nawabs in Lucknow. European furniture, mirrors, paintings and all the bric-à-brac that was bought in Lucknow looked better in a suitable European building, though in contrast to the pressure to buy such furnishings there does not appear to have been any pressure to build extravagant "country houses" in which to display Western acquisitions: in fact the idea of such houses seems to have sprung unprompted from the nawabs themselves. These houses were in the European style, since similar houses were not found among indigenous buildings in India, and indeed are seldom found even now.

The British conception of a country house is that of a large, free-standing house in its own grounds, often at a considerable distance from the nearest town, and where the owner would spend a good deal of time, the house being maintained during his absence by servants. This idea is quite foreign to India, where a lonely house or a house near a small village must either be fortified or self-supporting (which means a type of farmhouse) or a hunting lodge, often nothing more than a small square hut with a high parapet round the roof with embrasures for guns. The nearest approximation to the

[62] Oudh Company paintings in the State Museum, Lucknow. Uncatalogued.

British "country house" near Lucknow is probably the palace of Mahmudabad, owned by an eminent Muslim family, about fifty miles north-east of the city. This is a very large house with a series of courtyards, a separate zenana portion, and extensive stables and gardens, but is a palace which could be defended in times of attack and was originally called Mahmudabad Qila. A fair-sized village surrounds this palace and there are no extensive landscaped parks or fields which were so much a part of British country houses.

But just as the nawabs' propensities for European articles seem based on a superficial understanding and appreciation of Europe (Asaf-ud-daula's collection of worthless trinkets interspersed with valuable *objets d'art*, and Saadat Ali Khan dressed in his "canonicals") so does their building of "country houses" stop short of any real understanding of the *raison d'être* behind similar houses in Britain. Similarly, most European architects who designed houses for the nawabs or who sold houses already built lacked an understanding of the role such houses could play in India. P.C. Mookherji grasped this point precisely when he wrote, "It is easy to give a foreign turn to the ideas of a nation, in matters of luxury and the creations of fancy, not so as regards affairs of necessity and utility and religion." In Lucknow, he wrote, "its luxury was anglicised; in other respects it was as oriental as before."[63] The nawabs realized that a country house was to be something showy and impressive, but having gone that far they were at a loss to know what to use these houses for. While wealthy British owners would spend a considerable amount of time in their country houses, the nawabs spent most of their time in the city palaces, where the most elaborate Western furnishings were housed. All of their "country houses" were built in and around Lucknow – the most isolated is only three miles to the west of the city – and this means that such houses became town houses although they were built in a style more suitable for a large British estate than for the outskirts of an Indian city. Because these houses were built so near Lucknow it was not necessary for

[63] Mookherji, p. 203.

the nawabs to transport their retinue of servants and furniture to these houses when they visited them. Guests in these houses either "camped" in the large rooms, which were certainly not fully furnished, or stayed only during the day, returning to the comfort of the Residency or the city palaces for the night.[64] The houses were not used as places for lavish entertainment – all such recorded festivities took place in the public rooms of the city palaces. Neither were they used as hunting lodges, though they have sometimes been referred to as such. Hunting expeditions did go out from Lucknow, but they were not centred on such houses, being more in the nature of a "royal progress" through extensive tracts of land, taking several weeks. During these expeditions the nawabs and their nobles would live in large and splendid tents, a reminder that their predecessors had been fighting men who shunned town life and held their court in tented "cities" which could be speedily taken down when necessary; or they lived in hastily erected bungalows which were expendable as the party moved on.

The nawabs' country houses could not be used as a base from which to supervise large estates either, as was the case in Britain, for although the nawabs in one sense "owned" the whole of Awadh and the revenue which came from it, in another they owned no more than the sites of the palaces, houses, imambaras, etc. and small amounts of land round these buildings. Barowen, one of the larger country houses, had only a large walled garden behind it, which though originally set out in formal patterns speedily became overgrown and wild, so that visitors did not venture outside the house.[65] It is not surprising that many of these houses should have been little used

[64] The Khurshid Manzil, or Palace of the Sun, which had recently been completed when the Marquess of Hastings visited it in March 1818, appeared to have no place for any attendants, "so that I suppose it is only intended as a place at which a breakfast may be occasionally given. The building of it is just one of those expedients to which a person of unextended views is obliged to resort in order to get rid of superabundant wealth." *The Private Journals of the Marquess of Hastings* (London 1838), ii, p. 288. Hereafter Hastings.

[65] Spry, Henry, *Modern India* (London 1837), ii, p. 224. Hereafter Spry.

even during nawabi times since their function was not understood, and that having been built they were something of a white elephant. Some of these houses remained empty or tended only by caretakers, while others were given to relatives of the wives of the nawabs. The late Mohammad Ahmed Taqi, an eminent historian who lived in Lucknow and who studied the nawabi period extensively, believed that architecture for the nawabs was a hobby in exactly the same way that kite-flying, pigeon fancying and elephant fighting were.[66] This attitude, together with the large amounts of money,[67] cheap labour and materials that were available. would appear to be the main motive for the erection of many of Lucknow's non-functional buildings.

[66] Mohammad Taqi Ahmed to R.M. Llewellyn-Jones, Lucknow, 13 January 1975.

[67] *Asiatic Annual Register* (London 1807), p. 176; and idem (London 1808), p. 393.

4

Nawabi Buildings Erected for the British

APART FROM palaces and state buildings, any city where life is lived in a reasonably civilised fashion needs other public buildings in order to be a viable entity. Places of worship, jails, courthouses, shops, gardens, well, tanks, and serais all make up the structure of an Indian town and are considered functional buildings since they benefit the majority of the townspeople. But Lucknow was peculiar in that it contained a second strata of functional buildings which were erected by the nawabs in response to strong persuasion by the East India Company and its Indian collaborators. These included the Observatory, the hospitals, the Poor House, the canal, the Iron Bridge and the new Cawnpore road. The majority of these latter buildings were erected for the convenience of the British, and that some of them also benefited the inhabitants of Lucknow should be seen more as a secondary benefit rather than the prime reason for their existence. The various arguments advanced by the Company so that its motives should appear altruistic provide some choice examples of British hypocrisy in Lucknow.

The prime example is that of the Observatory or Tara Wali Kothi, a large building with extensive grounds set on a small hill between the south bank of the Gomti and Hazratganj, the long main street in the newer, eastern part of the city. The Observatory was a low, two-storeyed building with a semi-basement and two large central halls. It was designed in a plain neo-classical style. On the flat roof of the main building was a small circular room with a metallic hemispherical dome, with shutters round it that could be removed. The whole of this room and dome revolved on six large iron wheels operated by pulleys so that the giant telescopes in this circular room could be manoeuvred into any position. The main telescope was mounted on a massive unsupported masonry pillar, nearly sixty feet in height, which ran right up through both storeys of the building; other instruments were mounted on stone pillars.[1] The halls beneath the dome could be completely darkened by shutters which ran in vertical grooves cut into the walls, and these shutters descended into the basement when not in use. There was a great amount of equipment within the Observatory, including four telescopes, barometers, thermometers, magnetometers, and various "electrical and galvanick machines".[2] These were made "after the models of those formerly in use at the Royal Observatory, Greenwich."[3]

Where did the idea for such an institution come from? The first official intimation was in two letters sent to the British Government in Calcutta in October 1831 from Nawab Nasir-ud-din Haider to the Governor General and from the Assistant Resident at Lucknow, John Paton. The nawab's letter, with its high-sounding phrases, read: "As my mind is always bent on promoting divers enlightened arts and sciences which are replete with good and possess salutary advantages to the wise and to the public at large, it is my wish to establish an observatory in the metropolis of Lucknow and to appoint for its superintendence and establishment Captain Herbert."[4] Paton's letter in vague and equally grandiose terms said that the observatory was to be established "for the advancement of that noble science by new discoveries [and] for the diffusion of its principles amongst the inhabitants of India."[5] So far there is nothing remarkable about these rather pompous but apparently straightforward

[1] Foreign Con., 27 Feb. 1857, nos 176–8.

[2] Ibid., no. 168.

[3] Ibid., nos 176–8.

[4] Foreign Con., 28 Oct. 1831, no. 32.

[5] Ibid., no. 3.

letters. What is interesting, however, is to set alongside them a few pages of the diary kept by Captain James Herbert, the man referred to in the nawab's letter. The first entry, dated September 1831, reads: "The King of Oude and his new minister Hakim Mendi the richest man in India, are represented to be both of them very desirous of establishing an Observatory at Lakhnau not only as a means of establishing a series of observations of the heavenly bodies but more particularly as a school for the young courtiers in which some knowledge of Astronomy and general Physics might be taught. It is the Assistant Resident [Paton] who has the merit of having confirmed the King and his minister in so good a resolution."[6]

The nawab's proposal was not therefore made entirely unprompted; indeed the tone of the royal letter suggests most strongly that it was dictated to the nawab by someone who knew exactly the right terminology and phrases that would make an impression in Calcutta. The nawab's letter, which was dated 28 October, had been preceded on 7 October by one from Paton wherein the Assistant Resident reports that over breakfast with the nawab, "I took the opportunity of encouraging various projects in contemplation, especially the erection of the cast iron bridge over the Goomti with which I said His Majesty's name would be associated in after years."[7] The nawab took no further action over the bridge at that time, but Paton's advice, it will be noted, always encouraged royal attention to schemes which would benefit the Company and its servants. This was not the first time that Paton had dropped an encouraging word in the nawabi ear. A letter of his dated August 1831 described how during an evening drive with the ruler "His Majesty conversed upon the architectural improvements in progress in the Palace, and I took the opportunity, in passing, to suggest the completion of the street leading from the adawlut [Court of Justice] towards the Residency."[8]

[6] Diskalker, D.B., "Foundation of an Observatory at Lucknow", *Journal of the United Provinces Historical Society*, vol. x, part 1, July 1937, Allahabad 1936–7, pp. 10–11. Hereafter Diskalker.

[7] Foreign Pol. Con., 7 Oct. 1831, nos 24–5.

[8] Bengal Pol. Con., 12 Aug. 1831, no. 67.

Why was Paton so enthusiastic about the founding of an Observatory at Lucknow? Did he really believe, as he wrote, that it would advance "that noble science [astronomy] by new discoveries" or was it that the British government in India hoped to begin a series of astronomical observations and it would be extremely convenient to have a well-equipped observatory at Lucknow, especially one they did not have to pay for?[9] And why was Hakim Mehndi, the chief minister, bent on encouraging the nawab to set up an expensive observatory? In order to answer this question, or at least to postulate a convincing theory, it is necessary to look at the career of this man who had fallen in and out of favour with the nawabs several times during the previous twenty years. Originally rising to power as chief minister under Saadat Ali Khan, Hakim Mehndi was dismissed by Saadat Ali Khan's successor, and pursued "very extensive mercantile concerns at Futtyghur"[10] where he amassed a great fortune. In 1830, when finally recalled by Nasir-ud-din Haider to become chief minister again, Hakim Mehndi was probably, as Captain Herbert wrote, one of the richest men in India.

But on his reappointment Hakim Mehndi sought vigorously to cut down nawabi expenditure in Lucknow as part of a general programme of retrenchment throughout the whole province. The salaries of some Europeans at court were curtailed drastically and the minister stated publicly that it was his job "to check the extravagant expenses of the Palace expenditures."[11] All these economies delighted the Company, which was constantly urging thrift on the nawabs in order that its own enormous demands upon them could be met. But if Hakim Mehndi was so solicitous over nawabi expenditure, why was he at the same time urging expensive schemes on Nasir-ud-din Haider? The observatory was only one scheme promoted by Hakim Mehndi: others included a college, a hospital, a canal, and the erection of the Iron Bridge. The reason would seem to be that Hakim Mehndi, like other ministers before him, was in-

[9] In fact these experiments did not start until 1840. See Bengal Pol Con., 27 July 1840, no. 139.

[10] *Asiatic Journal* (London 1834), p. 222.

[11] Bengal Pol. Con., 29 July 1831, no. 58.

volved in the dangerous game of playing off the Resident (and thus the Company) against the nawab, while promoting his own interests as much as possible. Viewed more closely all the projects suggested by the minister, without exception, may seem to have been calculated to impress and please the Company. The college proposed by Hakim Mehndi, which was never realised, was to be "a means for improving the social condition of the natives of Oude; and thus by the introduction of sound information lead them to form a juster estimate of the [British] character."[12] The hospital, which was built and where Hakim Mehndi was a trustee, was an obvious blessing.[13] The canal (half-finished) was to be "a work of great advantage to the Country,"[14] and the Iron Bridge was one of the Company's pet schemes.

There is a touching little vignette, again by the garrulous Paton, in which he shows the old minister towards the close of his life saying "my aim is to do good while I live, and to leave behind me traces of my labours, amongst which I wish to number the endowment of colleges, the erection of a bridge and the foundations of an hospital."[15] Nice sentiments indeed, and ones which accord so well with Paton's own ideas that one strongly suspects they were calculated to have just that effect. Of course there was an element of the minister genuinely wanting to be remembered in practical ways by the erection of buildings, but by far the most important element was his wish to ingratiate himself with the British, who, he thought, were less fickle masters than the nawabs. Unfortunately when Nasir-ud-din Haider dismissed Hakim Mehndi in 1832 in favour of another wealthy minister, Roshan-ud-daula, the Resident proved powerless to do anything about the old man's dismissal. But this does not weaken the case made out. What mattered was that Hakim Mehndi had had before him the example of his rival Agha Mir, who, having urged his master Ghazi-ud-din Haider to make

[12] India Pol. Con., 16 Oct. 1837, no. 135.

[13] Foreign Con., 12 May 1854, no. 98.

[14] India Pol. Con., 3 Jan. 1838, no. 9.

[15] Bengal Pol. Con., 12 Aug. 1831, no. 67.

a considerable loan to the Company,[16] won for himself the protection of the Company – to the extent that he was able to seek refuge in the British Residency from the furious Nasir-ud-din Haider and was finally escorted to the safety of British territory in Cawnpore by a Company cavalry regiment.[17] Hakim Mehndi had no reason to expect less, especially after his assiduous cultivation of Paton, but he had miscalculated the influence of the Assistant Resident and the Company, whose championship of the corrupt Agha Mir had caused the greatest scandal and concern. The Company was not going to risk more scandal by being seen to support another chief minister against the nawab. The old man was exiled again, though on the death of Nasir-ud-din Haider in 1837 he briefly held office for three months under Muhammad Ali Shah, until his own death in December 1837.

The building of the Observatory began in 1832. Captain Herbert was by now living in Lucknow, in a house selected for him by Hakim Mehndi to whom Herbert had submitted plans for the Observatory. "One of them being a lower storey, was approved of and orders given to Buctour Sing [Raja Bukhtawar Singh][18] to commence on it immediately."[19] In the autumn of that year, however, Hakim Mehndi fell from grace and shortly afterwards Herbert died. But unlike the minister's other project, to move the Residency quarters to the Dilkusha Park, south of Lucknow,[20] the Observatory was not abandoned – although it was not until February 1835 that a note came from Nasir-ud-din Haider asking Sir William Bentinck, the Governor General (who strongly advocated the Observatory) to appoint another British astronomer in place of Captain Herbert.[21] A highly critical minute by Bentinck was attached to the nawab's request, which spoke of "a corrupt Court, where it

[16] Bengal Pol. Con., 23 June 1826, no. 8.

[17] *Asiatic Journal* (London 1834), p. 221.

[18] See Chapter 8 for a note on Bukhtawar Singh.

[19] Diskalker, p. 14.

[20] See Chapter 5.

[21] Foreign Pol. Con., 5 Feb. 1835, no. 1.

is so necessary to exercise the strictest supervision and vigilance over every European of whatever description to guard against the inconvenient consequences of intrigue and interference" and where "this weak prince [Nasir-ud-din Haider] thinks of little in the appointment of an Astronomer but the presumed augmentation of his own State and dignity which he hopes to acquire by it."[22] Nevertheless Bentinck hoped at that stage that the Observatory would be completed as soon as possible and that when fully operational it would lead to "the advancement of Science".[23] Bentinck's strictures on the nawab were obviously prompted by a report from the Lucknow Resident, Col. John Low, who wrote: "all that my silly King thinks of is that it adds to his dignity to have an astronomer and to have an English engineer for the Court but he is indifferent whether that officer will do the dutys [*sic*] of the office or merely attend his Court."[24] Despite the nawab's frivolous attitude, the Company was still anxious to have the Observatory opened and working as soon as possible, and within six weeks of the nawab's request Bentinck had appointed Lieut. Col. Richard Wilcox "to superintend the erection of the Observatory in Lucknow."[25]

By April 1835 Wilcox had already taken up his job, though he was to meet numerous delays before the completion of the Observatory almost five years later. One such setback was that on the death of Nasir-ud-din Haider in 1837 and the accession of Muhammad Ali Shah, the latter nawab endeavoured to stop the whole project and to dismiss Wilcox because he could not afford the scheme. But the Resident would have none of this and told the new nawab that the Observatory was "the only thing in His Majesty's dominions which attracted the attention of Europeans and it would therefore be a pity for such an institution, the only one of the sort in Hindostan, to be broken up during the reign of so just a Sovereign as His Majesty."[26] These lies and shameless cajoleries succeeded.

[22] Ibid.

[23] Ibid.

[24] Ibid., no. 2.

[25] India Pol. Con., 23 March 1835, no. 35.

[26] India Pol. Con., 6 Oct. 1849, no. 135.

The project limped ahead again with Wilcox meeting severe difficulties on site, and also being severely rebuked by the Company in Calcutta for letting these delays occur.

Meteorological observations which had been carried out in a separate building were discontinued and when the Company complained from Calcutta, Wilcox pleaded pressure of work, for he had been "much occupied in making drawings for their guidance and in superintending the workmen."[27] Another drawback was that Wilcox was merely the superintendent of the site, as the Resident explained, and that "as the building is being erected by contract it is quite out of his [Wilcox's] power to do more than urge the Contractor to complete his engagements without delay."[28] Wilcox reiterated this – "I am not charged with the execution and I have no control beyond that of merely directing what is to be done, and of furnishing plans."[29] The answer from Calcutta was extremely sharp, the Governor General threatening to sack Wilcox and hand the whole project over to another British officer working at that time on other buildings in Lucknow.

The following year, 1841, Calcutta was still urging speed on Wilcox and in his defence the Resident John Low wrote about his difficulties, saying that Wilcox "has been subjected to very frequent and vexatious disappointments, by repeated failures in the promises of the Native Builder (who has many other occupations besides that of constructing the Observatory)" and at times the "Builder has declared that he could not get funds to go on with from the Durbar, and at other times the King himself has rather capriciously put a stop to the work" while on site "many large beams procured from a great distance expressly for the Observatory . . . have been suddenly carried away and applied to other purposes." The same thing happened to the scaffolding, which Wilcox got erected after "much solicitation" only to have it taken down and used for other buildings in the city which the nawab was more anxious to see completed. It was not, Low explained, that the nawab did not want the Obser-

[27] India Pol. Con., 22 June 1840, no. 57.
[28] Ibid.
[29] Ibid.

vatory finished; "far from it: he is proud of having the name of encouraging Science and is flattered at the notion of having a Royal Observatory at Lucknow which there is not at any other Native Capital on this side of India: but on the other hand he evidently considers the construction of the building to be an affair of his own. he does not think it quite fair that any-one should interfere in this matter."[30] As the nawab was bearing the entire cost of Col. Wilcox's salary, the building and the expensive instruments within it, one could well believe that he rightly considered it "an affair of his own".

By the end of 1841 Wilcox had completed the building in spite of setbacks and delays, and until his death eight years later he regularly submitted half-yearly reports to the British government in Calcutta. There were minor irritations still. The astronomy classes were discontinued through lack of interest and application on the part of the young courtiers and there were numerous delays in the printing of works from the Observatory because the printing presses used were busy producing official forms for the nawab's Revenue Department and "books patronised by the Nawab"[31] instead of more serious works like Lord Brougham's translated *Treatise* on astronomy. The Governor General was still talking hopefully about the benefits of the Observatory, and he requested copies of translations of the astronomical works produced to be forwarded "to Egypt and else where, where the merit of such works will be duly prized."[32] But in fact *The Lucknow Almanack*, which seems to be the last volume produced by the Observatory, is a strange amalgam of the ascensions and declinations of the sun and the planets in 1849, horoscopes cast for the Residents of "the English Company Bahadur", and a "summary of the condition of the Kingdom of London" [*sic*] – including lists of English kings from AD 1660 onwards, with their potted biographies. Possibly this might have gone down well in Egypt, but it is a far cry from the advance of the

30 Foreign Con., 28 June 1841, no. 161.
31 India Pol. Con., 25 Oct. 1841, no. 57.
32 India Pol. Con., 28 June 1841, no. 159.

"noble science of astronomy by new discoveries" which had been set as the original objective of the Observatory.

Work continued after Wilcox's death in October 1848 until August of the following year under the two senior assistants, Kala Churn and Gunga Persaud. But on the publication of Kamal-ud-din Haider's book on the *History of Oude*[33] Wajid Ali Shah abruptly shut down the Observatory and all private printing and lithographic presses in Lucknow. The reason for this move was that Haider's work had omitted to "flatter the King"[34] and had included an extremely amusing article which showed the nawab in a bad light. Because Haider had worked for Wilcox at the Observatory and had his scurrilous book printed in Lucknow, the nawabi revenge was to shut down those establishments whose workers had given such offence. William Sleeman, the British Resident at the time, strongly urged that a successor to Wilcox should be appointed but he found that "a strong disinclination on the part of the Court had been manifested to the nomination of a successor."[35] Various official reasons were offered by the court for this disinclination, the chief one being the plea of economy – despite Sleeman tartly pointing out that the nawab "lavished every month more than enough to support a dozen such observatories among persons who have no claim whatever upon his bounty . . . or service."[36] Sleeman said the real reason behind the reluctance to appoint a successor to Wilcox was that the Governor General would want a say in the choice of the next astronomer and would doubtless pick an upright European, so there would be no money to be made out of such an appointment by the court. If on the other hand an Indian were to get the job, the amount he would have to bribe influential courtiers would be immense; the European principal of La Martinière School, on applying rather naïvely to the court for the job of astronomer, was asked how much he would pay the court for

[33] Bengal Pol. Con., 6 Oct. 1849, no. 130.

[34] Ibid.

[35] Ibid.

[36] Ibid., no. 132.

the job. Sleeman also wrote that a minister (unnamed) wanted the Observatory and gardens attached for himself for the site was "among the best, and best situated at Lucknow."[37]

The court's own explanation for the closure of the Observatory was that "it has produced no advantage whatever either to the state or to the people and learned of Oude," which indeed had more than a grain of truth in it. In 1852, two years after the closure, the Surveyor General of India, Lieut Col. A.S. Waugh, sent to the Under Secretary to the British Government in India a letter which was a masterpiece of expediency. The Surveyor General suggested that the valuable instruments in the Observatory, made by Troughton & Simms about 1833, should be moved to Calcutta to the Mathematical Instrument Makers Department, adding with quite splendid effrontery:

> I have assumed . . . that these instruments however valuable *per se* and useful to those skilled in their management, are perfectly worthless to the Lucknow Government and in fact so much lumber occupying a valuable house. I suppose therefore that the King would be very glad to be relieved of them and would transfer them *free of expense* to my Department . . . if it be merely a question of transference free of expense I consider the Lucknow Instruments valuable and perfectly sufficient for a first class Observatory . . . It will be remarked that the question of the removal of these important Astronomical instruments can be made to rest solely on considerations affecting their preservation and the relief of the King's Government from the embarrassment caused by their custody.[38]

For sheer nerve this letter is quite unequalled – not only were the nawabs encouraged to set up an observatory, to equip it in a most lavish fashion, and to pay the salary of the astronomer who regularly reported his observations to the Company for their purposes, but they were now being asked to donate the valuable instruments in the building and bear the costs of moving them, the whole business

[37] Ibid.

[38] India Pol. Con., 10 April 1852, no. 177.

being engineered to make it seem as though the Company were doing the nawab a favour by clearing out "so much lumber occupying a valuable house." The Surveyor General's letter proved too much for the Governor General, Dalhousie, who said that he "could not consent to ask for them as a free gift from the King,"[39] though it may be wondered whether his refusal was occasioned by a pang of conscience or by a reluctance to be put under an obligation to the nawab by the acceptance of such a gift.

Indeed the tone of British correspondence on the Observatory after its closure was one of pained surprise that the nawab should not be using the equipment on which his predecessors had spent so much money. An inventory made of the equipment in 1852 was preceded by the remark that "Neither he [the nawab] nor any of his people can appreciate or understand the advantages of such observations or be made to take any interest whatever in them."[40] The last comment on the Observatory, in 1857, when the British having annexed Awadh were compiling inventories of the contents of buildings in Lucknow, brings the wheel full circle. Major Strange, an assistant astronomer, stated that Col. Wilcox had been appointed astronomer "only in a spirit of imitation of European governments" and that "the magnificent instruments, made after the model of those formerly in use at the Royal Observatory at Greenwich [were] thus doomed to an ignoble repose."[41] The British had managed to convince themselves that the whole idea of the Observatory had been just a whim of Nasir-ud-din Haider's who was playing at being European by setting up his own Observatory, and that he employed a British astronomer merely as a symbol of his "Westernisation". The whole range of subtle pressures brought to bear on the nawab were conveniently forgotten, Paton's behaviour as an "adviser" ever at hand to whisper a few more flatteries in the royal car was discounted, Hakim Mehndi's subtle cultivation of the British ignored, and in short the whole exercise was seen as one

[39] Ibid., no. 178.

[40] Foreign Con., 27 Feb. 1852, no. 168.

[41] Foreign Pol. Con., 27 Feb. 1857, no number given.

more proof of nawabi extravagance and stubborn refusal to benefit from superior Western technology. The same pattern was to be repeated to a greater or lesser extent whenever other functional buildings were erected in Lucknow with British help or encouragement.

In the 1830s both Paton and Hakim Mehndi were pressing for the Iron Bridge over the Gomti as a desirable addition to the city. Though the history of the bridge, like that of the Observatory, was somewhat chequered, the idea of such a structure appears to have sprung unprompted from Saadat Ali Khan. In July 1810 he requested the Governor General's help in sending "professional Gentlemen" to Lucknow to measure the breadth of the river and to determine the best site, saying: "For two or three years past I have had it in contemplation to send for an Iron Bridge to be laid over the River Goomti."[42] There was already one bridge over the river, erected by the minister Abdul Mansur Khan in the 1740s, which was a brick-built structure, but with a stone facing and coping so that it was always, though erroneously, known as the Stone Bridge. It stood in the older, western part of the city, very near the Macchi Bhavan fort. Saadat Ali Khan received his "professional Gentlemen", or rather gentleman, in the shape of the Scots engineer, Captain Duncan MacLeod, who surveyed the river and sent his measurements and specifications to John Rennie in England, then engaged in designing Waterloo Bridge and the iron bridge at Southwark. Rennie suggested an iron bridge with a single span of two hundred feet for the Gomti, and the Captain made a model and drawings for the nawab, who was highly delighted.[43] In 1812 Captain MacLeod suggested, for what reason is not known, that the bridge should have three spans, not one, and this was the pattern finally adopted. The iron superstructure was cast in Britain, despatched to Calcutta, and sent up river to Lucknow, arriving there in August 1816.

But by this time Saadat Ali Khan was dead and his successor Ghazi-ud-din Haider was forced to pay £12,822 for the bridge, a

[42] Foreign Pol. Con., 14 July 1810, no. 138.
[43] Foreign Pol. Con., 29 Feb. 1812, no. 70.

steam engine that had also been ordered, and a further £676 for a British engineer and two British workmen. The nawab objected vigorously to the presence of the workmen, which he thought unnecessary as "persons of that description may be procured at this place,"[44] but the Resident, Richard Strachey, insisted that the skilled British workmen should put up the bridge. However, a year later the bridge had still not been erected and the nawab told Strachey that he was abandoning the idea because of the great expense of the foundations. (The superstructure, which had come out in separate panels, was to be riveted together with iron bolts and erected on brick piers.) "I have observed that His Excellency [the nawab] never showed much Interest about it," said the Resident dryly and added that the nawab was preparing traditional floating bridges (a series of barges lashed together) which were to be situated directly south of the Badshah Bagh, a pleasure garden on the north bank of the Gomti.[45] The sections of the Iron Bridge lay on the banks of the Gomti for thirty years before being erected in 1846 and the British workmen who were under contract to the nawab for a year were employed in other projects. Two unsuccessful attempts were made to persuade successive nawabs to erect the bridge, in 1823 and again in 1828.

On the first occasion the Governor General, Lord Hastings, suggested that the British should take it upon themselves to erect the bridge over the Gomti. This proposal, he wrote, "was intended to induce His Majesty to allow us to erect in His Majesty's Dominions this Striking Specimen of British Art and Skill, an undertaking which from Superstitious Motives it was understood His Majesty had himself abandoned, and Consequently the Materials of the Bridge being unemployed, and likely to be soon buried in the Sands."[46] The "superstitious motives" were reiterated, however, by the nawab, who while replying to this proposal wrote that it was

[44] Letters from Richard Strachey, Resident at Lucknow 1815–17, Eur. D. 514, 6.20. I.O.L. Hereafter Strachey.

[45] Strachey, ff. 390 and 391.

[46] Bengal Pol. Con., 5 Dec. 1823, no. 26.

"the Opinion universally entertained by Musulmen that to complete a work commenced by their Predecessors was Namobaruck [i.e. unlucky] that this feeling which precluded the possibility of His Majesty carrying into effect the proposed plan of his Father was equally applicable to the Governor General in Council doing so, he could not therefore allow the Governor to put up the Bridge anywhere within his Dominions."[47] The nawab went on to offer that the bridge be erected elsewhere in India. Hastings replied with an astute mixture of flattery and tact that he still believed "the persuasion that His Majesty's liberality of Sentiment and known patronage of Science and the Arts, [would] induce him to rise Superior to the influence of a prejudice, Originating in the mistaken notions of a less enlightened age and to resolve either to erect the Bridge himself, or to Consent to allow the British Government to undertake the work."[48] But Hastings' letter could not budge the nawab from his position and the Governor General for his part did not take up the offer that the bridge be erected outside Awadh.

The Company was particularly keen to have the bridge erected on its selected site in Lucknow because the cantonment at Mariaon to the north was extremely isolated. "The British subsidiary force," wrote Bishop Heber in 1825, "is by a strange choice, placed in a cantonment five miles from the town, separated by the broad and rapid stream of the Goomti."[49] The Iron Bridge when erected would shorten considerably the distance between the British forces and the town, an important military consideration, as well as provide a vital alternative crossing point should the Stone Bridge ever fall into enemy hands or be rendered unfit for use. Hastings was said to have offered the Lucknow court three lakhs of rupees to have the bridge erected, but money was not sufficient incentive for Ghazi-ud-din Haider to accept the offer. The nawab's own reasons for not wanting the bridge to be put up are less clear. The superstition theory can be discounted because it is known that the nawab

[47] Ibid., no. 25.
[48] Ibid., no. 27.
[49] Heber, i, p. 383.

was not averse to adding to and altering his father's buildings in the Chattar Manzil palace complex. No doubt he was reluctant to see "this Striking Specimen of British Art and Skill" erected in a prominent place in his own capital where it would serve as a constant irritating reminder of the British presence in Awadh. His father Saadat Ali Khan had been at pains to keep the British military force as far away from the city as possible and the erection of the bridge would to a large extent nullify this policy. With the accession of a new ruler, Nasir-ud-din Haider, however, the British again began prompting and by 1828 the nawab was requesting the services of "Lt. J. A. Crommelin of the Corps of Engineers"[50] since he wished to "erect several public Buildings" and "put up the Iron Bridge strongly recommended by Govt [the British] to his late Majesty." Nasir-ud-din Haider sang the praises of Lieut. James Crommelin who he had heard was "a good Man, and a Mathematician," but did not draw attention to the fact that Crommelin was "a near Connection" of the Resident, Mordaunt Ricketts, who was later named on several corruption charges though he was never prosecuted for want of conclusive evidence.[51] The British officials in Calcutta perhaps suspected nepotism or something shady, for their reply to the nawab is sceptically phrased: "presuming that the King of Oude is really desirous of employing the above officer, and has not made the present application merely in compliance with any solicitation which may have been addressed to him, the Governor General in Council naturally feels disposed to gratify His Majesty's wishes."[52] The reply also recalled "the interest which Govt. has so often expressed in the final completion of that work [the erection of the bridge] after the large expense incurred in bringing the materials from England." Unfortunately, at the end of 1828 Lieut. Crommelin who had been appointed by the nawab had to resign from his work in Lucknow because of ill-health brought on, as he wrote, by "the daily exposure

[50] Bengal Pol. Con., 3 April 1828, no. 6.
[51] India Pol. Con., 28 May 1852, no. 116.
[52] Bengal Pol. Con., 3 April 1828, no. 6.

to the sun, without protection attendant upon the nature of the duties here required of me."[53] The project then languished until 1831 when Paton, as Assistant Resident, borrowed the nawab's steam vessel to entertain its owner with an evening trip on the Gomti. Paton reported that "the building and alterations going forward led to the subject of the cast iron bridge the erection of which over the Gomti I did not fail to urge as a noble undertaking."[54] The cynical might well feel here that Paton had arranged the river trip for the express purpose of urging the bridge on the nawab, not hesitating to point out how well it would look spanning the river near the British Residency. Two weeks later Paton had breakfast with the nawab and again brought up the subject of the bridge: "I recommended the construction of a substantial road of communication between the Residency and the old bridge, a road which would unite the two bridges when the cast iron structure should be put up. It is a splendid bridge and its erection is worthy of all encouragement."[55]

Hakim Mehndi it will be recalled was also keen on the erection of the bridge and doubtless was on hand to persuade the nawab on Paton's behalf. With so much pressure on him the nawab consented to the sinking of foundations for the bridge by an English engineer, but for some reason the project was abandoned. It is possible that technical problems intervened or it may be that on Hakim Mehndi's fall the idea with which he had been closely associated was shelved. Certainly when the minister was trying to move the Residency to the Dilkusha he also planned the building of a splendid palace on the Residency site which was to have "an avenue of trees from it to the new Iron Bridge."[56] The collapse of Hakim Mehndi's plans meant that the palace was never built, and the avenue never planted, so the bridge was no longer thought appropriate. It was not until 1840 that Muhammad Ali Shah, the next nawab, gave £10,000 for the construction of the brick piers, and 1843 when an

[53] Bengal Pol. Con., 26 Dec. 1828, no. 20.

[54] Foreign Pol. Con., 23 Sept. 1831, no. 59.

[55] Foreign Pol. Con., 7 Oct. 1831, nos 24 and 25.

[56] Foreign Pol. Con., 2 Sept. 1831, no. 14.

engineer, Captain Hugh Fraser, began work. He completed the bridge two years later after a further large sum had been given by Muhammad Ali Shah's successor, Amjad Ali Shah.[57] The bridge was described at its opening as a "conspicuous ornament to this city and promising to be of the greatest utility to its population."[58] Certainly the bridge made life easier for the British and Dr Login, the Residency surgeon, noted that accommodation in the Cantonment began to be regularly used after the opening of the "Bridge and the direct road to Cantonments".[59]

When Hakim Mehndi was talking to Paton of the projects he wanted to see established, he mentioned setting up a college on British lines and about 1836 this was proposed by Nasir-ud-din Haider and was enthusiastically taken up by the British. Sir John Hobhouse in particular had urged "the introduction of useful knowledge among his [the nawab's] subjects"[60] by means of a college, and the nawab had been persuaded to write to the king of England requesting a suitable principal, whose salary of Rs 1000 per month had been guaranteed for three years by the British Government in India. Professor Seddon who was teaching oriental languages at King's College, Cambridge, applied for the post and was appointed head of the proposed college in 1836.[61]

Unfortunately the professor never got a chance to prove himself, for by the time he arrived in Lucknow Nasir-ud-din Haider was dead, and his successor Muhammad Ali Shah said he could not afford a college, and promptly dismissed Seddon. The Resident John Low interceded on his behalf, but in vain, and the *durbar vakil* (court official) who was present at the meeting "remarked that the late King [Nasir-ud-din Haider] had applied for a professor merely from motives of vanity and to get a *'name'* in England by making

[57] Foreign Con., 1 Jan. 1840, no. 70.

[58] Foreign Con., 29 Nov. 1845, nos 190–1.

[59] Foreign Con., 24 March 1853, no. 54.

[60] India Pol. Con., 16 Oct. 1837, no. 135. Sir John Hobhouse was the Minister for Indian Affairs at Westminster at this time.

[61] India Pol. Con., 16 Oct. 1837, no. 135.

such a request to the late Sovereign of Great Britain and that in his [the vakil's] opinion the late King had not the most distant idea of Establishing a College at Lucknow, even if Mr Seddon had arrived during His Majesty's lifetime."[62] The pattern of events here is closely paralleled by those in the Observatory case. The nawab is persuaded that an expensive project will bring him credit and renown, the British stand to gain with no financial responsibility, and when the project is abandoned the nawab is roundly abused for his frivolousness and accused of "showing off".

In the case of the Hospital, the third project cherished by Hakim Mehndi, it is less easy to gauge the amount of pressure that was put on Nasir-ud-din Haider. But the fact that the Hospital was established in 1831 along with proposals for the Observatory, the erection of the Iron Bridge, the canal which was to link the Gomti with the Ganges, and the building of a new palace on the Residency site, indicate that the same measure of persuasion was applied to the nawab both by the minister and by Paton, as had been in the other projects. The nawab's letter of 1828 to Calcutta in which he requests an English doctor is couched in the same formal language as that in which he applied for an astronomer. "As my attention is always directed to the welfare and prosperity of my Subjects," he wanted "an English Doctor, who is well versed in the Science of Physics and Medicines for diseases for the Cure of the Many Sicknesses with which the bodies of the generality of people in the City of Lucknow as well as the Military, are afflicted."[63] The need for a hospital could certainly not be denied. The Resident, Mordaunt Ricketts, reported that "Mortality in Lucknow and its environs has been excessively great of late, from serious diseases, which would have been greatly checked by the Active and Constant attendance of a Medical Man."[64]

The nawab's proposal was accepted and by 1830 it had been decided that the new Hospital should be under the charge of a

[62] India Pol. Con., 3 Jan. 1838, no. 9.

[63] Bengal Pol. Con., 11 April 1828, no. 29.

[64] Ibid.

doctor currently stationed with a regiment in the Cantonment at Lucknow, Dr Stevenson. Money for the Hospital was to come from the interest on a loan made to the Company by Ghazi-ud-din Haider. The original amount on loan was three lakhs of rupees[65] and the interest on the loan, when re-invested in British government securities, was Rs 17,244 per year.

Although Dr Stevenson got more than this amount alone in salary from the nawab yearly (his total salary was Rs 32,880 per annum),[66] the Hospital staff, whose wages came out of the Rs 17,244, received a monthly wage of Rs 138 shared between a dozen of them. The lowest paid, the *chowkidar* or watchman, got three rupees a month. Food and medicines for the three hundred patients at the Hospital also came from the interest on the loan, the sum of Rs 300 per month being expended on staples like *atta, daal,* rice, sago, sugar, milk, salt, wood, ghee, spice and tobacco.

The diseases treated remain distressingly similar throughout the period 1839 to 1850, the commonest illnesses being rheumatism, cutaneous afflictions (skin diseases), fever, syphilis, ulcers, and dysentery. Both the rheumatism and "cutaneous afflictions" were "connected with syphilis complicated with Venereal taint"[67] and these diseases were treated with mercury and iodine of potassium, both standard remedies for many years.

By March 1835 when the Hospital had been established for just under four years, Dr Stevenson requested an Indian assistant "not only to assist him in the general duties of the Residency but especially in the diffusion of vaccination while the season is favourable"[68] but his request was turned down although the number of patients treated continued to grow. Sometime between 1835 and 1840 the Hospital, which had been housed in a building off the Chauk, was split into two – the *unani* or native section where tradi-

[65] Foreign Pol. Con., 12 May 1854, no. 98.

[66] Bengal Pol. Con., 22 Jan. 1830, no. 11, and India Pol. Con., 8 Jan. 1840, no. 37.

[67] India Pol. Con., 8 Feb. 1850, no. 150.

[68] India Pol. Con., 5 March 1835, no. 93.

tional methods of treatment were used, and the European section. The unani section stayed in the original building near the Chauk and the European section moved to the Residency area in a two-storey building known as the Kings's Hospital. The unani section stood off the Cawnpore road and was used as a place where the old and sick lived and died. In 1975 the frontage of the building had been demolished and rebuilt but the two original courtyards were quite unchanged, the main one being a large square of beaten earth surrounded by a verandah and a series of small dark cells. The verandah roof was supported by thick stumpy pillars and there were no traces of decoration. Many of the "miserable objects picked up off the streets in the last stage of disease"[69] were sent, if they recovered in the Hospital, to work in the Poor House for a short time as a means of rehabilitation.

It is not known how far the nawabs who funded the Hospital and the Poor House were genuinely activated by humanitarian concepts or whether they felt it was their duty to support such enterprises. It is part of the Islamic tradition that a portion of income should be devoted to charitable works, and it is probably in this light that the nawabs regarded money given to the Hospital and the Poor House. Even so, they came low on the list of priorities and two reports from 1843 and 1844 show that the nawab wanted expenditure to be cut and contained within a fixed sum every month.[70] It is significant that Wajid Ali Shah, in his reply to British charges brought against him at the time of his deposition, did not mention that he had supported hospitals and the Poor House in Lucknow when this was one factor that might have carried some weight among the British and provided a small counterpoint to charges of his selfishness and blindness to the sufferings of his country's people.

Another project strongly urged on Nasir-ud-din Haider by Hakim Mehndi and again superintended by the British was the Canal which was to link the Gomti with the Ganges. When the idea had

[69] India Pol. Con., 3 July 1847, no. 69.

[70] India Pol. Con., 14 June 1843, no. 457, and India Pol. Con., 6 Jan. 1844, no. 105.

been first mooted in 1831 Hakim Mehndi had chosen two men to start work on the site – the Raja Bukhtawar Singh, superintendent of nawabi buildings, and William Trickett, who had accompanied the Iron Bridge out to Lucknow. Funds had already been allocated by the nawab, the direction marked out and the ground levelled and cut by 1832 when, for some reason, the minister persuaded the nawab to appoint a European engineer to finish the scheme. A meeting was arranged between the Resident, John Low, the minister, and the nawab, in which the latter was persuaded by Hakim Mehndi to apply for an Engineer Officer from the British Government.[71] Col. Davidson was appointed but by the time he arrived Hakim Mehndi had fallen from grace and Davidson was never allowed "to exercise that degree of control over the construction of the work which was indispensable to its efficient completion."[72] Representations were made to the nawab who had, according to the Resident,

> with his usual caprice . . . lost all feeling of interest in the matter: but I imagine that he was ashamed to say so, as he had applied to the British Government for an Engineer, and had affected publicly to be anxious to confer a lasting benefit on his subjects by the construction of so useful a public work. So far as the King of Oude's reputation is concerned, the Canal, like the half finished iron bridge . . . is chiefly remarkable as a conspicuous monument of His Majesty's folly.[73]

The half-built project was abandoned shortly afterwards "partly from the ignorance and obstinacy of the Chief Natives employed on the work . . . and partly from their corrupt conduct also, as connected with some of the zemindars through whose estates the Canal should have been cut" and lack of nawabi funds.[74] The abandoned project had cost twelve lakhs of rupees and had taken a large tract of land out of cultivation but, Low argued, if the money had not been spent it "would sooner or later [have been] thrown away

[71] India Pol. Con., 27 Feb. 1837, no. 36.
[72] Ibid., no. 36.
[73] Ibid., no. 37.
[74] Ibid., no. 38.

chiefly among menial servants and prostitutes about the Palace, whereas a large portion of it has been paid to labourers in the country – a far more deserving class of people."[75] Because of the clumsy construction of the Canal it *held* water which could be used for irrigation in the dry season, and during the rains, people were able to float down it grain, timbers and firewood, thus saving the cost of transporting these by road. A postscript to the Canal was written in 1838 after the death of Nasir-ud-din Haider when an anonymous court official criticised his late master by saying that Davidson "was applied for by the late King ostensibly for the express purpose of constructing the Canal, which his late Minister said would be a work of great advantage to the Country and yet Major Davidson was never allowed to perform any Service at the Canal, and drew his Salary for four years doing no other duty than that of an Aide-de-campe."[76] This criticism, like that of Low's, conveniently ignored the part that Hakim Mehndi played in the affair and put the whole onus for the failure of the project squarely on Nasir-ud-din Haider. The fact that Davidson's presence was an embarrassment in Lucknow when he arrived after Hakim Mehndi's fall shows how closely this project and others were tied up with individuals at the court, and the fact that the British Resident was prepared to intercede on Davidson's behalf with the nawab shows that the British were not merely interested spectators in the affair. The failure of the Canal was thus summed up as one more example of the nawab's "usual caprice".

One important area where the British again took an active interest and succeeded in persuading the nawabs to pay for a scheme beneficial to the Company was the new Lucknow to Cawnpore road opened about 1842. The old road ran from the Macchi Bhavan fort, through the Chauk and out of the city in a south-westerly direction, passing through Alamnagar.[77] As long as the buildings

[75] Ibid., no. 37.

[76] India Pol. Con., 3 Jan. 1838, no. 9.

[77] Map in the National Archives, New Delhi, entitled "The City [Lucknow] surveyed in 1862/3 under the Superintendence of Lt Col. D.C. Vanrenan,

of Lucknow were concentrated around the Macchi Bhavan and Chauk areas this route made sense, but as the court and its attendant offices moved east a new, more direct road, was necessary. In 1840 it was proposed that the new road should run south from the British area, crossing the new Canal by the Charbagh bridge. A track along this route already existed and there was a kutcha road for some thirteen miles beyond the Charbagh bridge towards Cawnpore.[78] Muhammad Ali Shah offered to put up £3000 for building the road and asked the Company to supply him with a good engineer to superintend the road.[79] Lieut. Cunningham was appointed; he was also working on other projects in the city and started work in 1840.[80]

But by August 1841 Lieut. Cunningham had run out of money because of a miscalculation in the original estimate. He had only been able to survey the proposed route and make a road "*consisting of earth only* beat down into the proper shape,"[81] although he had erected some bridges along the route. The Political Department of the Company in Calcutta, on being informed that more money was needed, described the new road as being "an important line of communication" and they trusted that the nawab would find sufficient funds to complete it. More money was given and by July 1842 the engineer reported that the road was finished and was much used "by all European travellers" and some Natives, though other Indians who wished to travel at a more leisurely pace still used the old road "because there were more villages and bazaars along that route." The nawab proposed, however, to grant land along the new road to various individuals on which they would erect serais (wayside

---

Revenue Surveyor: The Environs Surveyed under the Superintendence of Capt. A.D. Vanrenan, Revenue Surveyor, in 1865/7". Hereafter Vanrenan.

[78] Foreign Con., 9 Aug. 1841, no. 43.

[79] Foreign Con., 1 Jan. 1840, no. 70.

[80] The Lieutenant was also responsible for the additions to Constantia (La Martinière) when it was converted into a school, and for erecting the brick piers for the Iron Bridge.

[81] Foreign Con., 9 Aug. 1841, no. 44.

inns or sheltered places) for travellers, so the new road could be fully utilised.[82]

Four years later the next nawab, Amjad Ali Shah, was writing to the Company in Calcutta that "The new road from Lucknow to Cawnpore . . . having become much out of repairs I am desirous that the said road should be repaired and well metalled and that Bridges should be erected and drains dug wherever they may be necessary."[83] The nawab specifically requested the services of Engineer Hugh Fraser (now a Captain) because he had given the nawab "much satisfaction in the manner in which he erected the Iron Bridge."[84] But by this time Fraser had resumed his job as executive engineer at Cawnpore for the Company and Lieut. George Sim, another engineer, was finally appointed. The road was now extended for a further section, linking the British Cantonment at Mariaon with the new Cawnpore road that started from the Residency in the town. The opening of the Iron Bridge had made this proposed road possible and the importance of a good direct route from the Cantonment through the Residency site in the city and straight to Cawnpore, the nearest large British garrison, can hardly be underestimated. Naturally the nawab was expected to pay for the privilege of facilitating British travel, although money for the upkeep of this road was given "reluctantly" and Lieut. Sim's wages were finally stopped by the nawab.[85]

The reaction from Calcutta was hurt – "The only object the Government of India had in view was to aid in securing to the public the great advantage of such a road, the only piece of metalled and bridged road in all his [the nawab's] dominions."[86] There is good

[82] Foreign Con., 6 July 1842, no. 43.

[83] Foreign Con., 6 June 1846, no. 223.

[84] Ibid., no. 224.

[85] For a fuller version of the story of George Sim, see R.G. Varady, "The Diary of a Road: A Sequential Narration of the Origins of the Lucknow-Kanpur Road (1825–1856)", *The Indian Economic and Social History Review*, vol. xv, no. 2, pp. 151–72.

[86] India Pol. Con., 9 Sept. 1853, no. 82.

reason for cynicism at the exchange between the nawab and the Company, for if, as the British claimed, their object was to aid the public by building a new road, then there were many other roads that would have afforded much greater relief to the public than the one they chose to build. Two years after the new Cawnpore road was opened Dr Login's half-yearly report on the city Hospital contained this passage: "It can be a matter of astonishment to no-one who has frequently passed through the crowded narrow and filthy lanes of this city in the months of August or September, that upwards of 1000 deaths should occur in the city, in one day, during an epidemic as was the case in August 1842,"[87] and the doctor further complained that during the rainy season when illness was at its worst it was impossible for patients to travel through the city except in a palanquin (which most patients could not afford) "in consequence of the filth and mud of the streets after each shower of rain." The doctor's second report for 1844 continued to criticise the filthy streets and added: "there may be . . . cogent reasons, which prevent any attempts to remove so evident a cause of unhealthiness, but so long as the cause is permitted to remain but little comparative good can be accomplished by purely medical means, however zealously and skilfully they may be applied."[88]

Here was a most obvious need for a public amenity that would actually save lives, but perversely the Company chose to ignore its doctor's report and concentrated on building a road to Cawnpore which was "much used by all European travellers" and some natives. The reason is of course clear. No more than a handful of Europeans on business, like Doctor Login, travelled frequently between the old and the new areas of Lucknow, while there was a constant traffic between the Cantonment, the Residency and Cawnpore. (By 1848 for example there was a mail coach which ran between Lucknow and Cawnpore twice daily, taking eight hours for a single journey and "seven when the road is completed."[89]) Not only did

[87] India Pol. Con., 6 Jan. 1844, no. 105.
[88] India Pol. Con., 29 June 1844, no. 82.
[89] India Pol. Con., 28 May 1852, no. 120.

the new road make life easier for Europeans but it also meant that in an emergency troops could be moved quickly from Cawnpore to Lucknow and between the Residency and the isolated Cantonment. The British did not foresee that when the emergency came in 1857 the Cantonment would be completely gutted in a night, nor that the new Cawnpore road between the Charbagh bridge and the Residency would be held in a desperate resistance – but this does not weaken the force of the argument. As far as the British were concerned the new road, which was finally completed in 1849, opened up the British areas of Lucknow and facilitated communications between them, all at little or no cost to themselves. As for the nawabs, it was these very same reasons which produced their "reluctance" and general lack of enthusiasm for the new road. It is little wonder that Wajid Ali Shah did not welcome the prospect of Europeans travelling freely through his city: and even less wonder that a direct route to the British garrison in Cawnpore, for which his father had paid handsomely, should not fill him with the same joy as it did the British.

5

The Resident and the Residency

In October 1773 the Governor General, Warren Hastings, reported a conversation he had had with the nawab Shuja-ud-daula about the proposed appointment of a British Resident to the nawab's court, then in Faizabad. Hastings asked the nawab "whether it would be agreeable to him that a person in whom I confide should be appointed by me to reside near his Person for the sake of perpetuating and strengthening the good understanding so happily begun, as well as for the Transaction of such Ordinary affairs as might not suit the Formality of a Correspondence by Letter, but which in their Amount are always found to be productive of important Effects."[1] The nawab replied that "it would be entirely pleasing to him" and it was agreed that the Governor General should nominate a suitable Resident.

In January 1774 Nathaniel Middleton, an associate of Hastings and a merchant, was sent to the Faizabad court with a salary of Rs 1000 a month (about £100) and captain's double *batta* (a military allowance) as well as travelling expenses.[2] Middleton was recalled at the end of 1774 and John Bristow appointed in his place (for what reason is not clear) but this time a secretary was allowed to travel with the Resident; he received Rs 200 a month and double batta as salary.[3] The comparatively modest trappings of the first

[1] "Origins of the Residency", Home Misc. Series, no. 345, pp. 329–48. Extract from Bengal Secret Consultations, 4 Oct. 1773. I.O.L.

[2] Bengal Secret Con., 21 Dec. 1774, no number given.

[3] Bengal Secret Con., 28 Dec. 1774, no number given.

Residents at the nawabi court should not deceive one into thinking this was a position of little importance. As Bristow travelled to Faizabad his position was succinctly defined by Richard Barwell, a Company official and councillor to Hastings, as a "Weighty Charge which has for its Object the cementing of the Friendship between the Company and the Vizier [Shuja-ud-daula] and the obtaining of large Sums of Money said to be due from him."[4] Friendship based on such a premise is hardly likely to flourish and eighty-three years later, after the annexation of Awadh, an anonymous writer defined this "friendship" in a series of questions and answers thus:

> How did the East India Company acquire their power in Oude? By gradual encroachment and interference effected by means of Residents, a Resident being an officer appointed by the Company at the Court of a native Prince, ostensibly to advise him, but really, to promote mismanagement and confusion in his dominions, and thus afford plausible excuses and opportunities for the English taking possession of them. The friendship of the English to the Princes of Oude has been a fatal friendship.[5]

Thus the position of Resident in Awadh was from its very inception an anomalous one, the position of an unwelcome guest foisted upon a reluctant host (despite Shuja-ud-daula's initial reaction) by a third party, the East India Company. The cost of accommodating the Residents throughout the nawabi period rose steadily as the British entourage increased from Bristow's one secretary in 1774 to a great army of officials, clerks, messengers, and servants, so that by 1856 the last nawab, Wajid Ali Shah, estimated he was paying Rs 60,000 annually (£6000) merely for the Residency expenses and "the comfort and convenience of the British officers." This sum included the upkeep of Residency buildings requested by the Resident, which was estimated separately.[6]

[4] Bengal Secret Con., 28 Dec. 1774, no number given.

[5] Oude Catechism, p. 6.

[6] Reply to Charges, p. 3.

Here I am mainly concerned with the physical manifestations of the Residency in Lucknow, set up in 1775 after the court had moved there from Faizabad, and with the relations between the Resident and the civilian European population in Lucknow, rather than the political dealings of the Residents and the nawabs – an area which has received more attention.[7] Nevertheless the frictions between the Residents and the nawabs which were often exacerbated by the extreme proximity of the palaces to the Residency deserve to be fully examined, for did they not reflect in miniature the greater disputes that raged between the nawabs and the Company over the wider political spectrum? The nawabs' continued and well-founded complaints against the cost of maintaining the Residency buildings, while at the same time sensing the obligation of "host" to "guest", were equally matched by complaints over the cost of maintaining the Company troops in Awadh, troops which had originally been stationed there to protect the nawabs during the troubled eighteenth century. Similarly the defining and redefining of the Residents' role which continued during the nawabi period, particularly in relation to the supposed jurisdiction over European or Anglo-Indian civilians, reflect the anomalous position of the Residents, who were unsure as to the amount of power they held and could exercise in another man's province. Did an increase in the Residents' jurisdiction mean a decrease in the nawabs'? Constant bickering over such trifles may seem unimportant today when the whole sweep of British relations with Awadh is clear, but these daily aggravations should be examined as important symptoms of the malaise that was to end in annexation.

The increase in the Residents' establishments after 1775 and their corresponding increase in status and importance in the city of Lucknow can best be established by examining the few facts available on the Residency site at the end of the eighteenth century. The site, which lies to the south of the Gomti and the east of the Macchi

[7] See, for example, John Pemble, *The Raj, The Indian Mutiny and the Kingdom of Oudh 1801–1859* (London 1977).

Bhavan, covers an area of approximately thirty-three acres. It rests on a plain raised considerably above the surrounding land on the river side and slopes gradually down at the south-western side to mingle with the streets and houses round the Chattar Manzil palace complex developed at the start of the nineteenth century. The term "Residency" is now used to include all the buildings within this area, though the term appears to be a post-1857 description: the Residency itself is a single building to the north of the site. For the sake of convenience the term Residency complex will be used to designate the whole area.

The site was originally owned by the Sheikzadas,[8] but sometime during the late 1770s Claude Martin (who had been appointed Superintendent of the nawab's arsenal in 1776) bought a considerable amount of land here, extending east to the site of the later Chattar Manzil, north to the bank of the Gomti and south-west for an unspecified distance over the slope of the complex. The remaining land was bought by the nawabs at an unspecified date.[9] On this large site Martin began buying and renting houses to members of the Residents' staff, houses which may already have been standing or which may have been commissioned by Martin. At the same time Bristow, the second Resident, was presenting a bill to the East India Company in April 1777 "amounting to Rs 5500 for the Expense of erecting three Bungalows for Offices and his own accommodation, two Bungalows for his Assistants and repairing Buildings at Lucknow during the period of his Residency."[10] Bristow's staff now included not only a munshi who received Rs 100 a month (in addition to his secretary) but also *jamadars* and *harkaras*.[11] Bristow was, however, at fault in presenting his bill to the Company, for when it was re-examined two years later the Governor General noted: "It appears that Mr Bristow was reimbursed by the Company the

[8] *Gazetteer*, ii, p. 364.

[9] Claude Martin's Will.

[10] Bengal Secret Con., 25 Feb. 1779, no number given.

[11] Bengal Secret Con., 25 April 1776, no number given. *Jamadars* are superintendents, *harkaras* are messengers.

Expense of erecting Bungalows and repairing Buildings at Lucknow . . . which should have been paid by the Nabob, and the Board therefore direct that he [Nathaniel Middleton, reappointed Resident in 1776] demand from the Nabob the amount of such Sums as may have been disbursed on this account."[12] This was the first intimation that the nawabs were expected to pay for the accommodation of their Residents – a fact of which even the Resident was apparently ignorant. It was left to Nathaniel Middleton to press for payment of the Rs 5500.

Middleton also had some problems with the Lucknow buildings for in 1778 he reported to the Governor General that an item in the Residency Treasury accounts for Rs 499 was "incurred by a Fire which lately happened here and destroyed entirely the Straw Buildings where the Treasure had always been kept as well as every Chest and Package in which the Money was contained." The money, partly in gold, which was intended to pay for the troops of Sepoys and "lay in the open for many days." Middleton added that to prevent such an accident in future and to guard such money more securely "I have taken upon me to direct the Erection of a strong Brick Building to serve as well the purpose of a Treasury as a safe Repository for the Records of my Office, which is at present much wanted, having hitherto had no place but thatched Buildings to keep them in." As soon as Middleton knew the estimated cost for such a building he promised to forward "an accurate Plan and Section of the Work" to Calcutta for approval.[13] This building was subsequently erected and was considered part of the Residency proper in 1838, which suggests that it was not one of the peripheral buildings on the edge of the complex but quite near the Residency.[14]

The next year, 1779, Middleton was again requesting money from Calcutta, writing: "I have also been put to a very heavy Expense, in buildings and repairs for my own accommodation and necessary Offices for the extensive business of my Department. These

[12] Bengal Secret Con., 25 Feb. 1779, no number given.

[13] Bengal Pub. Con., 28 July 1778, no number given.

[14] Foreign Con., 24 March 1853, nos 45–59.

consisting chiefly of Bungalows and thatched Places and having required continual repairs."[15] The Residency complex at this time can be seen as a rather ad hoc arrangement of bungalows with thatched outhouses situated between the trees on the wooded hill. The fact that the Treasury was to have plans and elevations drawn up which had to be approved by Calcutta implies that this was the first Company building of any note to be erected on the site, and would indicate that the idea of a Residency had not yet been mooted. Unfortunately Middleton's note on the treasury is almost the last mention of buildings in official documents until well into the nineteenth century. There is no mention of the construction of the Residency itself, nor the huge and splendid Banqueting Hall nearby, nor indeed scarcely any of the numerous buildings on the site until the proposed erection of a church in 1845. It is true that the Residency records were destroyed in 1857 but the fact that there is no mention in Company documents of any erection of important buildings here strongly suggests that such buildings were put up by the nawabs and leased to the Resident and his staff for a sum so nominal it was not deemed worthy of note.[16]

The next evidence available on the site's development is particularly valuable for it is pictorial as well as written. Ozias Humphry (1742–1810), a British artist, spent four-and-a-half months in Lucknow in 1786 sketching notable figures at the nawabi court. Humphry also kept some sketchbooks where he drew buildings in and around the Residency area as well as some general views of the city.[17] During this period he stayed with John Wombwell, the Company's accountant, in a house which can be positively identified as the one called Innes Garrison during 1857. This house, or

[15] Bengal Secret Con., 18 Feb. 1779, no number given.

[16] In 1854 the Resident, Col. J. Low, stated that houses for two Company assistants and the Company medical officer were "in the city, and close to the Residency, in fact they are all considered within the limits of the Residency grounds. Those houses are the property of the King, as is also the house occupied by the Resident himself." Foreign Con., 21 July 1854, nos 9–12.

[17] Ozias Humphry's sketchbooks, Add. 15,959, 15,962, 15,965. B.L.

rather large bungalow, was at the northernmost tip of the Residency complex, on a mound overlooking the Gomti. To Humphry it provided a "comfortable existence . . . in the violence of this season [May] where House and enclosures bring to one's mind the comforts of England with trees and Lawns forever green whilst all the lands surrounding Lucknow seem like an Arabian desert." A less pleasant experience happened in the same month when Humphry wrote: "whilst we were seated at supper upon the Mound before Mr. Wombwell's a wolfe on the opposite side of the river seized a child."[18]

Humphry's sketch of Wombwell's bungalow shows a pleasant one-storeyed structure with a tiled veranda roof supported by plain wooden columns. To one side are two blank brick towers, no higher than the roof of the bungalow, containing the stairwell. There is no architectural merit attached to the building and it required no elaborate elevations to be drawn up, being easily constructed from local materials by local workpeople. From Wombwell's garden Humphry sketched "The durgah or burying place of Meer Shuruf ula" and "the Zinana in Mr. Wombwell's garden," an undistinguished low brick building.[19] The interest of these last two sketches is not architectural but provides valuable evidence of the mixed character of the Residency site – it was never a clearly defined area made over to the British to be laid out in a formal style suited to the status of the Resident at an important native court. It was instead an area which contained some Muslim buildings picturesquely sited among the trees, for Humphry's sketches show the area to have been quite heavily wooded. Only three distinguished and substantial buildings on the Residency site are shown in Humphry's general views of Lucknow. These brick-built dwellings rise up above a forest of trees and were at least two-storeyed. One appears to stand where the Residency is now situated but there is not enough evidence to claim that it is the same building.

[18] Diary of Ozias Humphry.

[19] Humphry's sketchbooks, Add. 15,965, f. 1.

By 1786 the nucleus of the Residency site was well established – an informal mixture of thatched houses, brick-built bungalows with flat roofs, Muslim shrines, zenana buildings, and a few substantial buildings for the highest Company officials. A list for April 1785 gives the Resident's staff and their monthly salaries as follows:

	Rs per month
Major Palmer, the Resident	19,000
Robert Gregory, Assistant Resident	2000
John Wombwell, Accountant: no figure given	
Col. Claude Martin, Arsenal Superintendent	3730
William Blane, Surgeon to the Civil Establishment and the Nawab	5000
Robert Bruce, Surgeon to the Military Establishment	2000
Mr Scawen, Auditor General	2000
Mr Gale, Assistant to Auditor	1000
Mr Grant, Assistant to Robert Gregory	2000
Mr Johnstone, Assistant to Robert Gregory	2000
Sacville Marcus Taylor, Post Master	2000
James Orr, employed by John Wombwell (not in the Company)[20]	2000

The great increase in staff during the eleven years since John Bristow was sent to Lucknow is matched by a corresponding increase in salaries – Rs 19,000 monthly compared with Rs 1000 monthly for the Resident, for example. Although the salaries of these officials were paid by the Company a list of allowances was made to them by the nawab, though it is neither clear from these records what percentage of these allowances made up their salaries nor whether they were considered as extras. It is also not clear if all the officials knew where their allowances came from; a note accompanying the list of salaries states "the allowances that are granted are to be considered as Allowances from the Company and in Lieu of all others; they are to

[20] Home Misc. Series, 345/1–5, f. 125. I.O.L.

be paid by the Accountant at Lucknow and charged in the Public Account to the Nabob's Debit." This secrecy would imply that the Company was trying to appear more generous than it actually was while not being out of pocket.[21]

There was no secrecy about who paid for the upkeep of the Residency staff's houses and bungalows though, and the procedure that was to annoy future Residents so much in the nineteenth century was firmly established by 1787 when Col. Gabriel Harper wrote to the Governor General that "The Vizier's [nawab's] Ministers have constantly provided for the repairs of the habitations of your Resident and other Servants at Lucknow . . . the whole being conducted under the inspection of a Servant of the Vizier, whose accounts I have examined and checked at the expiration of each Month. These combined charges have amounted from June 1785 to March 1787 to something more than Rs 17,000 – 6000 of which are now in arrears." The nawab also "paid the wages of the people employed for the service of most of these Places; such as watchmen, Gardeners, Hircarrahs, and Artificers."[22]

Further information on the site appears in Claude Martin's Will of 1800. Martin had bought a large piece of land here, including part of the Residency site, and rented houses to Europeans like Lt Bellas, an engineer from Cawnpore who had been invited to Lucknow by Asaf-ud-daula.[23] Martin had also bought the house of the Assistant Resident, Robert Gregory, and two more houses belonging to Europeans in the area. In all, Martin owned eleven houses in Lucknow (in addition to his mausoleum palace, Constantia or La Martinière, an area in Gola Ganj, two gardens, and three extensive tracts of land, two to the south of the city and one on the north bank).[24] One of the Lucknow houses, the Château de Lyon, later known as Farhad Baksh and incorporated into the Chattar Manzil

[21] See for example the discussion on the salary of Dr Stevenson, Superintendent of the Lucknow Dispensary. Bengal Pol. Con., 22 Jan. 1830, no. 11.

[22] Bengal Secret & Pol. Con., 23 May 1787, no number given.

[23] Claude Martin's Will.

[24] Bengal Inventories 1801, range 1, vol. 24, no. 75, I.O.L. Hereafter Bengal Inventories.

palace, was Martin's town house. A considerable amount of land was attached to this house, including a bazaar which was rented out and known as Captain Bazaar.

Captain Bazaar was situated between the Farhad Baksh and the most northerly point of the Residency complex where it sweeps down to the river. It was separated from the Gomti only by a small area of low-lying cultivated ground flooded during the monsoon. It is tempting to imagine that Martin's bazaar, so conveniently situated next to the houses of the European community, must have provided luxuries and European goods not readily available elsewhere. Apart from the houses rented out by Martin or bought by him in this area were three others belonging to Europeans – the large house of Col. John Mordaunt, a close associate of the nawab, which was taken over by him on Mordaunt's death in 1791,[25] the house of Andrew Pringle, a trader in sugar and saltpetre, and the house of Mr James Paull, another trader, and his Indian wife.

It is obvious that Martin exercised considerable control over the early European residents in Lucknow, and on his death in September 1800 nineteen Europeans still owed him money, including more than £ 8000 in rent for houses in the Residency area.[26] The European community was a close community, both physically from the proximity of their houses and socially, as is evident from relationships and cross-references in contemporary letters. There is no doubt that the houses of these Europeans, together with those already erected by earlier Residents or by the nawab for the Residents, formed the basis of the Residency complex which developed piecemeal among existing Muslim and Hindu buildings over the next fifty years.

[25] Col. John Mordaunt was the illegitimate son of the Earl of Peterborough. He was taken into Asaf-ud-daula's service as an aide-de-camp and died in 1790. A picture by the artist Zoffany, begun about 1784, depicts Col. Mordaunt's cock match which took place in a large tent and shows the nawab with twelve other Europeans, including John Wombwell, the Company accountant, and Claude Martin. It is said that Asaf-ud-daula "never enjoyed himself after the Col's [Mordaunt] death, as he had done before." See Daniel Johnson, p. 162.

[26] Bengal Inventories.

The Resident's relationship with the nawabs was bound to be a strained one for reasons already discussed, but his standing among the Europeans in the city was also open to question, not least because of the activities indulged in by early Residents. Until 1788 when a commercial treaty was signed between the nawab and the Governor General, "trade was mostly in the hands of the army officers attached to the British brigades or of the Resident at Lucknow and his entourage."[27] Nathaniel Middleton was able to set up his own monopoly to supply saltpetre (which Awadh was rich in) to the Company by offering patronage and protection to two merchants, John Scott and John Hyde, who in turn employed people to help them. The 1788 treaty put a stop to the Resident's commercial speculations, not because anyone thought it immoral that he should be engaged thus but because it was thought trade would be more profitable in a free market.

The implications of the Residents' trading interests for fifteen or so years offer alarming possibilities of bribery, abuse of power and deals with other Europeans, many of whom had their Lucknow homes in the Residency area. Merchants such as James Orr, James Paull, Andrew Pringle, H.J. Clark, George Prendergast, and Claude Martin all had houses here within easy walking distance of each other. How much the Residents' commercial enterprises detracted from the political authority which they undoubtedly sought among the Europeans cannot easily be answered, nor indeed the extent to which political power aided commercial concerns. An indication might be given by the letter written from the Governor General in 1791 to the Resident, Edward Otto Ives, that he was "determined no European who shews a disposition to insult the Resident of this Government shall . . . be permitted to carry on Commerce or to follow private pursuits of any kind in the Dominions of Oude."[28] To fall foul of the Resident, for whatever reason, was bound to lead to all kinds of annoyances, restrictions, and sometimes acute harassment.[29]

[27] See P.J. Marshall.

[28] Bengal Pub. Con., 12 Oct. 1791, no number given.

[29] See for example the complicated case of Thomas Hare, when the Asst. Res.

Yet despite the opportunities for corruption and abuse which the Residents utilized, they were still seen by the majority of the European community as protectors and arbitrators in civil and criminal cases. Although a ruling of 1791 stated categorically that the Resident could not interfere with "persons who are not British subjects who must seek redress from the Nawab's Government,"[30] it was found that by 1831 the "East Indian Christians [people of mixed race, usually Portuguese and Indian] invariably . . . look up to the Resident for protection, and are ready to refuse compliance with a summons from the Nawab's Court. Europeans out of the Company's service, residing in Lucknow, not being servants of the [nawab] always claim the Resident's protection"; and for Europeans in the Nawab's service it could lead to an embarrassing situation. "It would appear expedient," Paton added, "to make all Europeans at Lucknow, entirely amenable to the Resident's authority when he saw fit to exert it, as regards civil or criminal complaints against them, thus more fully to have them under control and to save that degradation of character which would arise from liability to be summoned before the native courts."[31]

Five years later the Court of Directors of the Company was obliged to make a further ruling because a number of cases had arisen over Anglo-Indians in the nawab's military service. There had been, they admitted, "an ill-defined but generally *supposed* right of jurisdiction vested in the Office of the Resident over Europeans living at Lucknow, but it was now to be understood that all persons who enter the [nawab's] service are *exclusively* under the jurisdiction of the native Government" and that even British-born subjects

---

George Johnstone was accused of inciting a Mughal prince to surround Hare's house because of non-payment of a debt by Hare. The prince prevented food being sent in for Hare's wife and daughter. When asked to intercede Johnstone claimed he could not because he did not believe that Hare was married until shown the marriage certificate. Bengal Pol. Con., 11 April 1794, no. 16. 30. Bengal Pub. Con., 22 June 1791, no number given.

[30] Bengal Pub. Con., 22 June 1791, no number given.

[31] Bengal Pol. Con., 26 Aug. 1831, no. 30.

living in Awadh and not in the Company were under similar jurisdiction: in fact all Europeans engaged in business should be treated as natives of the country.[32] After this directive it appears that British subjects in Awadh who were not in the Company were habitually tried by the nawab's judicial courts, as for example the two British burglars, Stewart and Anderson, tried in 1852 without reference to the Resident.[33] But the question of trials of such people before the 1836 ruling remains unsolved. If British and European people refused to go to the nawab's courts, as Paton claimed, then did the Resident hold his own judicial court? But no records exist of such courts being held in Lucknow; in fact the only criminal case recorded before the 1836 ruling was that of a British subject, Japhet Hill. He was accused of murdering an Indian in 1791 and sent to Calcutta to be tried by the Supreme Court, set up there under the Company's auspices.[34] Neither are there any reports of British subjects being held in a Company jail in Lucknow, the jail in the Residency complex being used exclusively for thugs and dacoits. Obviously the European community was not entirely law-abiding. There are several recorded cases of murder among Europeans and in a case in 1824 the statement of a self-confessed murderer was taken down, witnessed by two Europeans in the nawab's service and recorded in the Company records, but there is no report of how the murderer was dealt with or by whom.[35]

Apart from the Resident's function as an arbitrator, which many people believed him to possess – no matter on what vague grounds – he was also regarded as a stand-in for religious authority and performed baptisms and marriages for the European and Anglo-Indian community in Lucknow before a Residency clergyman was appointed in 1832.[36] On the death of a British or Anglo-Indian inhab-

[32] India Pol. Con., 21 Nov. 1836, no. 46. I.O.L.

[33] India Pol. & Foreign Con., pt 1, 30 Jan. 1852, no. 103. I.O.L.

[34] Persian Correspondence, ix, pp. 252–3.

[35] Bengal Pol. Con., 18 June 1824, no. 54.

[36] Bengal Pol. Con., 12 March 1832, no. 61. See also Bengal Pol. Con., 15 Feb. 1828, no. 23, for the only record of baptisms and marriages noted. These were

itant of Lucknow it was the Resident's job to attach seals to the property of the deceased until the Will of that person was proved or the disposition of the property agreed on, which often involved lengthy letters to the Resident by aggrieved relatives who felt they were being unfairly treated.[37] Some Residents did not hesitate to become involved in domestic disputes among the European community, and in 1835 John Low prided himself on the fact that in several cases he had been able to persuade erring wives to return to their husbands "with some success". In a particular case the Resident persuaded an Anglo-Indian woman to return to her British husband, born in India, and an unnamed nawabi minister said of this case that "Europeans [*sic*] were considered as being chiefly under the jurisdiction of the Resident," showing the confusion existing in both Indian and British minds about the Resident's extent of power, and the definition of Europeans.[38]

Another of the Resident's functions was to act as a filter between the European community and the nawabi court, and it became customary for Europeans who were petitioning the nawabs for a job or for some real or imaginary grievance to address their petitions to the Resident for forwarding to the nawab. The Resident had the right to veto such petitions, which he frequently did, and one Resident, Col. William Scott, was accused of prohibiting all such letters to the nawab and of trying to prevent Europeans from visiting the nawabi court at all during his period of office (1799–1802).[39] It was also the Resident's duty to co-ordinate the spies, or "newswriters" as they were called, who were stationed at various points around the city, including "one Khuburdar at the King's Deoree"

---

performed by the Resident Mordaunt Ricketts, who admitted no previous records had been kept, nor of burials either.

[37] Bengal Pol. Con., 5 July 1822, no. 64.

[38] India Pol. Con., 17 Aug. 1835, no. 30. I.O.L.

[39] Bengal Pol. Con., 10 May 1822, nos 73–5. See also the Pogson case when the Resident Major Roper was instructed by the Governor General to forward Capt. Pogson's petition to the nawab after complaints that the Resident was blocking access to the nawab. *Asiatic Annual Register* (London 1807), p. 183.

(i.e. a news-writer at the nawab's palace gateway) and one in the house of Husain Reza Khan, the nawab's chief minister.[40] There was no secret about the fact that both Residents and nawabs had an extensive network of spies established in the others' quarters, and nawabi ministers had their own spies. Information that could not be obtained by spying was got by bribing the servants of each party. "There is nothing I believe unusual in bribing the servants of the Resident, except in its detection," wrote one Resident dryly in 1830; and similarly Residents had no scruples about how they obtained their information, which was then sent to Calcutta for analysis and comment.[41] To sum up, the Residents enjoyed among the European community immense power and authority, some of which was presumed by the community and not in fact possessed by the Resident, but which nevertheless did not detract seriously from his status. It is no exaggeration to say that from about 1800 onwards there were two courts in Lucknow, that of the nawab and that of the Resident, and both by chance situated so near each other that the inhabitants of each claimed they could overlook the dwellings of the other.

It is interesting to turn back to the Residency site itself, having discovered the confused boundaries of the Resident's authority, to find that in this complex too there were few clear guidelines. It was inevitable that conflicts should arise over the Residency site between the Company officials and the nawabs, for given that the former felt they had an almost divine right to meddle in the internal affairs of Awadh it must have been perpetually galling to know that they only occupied their houses and offices by the grace of the nawabs. During the British occupancy of the site both the nawabs and the Residents sought to define and redefine the extent of authority each possessed over the area. Even in the time of the penultimate Resident, William Sleeman, there were difficulties in assessing the amount of control the nawabs had, although nominally they owned

[40] Bengal Pol. Con., 9 Aug. 1822, no. 28.
[41] Bengal Pol. Con., 24 Sept. 1830, no. 28.

all the land on which the buildings stood. Sleeman had asked the Company doctor, John Spencer Login, to write a short account of the area since 1838, when the doctor had arrived in Lucknow. It was revealed that when houses in the Residency complex became vacant these were not considered to be at the disposal of the Resident. But he could apply to the nawab to allow them to be occupied by gentlemen attached to the Residency when they were not required by the nawab. An officer did not automatically succeed to a house occupied by his predecessor, and the nawab treated the allocation of a house as a personal favour, although the formality had been neglected owing to frequent changes in the Residency staff. Dr Login stated that six houses were considered to be part of the Residency proper – the Residency itself, the Banqueting Hall with its attached houses for officers and servants, the Yellow House built originally for the Residency surgeon but now reserved for visitors, the Treasury and Guard rooms, and the Residency School. Seven more houses in the area were occupied by Europeans attached to the Residency and by a Muslim clerk.[42]

Wajid Ali Shah wrote after the annexation of Awadh that the nawabs considered it their "duty to make those attached to the Residency, who were deemed as our guests, as comfortable as we could,"[43] but the history of the site shows "guests" who not only assumed privileges far beyond their status but who also showed a certain tenacity in clinging to their houses when twice asked to vacate the property of their host. The proposed removal of the Residency to a new site is discussed later, but one of the reasons given for not wanting to move reflects again the supposed power of the Resident among the European community. If the Resident left, Paton argued in 1831, "a great number of the inhabitants of Lucknow who were dependants of the British Government would be deprived of the security which they derive from the immediate presence of the

[42] Foreign Con., 24 March 1853, nos 45–59. National Archives, New Delhi.

[43] Reply to Charges, p. 3.

Resident in the city [and] those who from the convenience of proximity to the Residency have purchased houses near at hand would suffer loss by the removal of the Residency office to a distance" – although the number of people that enjoyed this vicarious security was left vague. Paton went on: "there are no specific limits within which the occupants of houses are entitled to the jurisdiction of the Resident. The individuals attached to the Residency have either purchased or rented houses in its neighbourhood promiscuously chosen from amongst the houses of the city." He then listed seventeen houses which were "attached to the Residency" and occupied mostly by Indians working in the Persian Department and the Intelligence Department for the Resident.[44]

The advantages that these people derived were never clearly defined except in one curious case which adds more mystery than clarity to the situation. In 1826 Lalji, the Residency superintendent of news-writers, asked for a Residency *chaprasi* to be stationed at his house in the complex. This he claimed would allow the Resident "to interpolate against the Nawab's officers and to give a power and consequence to the Members of that House."[45] The request was vetoed by the nawab, who had been informed of it by the Resident, because he was afraid it would set a precedent, although from the manner in which the request was phrased it seems obvious that chaprasis were stationed at some of the Residency houses, and that Lalji, seeing them, also wanted some of the "power and consequence" that was conferred by their presence. Despite nawabi disapproval, chaprasis were employed by the Resident and three years later it is recorded that James Martin, Claude Martin's adopted son, who was an auctioneer and lived in the Residency complex, had a chaprasi stationed outside his house.[46] The fact that the Resident, who nominally could not even assign houses to his own officers in the area, could appoint watchmen to "interpolate against the

[44] Foreign Pol. Con., 14 Oct. 1831, nos 45–6.

[45] Foreign Pol. Index, 26 May 1826, no. 77, National Archives, New Delhi.

[46] Foreign Pol. Con., 4 Sept. 1829, nos 30–2.

nawab's officers" again demonstrates the anomalous position that the British enjoyed here before 1856.

In such a situation other anomalies arose too, one of the most bitter disputes being over who should pay for repairs and new buildings in the complex. The custom whereby the nawab paid for such things having been established from 1775, the system was that the nawab's *daroga* presented his bills for the Resident's approval, the sum being then added to the nawab's debt to the Company. A dispute began in September 1829 when the Resident, Thomas Maddock, became alarmed both by the excessive bills presented to him and the fact that little work was being done. "The charge for the past month," he wrote, "was Rs 3230 and this is the more remarkable as the Residency is totally out of repair."[47] The daroga at the time was Mir Hussein Ali Londoni, who was described as "an old man enmeshed in greed,"[48] a remark confirmed by the Resident's complaints that the large sums of money extracted from the nawab were obviously not being spent on repairs. The fact that Mir Londoni was arrested by the nawab's guards early the following year, with some force, implies that the nawab realized he was being cheated too.[49]

The matter came to a head and by February 1830, the officiating Resident, Lieut. Col. Abraham Lockett, who was temporarily replacing Maddock, wrote curtly to Calcutta that "all fixed establishments of the Residency of every description under the Nawab's Darogha have been discontinued by me. The Resident will not acknowledge any fixed Residency Darogha because of previous abuses in this system."[50] But what was to replace the old daroga system?

[47] Ibid.

[48] Ahmad, Safi, *Two Kings of Awadh* (Aligarh 1971), p. 50. Hereafter Safi, Ahmad.

[49] Bengal Pol. Con., 3 April 1830, no. 14.

[50] These "fixed establishments" included servants supplied by the nawab for the Residency complex – among them were two carpenters, eight "furrashes" or house-servants, three blacksmiths, and ten gardeners. Foreign Pol. Con., 19 Feb. 1830, no. 32.

Maddock had suggested in September 1829 that the nawab should cease to do any repairs at all in the complex and that the British should have them executed by a public officer of the Company and expenses charged to the Company. But Lockett disagreed and suggested that since the "Residency Buildings and grounds are the property of the Oude Government they should continue to be repaired and kept in order at the Nawab's expense," although they should first be surveyed and costed by a British officer, unless the nawab objected, "as he probably will". The repairs, Lockett thought, could then "be superintended in the same manner as the Nawab's other public Buildings by one of his own Daroghas." The nawab's reply to this, as Lockett had anticipated, was not favourable. The nawabs had always done the repairs and had darogas ever since the British representative was established in Lucknow and he (the nawab) would not have a British officer doing the surveying.[51] The tone of the nawab's letter was so strong that Maddock, by now back in office, had to write again to Calcutta saying that "if the Nawab was going to pay for repairs to the Residency the East India Company could hardly insist on executive officers preparing plans and estimates, because the Nawab's head builders would probably not work under estimates prepared by someone else [and] the houses and gardens being the Nawab's it was hardly necessary to dictate to him what number of servants he should maintain for the care of them."[52]

This report was a reversal of Maddock's previous idea that the British should take over repairs of the Residency, and while his new attitude may have been in some measure tempered by the nawab's indignant letter, it should also be seen in the light of a request he had recently made to the nawab for a country house. The Residency "is surrounded by a populous city," which made it hot, and "I suffer from a dread of excessive heat." Maddock had already chosen a site to the south of the city for his country house and estimated that it would cost about £3000, which the nawab had offered to pay. The

[51] Foreign Pol. Con., 19 Feb. 1830, no. 32.

[52] Ibid., no. 33.

response from Calcutta on both points could not have been pleasing to the Resident. The Governor General wanted to do away with the daroga system entirely and laid down that "petty repairs, such as mending of doors, windows, white-washing and cleaning parts of the premises were to be executed by the Resident himself at the Nawab's expense" while major repairs and alterations were to be superintended by the Resident and carried out by "the officer or officers instructed with the care and repair of the King's Palaces and other Public Buildings." As for the Resident's proposed country house, the Governor General replied: "if you require accommodation of that description, the cost thereof had better, on every account, be defrayed from your own personal funds," indicating that officers of the Company were not to put personal considerations above the feeling of obligation that would certainly be incurred if the nawab began making gifts of houses to them.[53]

The dispute over the repairs was finally settled by entrusting the repairs to the nawab's *vakil*, an administrator or factor, under the supervision of the Resident, though the nawab still paid for all the work. This meant that the British were still under a financial obligation to the nawab; this they tried again to shake off in 1853 when the nawab, Wajid Ali Shah, was urged to let the occupants pay for the repairs to their houses. The nawab sidestepped this proposal most adroitly by saying that this would "detract from his dignity" and that "the buildings are his own and he must be allowed to keep them in repair for his guests."[54] There was no doubt that both sides appreciated the tactical importance of who paid for the Residency repairs. Lord Dalhousie, the Governor General, had himself written in 1854 that "It is the general desire of the Government to shake itself free from all obligations to the Court of Lucknow in respect of its officers and this has been done (except in the case of residences) in all respects." He added however that "the relinquishment of the present residences must involve the building of a new

[53] Ibid., no. 34.

[54] India Pol. Con., 10 June 1853, nos 128–32. I.O.L.

Residency,"[55] a topic which had caused much controversy already between successive nawabs and Residents.

In 1820 the nawab Ghazi-ud-din Haider had written to the Governor General:

> Let it not be concealed from your Lordship – the spot selected for the residence of the British representative was originally at some distance from the dwelling houses of the principal People of my family, but when my revered father [Saadat Ali Khan] extended the City to the East and fixed his residence there, by degrees buildings grew up round the palace till at length they came to be close upon the house of the British representative, in so much that my father intended to have assigned a different house for his residence. Since his decease a new gateway has been erected beyond the boundary of the grounds originally attached to the house and there has not remained sufficient space for many necessary transactions.

The nawab stated that the Residency overlooked the Farhad Baksh and that when the Residency was vacated he proposed to incorporate it into the enclosure of that building. The nawab wanted "to allot in lieu of them [the Residency buildings] the House and Ground of Beroun [Barowen],"[56] which the Resident immediately rejected as being too far away, and he added that the gift of Barowen would only compensate for the loss of Bibiapur, given up to Saadat Ali Khan by a former Resident. The Resident further said that "the Residency was established in its present spot for nearly fifty years [i.e. the mid 1770s] and the late Vizier [Saadat Ali Khan] established his residence in the vicinity of the Residency with a full knowledge of its commanding situation. Twenty years have elapsed since the late Vizier and His Majesty have successively resided at Furuh Buksh." If, however, the nawab insisted on taking over the Residency site he should pay compensation to the people living and working in the area, added the Resident – an odd statement to make if the Residency staff had really seen themselves as guests of the

[55] Foreign Con., 21 July 1854, nos 9–12.
[56] Foreign Pol. Index, 17 Feb. 1821, no. 45.

nawab who were allocated houses by him "as a personal favour".[57] But the nawab abruptly dropped the subject of a move and the Resident was able to report back to Calcutta that the nawab had "either abandoned the wish of obtaining the Residency houses and grounds" or that he wished to put off finding a new spot for the Residency to "some future period".[58]

The second proposal to move the British out of the city came in the autumn of 1831 from Nawab Nasir-ud-din Haider who sent an official note to the Resident, Col. John Low:

> As the House in which you live is situated very close to the Palace of Kusur oos Sooleman [in the Farhad Baksh enclosure] and in consequence of its elevated situation, many of my houses are overlooked which for many reasons is inconvenient and troublesome, and as also it is improper for certain reasons that the Residency House should be so near to the Government Houses, in consequence of which his late Majesty [Ghazi-ud-din Haider] addressed the Most Noble the Marquess of Hastings to remove the Residency and His Excellency's acquiescence in this purpose is evident and as moreover from the concourse of the people of the city round the House, and from the public thoroughfare, and the proximity of filth and dirt, you must also feel inconvenience, under these circumstances it is my wish that a Residency House should be built, on my part, in Char Bagh, which, on account of its extensive grounds is a delightful place, and the water and air of which is pure, and near which the Canal from the river Ganges will pass. It is besides not very distant from my Houses and I wish to join the Residency House to the Palace as it is very close, that it may obviate trouble to me, and you may receive pleasure by residing in that extensive and delightful place.[59]

This extract is interesting for two reasons. Firstly the nawab appears to overstate his arguments for wanting the Residency site vacated, suggesting four different reasons in almost as many lines, though the probable reason emerged later in the debate. Secondly, the suggestion of the Char Bagh site might well have been prompt-

[57] Ibid., no. 46.

[58] Ibid., no. 48.

[59] Foreign Pol. Con., 7 Oct. 1831, no. 23.

ed by Maddock's suggestion the previous year that a country house paid for by the nawab in this area would be very acceptable.

Col. John Low, who had replaced Maddock, had mixed feelings about the proposal to move to Char Bagh: "The change from a crowded city to the country and surrounding gardens would be most agreeable as regards the question of a dwelling house" but he foresaw difficulties as many people had business both with the Residency office and the nawab's neighbouring court. Lawyers and others who had houses round the Residency would be inconvenienced if the Residency was moved out, and even so, "the Resident would still need a house in the city as he has to be in touch with the Court."[60] There was also the element of "protection" assumed by people in the neighbouring houses which would be lost if the Residency moved. As for the real reason for the proposed move the Resident wrote, "His Majesty doubtless has in view that his rule and authority would appear more complete within his capital by the removal of the British representative to the country."

However, the Residency doctor was deputed to examine the site at Char Bagh and his report was unfavourable "on the ground that Europeans living in a situation that is lower than all the surrounding country would almost to a certainty be attacked with fever for several months after the rains each year."[61] This is a highly unconvincing argument, as a walk over the site shows that Char Bagh is certainly no lower than any other spot south of the city. The nawab on being told that Char Bagh was unhealthy according to the British did not attempt to argue the merits of its pure air and water again, but offered Barowen, which was rejected as being too far away. Later "a spot across the River Goomti, near to the King's racecourse" was offered and also turned down.[62] The nawab then suggested with some desperation "any house, even the Dilkoosha, though he wished to keep it for himself with the view of occasionally spending a day there." The Resident, however, selected three elevated spots in

[60] Ibid., no. 22.

[61] Foreign Pol. Con., 2 Sept. 1831, no. 7.

[62] Ibid., no. 8.

the Dilkusha Park which seemed to be suitable and plans were made for roads to the proposed new Residency.[63]

Meanwhile Col. Low had written to Calcutta analysing the reasons why the nawab and his ministers wanted the Residency moved, and giving reasons why he himself would not strongly oppose the change. The Resident was often bothered by trifles, he explained, especially by Anglo-Indians and Europeans, and he also felt the Resident interfered too much in the court. Ricketts, who had been Resident between 1822 and 1830, had lived entirely for the last three years in the Cantonment, and the Hyderabad Resident lived a long way outside the city yet could still intervene when necessary in court.[64] The nawab, moreover, planned to erect "a very large and splendid palace on the present Residency site and to plant an avenue of trees from it to the new Iron Bridge."[65] The Resident saw "no harm in the move" and added, "the proposed new . . . palace would overlook the whole city of Lucknow and would be finished in such a style (as the Nawab says) that the Palace of the King of Oude would become famous as one of the most spacious and elegant Buildings in all India."[66] But, Low added, the minister Hakim Mehndi wanted the British to go for political reasons, "leaving to the King and himself, both the name and reality of more complete power in this capital." Hakim Mehndi who was constantly bothered with petty affairs said that both parties in these local disputes sought support from the Resident against the nawab, and if the Resident was "out there", he, the minister, "could settle things himself in a few minutes."[67] A year later the nawab was pleased to learn that the Governor General had ordered the Residency House "should be vacated and made over to my control and that the Resident should reside in some other place." "The order," he add-

[63] Ibid., no. 11.
[64] Ibid., no. 12.
[65] Ibid., no. 14.
[66] Ibid., no. 15.
[67] Ibid., no. 17.

ed "has much exalted my dignity."[68] But the reason why the proposed move never took place comes not from official records but from a private diary for 1831–2 kept by James Herbert, the Company official appointed to superintend the new Observatory in Lucknow. Herbert described the coldness between the nawab and Hakim Mehndi and wrote:

> An additional cause of offence [to the nawab] was said to have been the Minister's having authorized the site of the new Resident [*sic*] to be fixed in the Park of Dilkhoosha which the King it is said considers his private residence and therefore strongly objects to being opened even to the Resident anxious as he is to see him moved. But however this may be it is certain that the first intimation the public had of the insecure ground on which the Minister stood was promulgated on the occasion of fixing the actual extent of the new Residency and putting up flags in the park to mark the boundary preparatory to its being surveyed. And one of the first consequences of the Minister's disgrace was the discontinuance of the survey, the removal of the flags and the total abandonment apparently of the question of a new Residency.[69]

This highly interesting statement is confirmed by the fact that after Hakim Mehndi's dismissal there was a severe retrenchment in nawabi spending, and it is likely Nasir-ud-din Haider found himself seriously embarrassed by his promise to provide a new Residency with all its attendant offices, not to mention the grandiose schemes for the new palace he had proposed. There is no further suggestion from any source that the Residency should be moved, and it remains to this day where it was established in 1775.

The site now consists of ruins, many of them substantial, established among trees and rich foliage. All the outbuildings, which made the site something of a maze, its passages and garden walls, have been swept away, together with the numerous native houses to the north, east and south of the hill. The ruins now stand isolated

[68] Foreign Pol. Con., 17 Sept. 1832, nos 74A & 74B.

[69] Diskalker, pp. 7–23.

from the streets of Lucknow by broad swathes of grass and a low wall, thus making it difficult to appreciate the scarcely tenable position of the area during its siege for five months in 1857, when the mutineers were able to stand at the windows of neighbouring houses and fire directly into the British buildings.[70]

The tremendous impact on European imaginations that the siege made has unfortunately tended to obscure the earlier history of buildings here and the names now given to private houses within the area show only who lived in them in 1857, e.g. Gubbins' Garrison, Anderson's Garrison, Innes' Garrison, and so on. The bungalows where the first Residents lived and worked seem to have disappeared some time before 1800 and the transition to large, solidly built houses by the Residency staff passed quite unremarked. Earlier visitors to the compound usually described the area in generalised terms – "a sort of close, with good-looking houses and small gardens round it and a barrack and guard house at its entrance" (1825),[71] and twenty years later Dr Hoffmeister wrote, "the street soon widened into a spacious square, a beautiful and verdant lawn and rich wood appeared before us on the other side of a lofty freestone arch. Passing through this gateway, we entered a sort of park, at the further extremity of which are several large yellow rough-cast buildings. Flat roofs with massive balustrades, lofty colonnades surround plain quadrangular boxes, and carefully closed jalousies, characterised it as the dwelling of the British Resident."[72] Between the larger private houses set in their small gardens were metalled roads laid down about 1853 at a cost of £400, an unusual feature

[70] See for example *A Personal Narrative of the Siege of Lucknow* by L.E. Ruutz Rees (London 1858), p. 195 (hereafter Ruutz Rees), where the author describes a sortie to Johannes House just outside the compound, from which an African eunuch of the court had been shooting at the British. This house was finally blown up by British engineers who were able to lay a mine in a passage under the narrow road between the Residency houses and those opposite.

[71] Heber, i, p. 377.

[72] Hoffmeister, Dr W., *Travels in Ceylon and Continental India* (Edinburgh 1848), p. 251. Hereafter Hoffmeister.

at this time when there appear to have been only two other metalled roads in the city.[73] After the siege the buildings became the subject of the most intense interest, even to the extent of a model being made of every building in the complex as it had been before;[74] but naturally this interest was directed to recent events, not to the origins of the buildings. From maps and plans made after the siege, which itself had radically altered the area, it can be estimated that there were at least eighteen major buildings standing in their own grounds, including ten private houses, and many outbuildings. There were also a number of houses belonging to Indians, but not surprisingly considering the emotive subject of the siege, they are not mentioned in any detail. The names of the buildings give an indication of the varied nature of activities within the complex and the self-sufficiency of the inhabitants.

There was the sheep house, the slaughterhouse, the two Sikh squares, the horse square, the post office, the barracks, the brigade mess, the racket court, the native hospital, the school, the Banqueting Hall, the church, two mosques, and the Residency. Apart from a small museum in an undamaged portion of the Residency, the only other building in use today (1975) is one of the mosques, though it is only visited during daylight because of the fear of ghosts. Visitors to the area approached it by the main road that led west from Hazratganj, through the clock-tower gateway of the palace and the Baillie Guard gateway. Through the gateway to the left stood the new treasury building finished about 1851 at a cost of Rs 16,897, a long one-storeyed structure with a verandah supported by plain double columns. The Banqueting Hall next to the

[73] Foreign Con., 10 June 1853, nos 128–32.

[74] There were two copies of this model made by the Rev. T. Moore. One was housed in the Residency Museum, Lucknow, but has been greatly mutilated by the glass case falling on it, and is now useless for the purposes of research. The other model was presented to Bristol Museum in 1908 but recent correspondence with the curator has revealed that this model was probably destroyed during the second world war by air-raids. See also the Rev. T. Moore's *Guide to the Residency Model* (Lucknow 1885). Hereafter Moore.

new treasury was probably the most imposing structure in the whole area, with its state apartments and "spacious salons, furnished with costly chandeliers, mirrors and silk divans" where the Nawab Amjad Ali Shah would attend dinners and breakfasts.[75] The fine furniture in the hall was complemented by the high quality of the workmanship in the building. A stucco fireplace at first floor level still retains a marble-like finish after nearly one hundred and twenty-five years of exposure to the elements, and a broken fountain in the main entrance hall exhibits a fine example of inlaid marble work in black and white. The date of construction is unknown; it has been suggested on no firm grounds that it was erected by Saadat Ali Khan, but this can be disputed by a piece of negative evidence. Richard Strachey, Resident between 1815 and 1817, in a report to Calcutta two years after that nawab's death, justified recent enlargements within the complex, claiming "the old Residency was quite inadequate to the Entertainment of the Vizier [the nawab] and his Court, as it contains no Room which will accommodate more than half the party on great occasions, when Tents were pitched or Tables spread for the remainder of the Guests in adjoining Apartments."[76] This statement could certainly not be true if the Banqueting Hall had then been standing with its huge state rooms on the first floor.

To the left of the Banqueting Hall lies the house of the Residency surgeon during the siege, Dr Fayrer, and directly behind it is the Begum Kothi which originally belonged to Asaf-ud-daula and was bought from him by Sacville Marcus Taylor, Assistant Resident, postmaster and merchant, who was in Lucknow between 1786 and 1802.[77] The house could not be bought outright from the nawab, presumably because he wished to retain a measure of control over it, and when Taylor sold it in 1802 to George Prendergast

[75] Von Orlich, Capt. Leopold, *Travels in India*, translated by H. Evans Lloyd (London 1845), ii, 4. Hereafter von Orlich.

[76] Strachey, Mss. Eur. D. 514, E. 243.

[77] India Pol. Con., Part 1, 16 Aug. 1850, no. 134.

he had to obtain the nawab's permission for the sale.[78] George Prendergast was also a merchant, with an English assistant, and they carried on "very extensive dealings" in Lucknow.[79] These included the setting up of a Europe shop business in the Begum Kothi. A few years later Prendergast sold the house and the business to John Culloden, a previous tenant of Claude Martin's who had occupied a nearby house. Culloden continued to run the shop and on his death in 1807 he left the entire property to his wife and children, specifying that the house was to be kept "for the purpose of bringing up the children under their Mother."[80] Culloden's daughter and granddaughter were buried within the compound of this house, a second daughter, Shurf-un-Nissa, building a mosque and mausoleum for them here. It is this small mosque which survives to the present day, and which is interesting in that it is built on the first floor and can only be approached up a narrow flight of steps.

To the north-west of the Begum Kothi lay the Residency which gave its name to this whole area. It was described as "an imposing pile of buildings . . . of three stories. Along the west front extended a wide and lofty columnaded verandah. The principal entrance was on the east side, under a handsome portico . . . a spiral stairs inside two turrets on the north and south sides led to the roof." There were "numberless lofty windows, and the roof was protected by an ornamental balustrade in the Italian style." Under the south side of the building were deep *tykhanas*.[81] The building may have been an imposing pile in sheer bulk, but architecturally it was unsatisfactory and disappointing. There was no overall style, either Indian or European, which can be perceived, and the two squat towers (one of which remains) contrasted uneasily with the portico and loggia of the west front.

[78] Sleeman, Sir William, *A Journey through the Kingdom of Oude* (London 1858), i, p. 326.

[79] *Memoirs of William Hickey* (London 1919–25), iv, p. 125.

[80] Foreign Pol. Index, 12 Oct. 1816, nos 30 and 38.

[81] Gubbins, M.R., *An Account of the Mutinies in Oudh* (London 1858), p. 162. Hereafter Gubbins.

To the north-west of the Residency lay the church, now standing only to a height of two or three feet and surrounded by a cemetery, first used during the siege. It had previously been considered unhealthy to bury the dead in a residential area, but the enormous number of casualties meant that the dead had to be bundled into the ground near the church after nightfall, often with no burial service other than a brief prayer.[82] There had been a request for a church as early as 1775 by the Rev. Johnson, the Residency chaplain, but it was not until 1837 with the opening of the small church in the Cantonment that Protestants found a permanent place to worship.[83] Those who could not make the long journey to the Cantonment contented themselves with "a long commodious room properly fitted up by private subscription for the celebration of Divine Service,"[84] in a large two-storeyed house owned by the nawab, which stood near the post office. This house was destroyed by fire in April 1844 along with several others in the area, including the buildings that housed the European Library and the Girls' School. It was subsequently agreed that the nawab should give the British some land for a proper church and a minister was deputed to pick out a suitable spot, choosing the area to the west of the Residency where the Boys' School (set up by Nasir-ud-din Haider) had been housed, together with the "compound, buildings, Bricks and wood etc. attached to it." By August 1845 the Resident was able to forward to Calcutta "2 coloured plans of the Church and a subscription list" and to report that the Church which was to be erected would be "handsome and spacious".[85]

[82] Hilton, E.H., *Guide to Lucknow and the Residency* (Lucknow 1934), p. 57 (hereafter Hilton), and see also the Rev. Henry Polehampton's *A Memoir, Letters and Diary* (London 1858), pp. 94–5 (hereafter Polehampton), where the clergyman wrote (in 1856): "Close to the Residency is the church, covered in with trees, standing in a large walled-in space, not a churchyard; we don't bury in or near churches in India."

[83] Press List, 1775–9. Item dated 20 March 1775. National Archives, New Delhi.

[84] Foreign Con., 14 March 1845, no. 131.

[85] Foreign Con., 29 Aug. 1845, nos 89 and 90.

The anticipated opening of the Iron Bridge encouraged the Resident to think that people from the Cantonment would come to the Residency church for the evening service as well as the teachers and pupils from the newly opened college of La Martinière (Constantia) who as yet had no chaplain. But the church also had to be something more than a convenient meeting place for Protestants in Lucknow; as the Resident explained "surrounded as we are by Muslims and Hindoos with their towering mosques and gilded temples, a Diminutive and unattractive building would prove to be an object of no other than very unfavourable comparison to the non-professors of our holy Faith, [therefore] we determined upon the plan of which a copy is forwarded and we humbly hope that its contemplated original will in some measure answer the objects which in its adoption we had in view."[86] The grammar here may be convoluted but the message is plain.

To the south of the church stood the sheep house and the slaughter house, both of which have vanished completely, and beyond them was the racket court and the house of Martin Gubbins, since 1856 the Financial Commissioner of the province.

Gubbins House (as it was called briefly) was an unusual building for Lucknow, but no information about it is forthcoming, apart from a statement that it was "built by the king as a concert room and cock-pit."[87] Which king or nawab is not stated and one can only deduce that it may have been Asaf-ud-daula who was inordinately fond of cockfighting,[88] and that because the house contained an octagon room (an uncommon feature in European-style houses) it may have been designed by Martin or copied from one of his buildings – as this was a peculiarity of both the Farhad Baksh and Constantia. One could further speculate that it was the house originally belonging to Col. Mordaunt, who was also addicted to cockfighting. To the east of Gubbins House and in the southern quarter of the complex were the military quarters of the Residency; the

[86] Ibid., no. 92.

[87] Moore, p. 29.

[88] See note 25 above.

horse square, the Sikh square, the barracks and the houses of the two celebrated Indian moneylenders Shah Bihari Lal and Ragbir Diyal.

Because comparatively little remains of the Residency buildings and because there are so few contemporary descriptions it is impossible to judge what architectural effect these buildings had in Lucknow. The British put up few brick buildings in the complex, the majority being erected by the nawabs for the British at unspecified dates and without consultation with Company officials. One must conclude that the Residency buildings therefore played little part in influencing Lucknow architecture, being themselves, as far as can be judged, an eclectic mixture of styles.

6

The Cantonment

IN 1807 THE British Cantonment at Lucknow underwent a radical change when it was transferred from the banks of the river Gomti to Mariaon, nearly four miles north of the city. From being a purely military area that was almost exclusively masculine and where there was no scope for social activities, it became a British enclave that aped the larger Residency compound in the city and a place where the wives and children of officers could live in reasonable comfort, with a range of leisure activities. In spite of the change in the nature of the Cantonment, the area was always regarded as being of secondary importance to the Residency compound in the city and was seldom visited by tourists to Lucknow. Although no drawings or photographs of the area exist, the growth of the Cantonment is worth examining not only for the light it throws on European life in Lucknow but also as a further example of the territorial battles between the Company and the nawabs.

The original reasons for the presence of the British Cantonment in Awadh were both political and military. One of the keys to Warren Hastings' foreign policy was the maintenance of an alliance with the nawabs of Awadh, both to protect the frontiers of British-controlled India and to reduce the expenses of the Company's army. To that end Hastings and Shuja-ud-daula agreed in 1773 that the nawab would bear the cost of maintaining British forces in return for their help in annexing the Rohilla kingdom on the western borders of Awadh, which was successfully accomplished the following year. From then on pressure was brought by the British on subsequent nawabs to maintain permanent forces in Awadh, and payments for these forces and the Cantonment needed for them increased rapidly. Although the Rohilla war was the first and last major engagement where British troops were used at the nawab's request, Asaf-ud-daula was forced to make large payments to the Company for troops he did not want and which the Company would not withdraw. In 1801 Saadat Ali Khan was forced to cede half his territories as payment for unwanted troops, and under threat of losing the rest of his kingdom agreed to the stationing of 10,000 Company troops on his remaining land. So there was a distinct change between the first troops sent in to protect a friendly ruler, Shuja-ud-daula, and the battalions of Saadat Ali Khan's time which were able to dictate terms to their reluctant ally.

As for the composition of the troops themselves and the nature of their housing, paid for by the nawabs, little information is available other than that the Indians in the battalions had with them their own carpenters, which suggests that in common with other sepoy battalions they built their own huts. The European officers and soldiers on the other hand were provided for by the nawab and his ministers – who also "built Artillery Sheds, places for Arms, Powder Magazines, Guard Rooms, etc., the whole being conducted under the inspection of a Servant of the Vizier."[1] In 1796 the British Cantonment was situated mainly on the north bank of the Gomti, almost opposite the Daulat Khana complex inhabited by Asaf-ud-daula. This bank was known as the "English side of the river,"[2] and the Gomti was crossed by "a crazy Bridge of Boats."[3] By 1806 the British Resident Col. John Collins was writing to the Governor General in Calcutta,[4] suggesting that a new and larger site should be found for the troops, who needed additional buildings including a "store room, Hospital, publick Cattle and private stabling."[5] The estimated size of the enlarged Cantonment area was 1560 bighas of land,

[1] Secret and Pol. Con., 23 May 1787, no number given.
[2] Haider, S.K.U., *Tarikh-e-Awadh* (Lucknow n.d.), p. 170.
[3] Foreign Pol. Con., 12 Feb. 1807, nos 4 and 20.
[4] Foreign Pol. Con., 19 June 1806, no. 11.
[5] Foreign Pol. Con., 11 Dec. 1806, no. 35A.

which Saadat Ali Khan considered excessive.[6] It is clear from the nawab's response to the Company's request that it was not so much the position of the Cantonment that worried him as the greater amount of land demanded. The nawab saw any substantial increase in the Cantonment area as a further serious encroachment by the British upon his sovereign state. The presence of British troops was something that the nawab could not control, but he felt that by putting physical limits on the amount of land granted he could perhaps control their number. After much correspondence between the nawab, the Resident and Calcutta, Lieut. Col. Thomas – the officer commanding the detachment at Lucknow – was sent out to inspect an area of "elevated land South of His Excellency's Hunting Lodge called the ABC House, distant from the Eastern end of the pucka Bridge [the Stone Bridge] across the Goomtee, perhaps two miles."[7] In fact the area chosen was, as far as can be determined, slightly to the west of that proposed by Thomas, with the village of Subouli to the right of the Cantonment, though it was nearer three than two miles to the north bank of the river.

The Resident, Col. Collins, was able to report back to the Company in Calcutta in March 1807 that the nawab had agreed at once to the new site, making no objection to its size or position.[8] He may have felt that the situation of the site, which was difficult to reach from the city, in some way compensated for the disquiet he felt over the size of the new Cantonment. It was not until the opening of the Iron Bridge and the Cantonment road in 1846/7 that the Mariaon Cantonment became somewhat more accessible from the city, when troops no longer had to make the detour to cross the Stone Bridge. The nawab, having agreed to the site, nevertheless laid down

[6] Ibid., no. 30B.

[7] The ABC House was described in 1816 as a "hunting house, in an extensive rumna [park] near to the cantonments of Maneeown [Mariaon] . . . built by the late Vizier and whimsically ornamented round the freeze [*sic*] of each room with the alphabet, in Roman characters, A, B, C, etc. in repeated succession." *Asiatic Journal* (London 1816), p. 579.

[8] Bengal Pol. Con., March 1807, no. 74.

stringent conditions for the new Cantonment, which reflect both his fears about British expansion and about the possibility of his own people becoming too friendly with the British troops. A list of the conditions was sent to Col. Collins in March 1807 together with the nawab's agreement to the new site, and the Resident's acceptance of the conditions is also recorded. The documents are summarised below.[9]

1. Only the British troops and their followers were allowed to reside on the ground allotted for the new Cantonment.
2. No ganj was to be erected within the Cantonment area for *beparies* (*baipari*) traders or merchants, because such an area would have been detrimental to the markets in the city and the nawab would have lost revenue from the duties levied on the city markets.
3. There was to be no exemption of duty for the Cantonment except on articles actually required for consumption by British troops. Any traders who took such articles out of the Cantonment (i.e. unsold food, etc.) to other places had to pay duty on their goods sold elsewhere.
4. No moneylenders or inhabitants of Lucknow were to reside in the Cantonment without the previous consent and approval of the nawab.
5. There was to be no fortified building there, besides the officers' bungalows and the magazine for artillery.
6. No delinquents were to be given sanctuary within the Cantonment and any criminals who tried to hide there would be handed over to the nawab.
7. The exercising ground was to be distinct from the Cantonment, was to be kept clear and ready for exercising troops, and was not to be built on.
8. A ditch was to be dug round the Cantonment to define the limits, and no extension beyond that ditch would be allowed. The limits of the Cantonment were also to be marked out distinctly by a durable token.

[9] Ibid., nos 74 and 76, and Bengal Pol. Con., 5 March 1807, no. 74.

9. A *khubburder* (*khabardar*) informer, scout, or spy, was to be stationed in the Cantonment to bring news to the nawab, since the Cantonment was on land belonging to the nawab.

Clauses 7 and 8 show clearly that the nawab feared gradual encroachment by the British, and the ditch which he suggested was something of a Canute-like gesture – a futile attempt to limit British interference by a physical barrier. The flags the British had first suggested for defining the Cantonment limits could of course be uprooted and moved, but a ditch was the clearest possible boundary. The nawab was equally concerned both to keep the British confined and to make it as difficult as possible for his own people to enter the British zone. It will be seen later how this strict segregation broke down.

On 8th March 1807 Lieut. Phipps, Adjutant of the 2nd Battalion, 13th Regiment, met Paris Bradshaw, the Assistant Resident at the new site, "to measure the space given by His Excellency."[10] Lieut. Phipps, who had been left at Lucknow "for the purpose of constructing new Cantonments,"[11] found that as soon as he had measured out the ground the Hindu sepoys of the Company's troops were moved out to the site to avoid communal disturbances at the old Cantonment site. The pukka buildings for the officers, the magazine for artillery, tanks, etc., were erected in great haste (Lieut. Thomas had said as early as 12 February that "the season favourable for building is passing away"), and by June 1807 before the rains began the buildings were finished. At the end of June the nawab took a ride out to the new Cantonment and told the Resident that he had noticed that the four-mile ditch which had been dug round the Cantonment to define its limits was already filled up with sand, and he requested that eight or twelve masonry pillars should be erected as a more permanent boundary.[12] To this Paris Bradshaw,

[10] Bengal Pol. Con., 26 March 1807, no. 48.

[11] Bengal Pol. Con., 29 Jan. 1807, no. 93, and Foreign Pol. Con., 12 Feb. 1807, no. 20.

[12] Bengal Pol. Con.. 25 June 1807, no. 69.

the Acting Resident, who had taken over after Col. Collins' sudden death, agreed, and the site was declared completed.

No details survive of the actual materials used in construction, nor of the cost of building materials, but comparison with a similar Cantonment shows the kind of workers needed. They included carpenters, bricklayers of both sexes, smiths, sawyers, thatchers, lime makers, lascars, water carriers, buffalo drivers, watchmen, writers, messengers, coolies, and miscellaneous boys and women. A *sircar* (Indian superintendent or leader) supervised the work, and he was in turn responsible to a European captain of Engineers in charge of the whole site. (This would be the position that Lieut. Phipps held at Lucknow.) The wages of the sircar were the highest among the Indian workers, he got Rs 30 per month (about £1.10s) while the lowest paid workers, the women, got Rs 1.12 annas per month (about 1s. 9d). Work on the site included stone breaking, making lime and brick kilns, thatching, weighing and piling firewood, carrying limestone, and baking bricks. Bamboo and straw were used for thatching, and both iron and wood were used to make the moulds for bricks. Bricks were fired in kilns near the site, and stones, broken up by coolies, were burnt in kilns to provide lime for the cement and plaster. Crude scaffolding of bamboo lashed together with rope was erected so the thatchers could reach the roofs.[13]

The first description of the completed Cantonment is in October 1819 when Thomas Lumsden, a traveller, visited the area and described it thus –

> the general plan of a cantonment, on this side of India, is to have a good piece of ground for the exercise of the troops in front, with a line of small buildings for depositing the arms in the rear. Next to these are the huts of the sepoys and in their rear the bungalows of the officers, which are built in the cottage style, very well adapted for the climate, and each having a garden around it, with a range of out offices, consisting of a kitchen, stables and servants houses.[14]

[13] Secret and Military Con.. 10 Nov. 1790. No number given.

[14] Lumsden, Thomas, *A Journey from Meerut in India to London during the Years 1819 and 1820* (London 1822), pp. 14–15. Hereafter Lumsden.

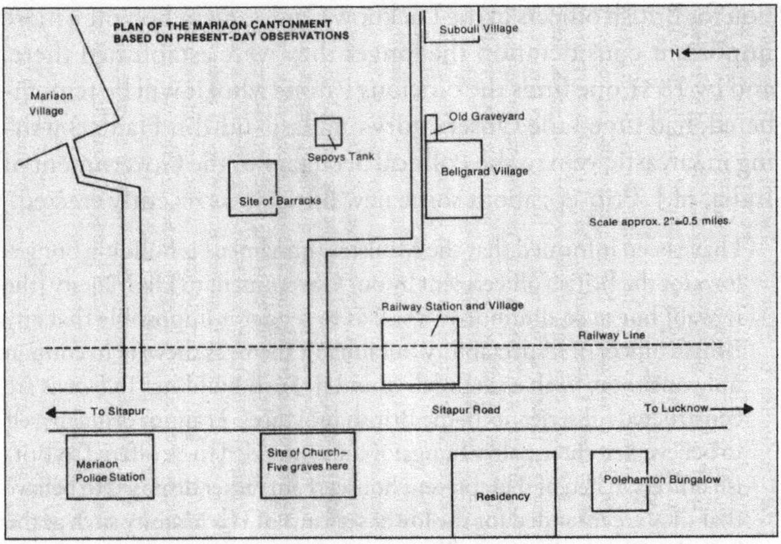

The bungalows of the officers were at this time developing from something more than the simple rectangular thatched or tiled huts that were common in Lucknow. By the 1820s the usual plan of a bungalow was to have one large high-ceilinged room in the centre and one of "a comfortable size" on each side, with a small room in each corner. The central room was for dining, the side rooms for beds and spare apartments, and the corner rooms for bath rooms, store rooms, etc. The apartments all opened out into curtains, or tatties, which could be rolled up when not in use. One important piece of information about the Lucknow Cantonment is missing, and that is who actually paid for the building of the bungalows and sepoys' huts. The Company had sanctioned payment for the ditch round the Cantonment and the masonry pillars, but it is not known whether they paid for the buildings and rented them to the officers and sepoys or whether the troops were expected to pay for their own accommodation, which they could sell when they were transferred elsewhere. Civilians living in the Cantonment certainly paid for the building of their houses but the initial arrangements for officers and sepoys' dwellings are unknown. Decent accommodation for British officers in the Lucknow Cantonment became a more important consideration the longer they were established there, and by 1831 one finds the officious Paton (who, it will be remembered, had urged the Observatory on Nasir-ud-din Haider) writing in sarcastic vein to the Political Secretary to the Government of India, H.J. Prinsep, about some new bungalows recently erected.

> I have been informed that the Minister [unnamed] is building bungalows for the British officers lent by our Government to His Majesty [the nawab] but of so diminutive a size as to render it impossible that any British officer of respectability can inhabit them, as they are to contain only one room with a verandah round it. Such buildings in fact as are constructed for serjeants in the British provinces. I cannot bring myself to believe that these paltry bungalows are intended to be offered to British officers in lieu of their present houses. I am rather disposed to believe that they are intended for the lower servants of His Majesty such as the hair-dresser, coachman etc.[15]

This was a clever letter as it allowed Paton to express his indignation at the insult offered to "British officers of respectability" while at the same time being rude about the nawab's hair-dresser, who was the famous Mr Derussett described in Knighton's book *The Private Life of an Eastern King*.[16] The coachman at that time was a Mr Joseph de Silva, a Portuguese or Indo-Portuguese.[17] It is interesting to note that the nawab's minister was now building diminutive bungalows for the British officers, for this represented a significant change from earlier policy on the Cantonment when the British had known exactly what they wanted to build, and had organised the work themselves. Certainly, local workpeople were employed, but it had been the British who were in charge, and Saadat Ali Khan's strict conditions had meant that the Mariaon Cantonment was effectively isolated from the mainstream of Lucknow life.

[15] Foreign Pol. Con., 16 Sept. 1831, no. 55.

[16] Knighton, William, *Private Life of an Eastern King* (London 1855), p. 17. Hereafter Knighton.

[17] Bengal Pol. Con., 25 Feb. 1831, no. 19.

The breakdown of this severe segregation had begun two years before Paton's letter in 1829, when Nawab Nasir-ud-din Haider had bought the bungalow in the Cantonment which had been built for Mordaunt Ricketts.[18] Ricketts had been the British Resident from 1822 to 1830 and during the last three years of his term of office he lived entirely in the Cantonment house.[19] A visitor in 1827 wrote, "in the cool of the day we drove to the country house of the British Resident where he generally resides in preference to the palace in the town."[20] Ricketts' country house or bungalow was evidently a fairly large building, for Henry Lawrence described it as being nearly as large as the city Residency building.[21] Together with the surrounding farm and dairy, with its imported English cows, it must have presented an exotic appearance to nawabi eyes, and proved irresistible to Nasir-ud-din Haider with his noted predilection for English things.

This house was subsequently known as the "King's House" or "Ricketts Sahib ka Bungalow" and was maintained by subsequent nawabs who considered it beneath their dignity to sell a house purchased by their ancestors.[22] There was, however, a tacit understanding that despite nawabi ownership of this house it would always be available for the Residents' use, though it never appears to have been utilised much for this purpose after Ricketts' departure. William Sleeman, the penultimate Resident, said: "I have made use of it occasionally for a few days at the close of the hot winds and commencement of the Rains, when epidemic diseases prevail in the City from accumulated filth, but even on these occasions I merely dine and sleep in it, returning except on Sundays to the Residency during the day for the transactions of business."[23]

[18] Foreign Pol. Con., 24 March 1853, no. 49.

[19] Foreign Pol. Con., 2 Sept. 1831, no. 12.

[20] Mundy, i, p. 35.

[21] Anderson, A.T., *A Short History of Lucknow* (Allahabad 1918), p. 15. Hereafter Anderson.

[22] Foreign Con., 24 March 1853, no. 49.

[23] Ibid., no. 45.

There is no further mention of the farm and dairy which had so delighted English visitors, and later the house was used as a theatre and ballroom, showing the substantial nature of the building.

Once a precedent had been set by the nawabi purchase of a British house in the Cantonment, the purchase of other buildings followed and a bungalow which had at one time been occupied by a Major Scott was, on his death "made over" to the nawab. This bungalow was very small and had been empty for some years, but the nawab had it repaired and enlarged and allowed the Rev. Dawson (the Cantonment chaplain) to occupy it. The clergyman reported that he regarded this "as a personal favour for which he felt greatly obliged" to the nawab.[24] This was the first house in the Cantonment "made over to Gentlemen about the Residency" and a similar transaction took place over the house built by J.M. Sinclair who had originally gone to Lucknow as an engineer and general mechanic to the Court. Sinclair had "built for himself a house in a garden in Cantonment, which he afterwards sold to the King." The house stood empty for three or four years and became much dilapidated but was then repaired and occupied by Dr Login, the Residency surgeon. The nawab, Muhammad Ali Shah, said Dr Login "wanted me and my family to be as comfortable as possible so he had glass doors fitted to it [the house] to make it habitable during the cold season."[25] When Dr Login and his family left this house it was improved and repaired even further at a cost of Rs 10,450 (£1045) and allocated to Captain R.W. Bird, the Assistant Resident, in 1848.[26] Three years later William Sleeman, Resident at the time, began to object strenuously to the fact that Captain Bird, his Assistant, had been allocated such a fine house instead of the usual bungalow allowed the Assistant in the Cantonment.[27] The Captain retaliated by claiming that the nawabs had always provided a house in the Cantonment for the Assistant Resident, just as a town house

[24] Ibid., no. 47.

[25] Ibid.

[26] Ibid., no. 52.

[27] Foreign Pol. Con., 24 March 1853, no. 49.

was provided too, and that both were "kept in repair, cleaned and otherwise attended to" by the Court officials. But Sleeman angrily refuted this, saying Captain Bird was the first Assistant who had ever got a country residence and that the upkeep of the Cantonment house had amounted only to "common floor cloths [probably *durries*, or cotton carpets] placed by his Majesty's servants, as in all of the King's houses" and the provision of ceiling fans (*punkahs*) and venetian blinds (*chicks*).[28]

But the reason for Sleeman's anger over what seems a fairly trivial matter becomes more explicable when it is learnt that Captain Bird, who was a keen racing man, only lived in his Cantonment house "during the training and racing season" in order to be near the racecourse, just south of the Cantonment. Captain Bird claimed that the Lucknow races "tended to bring together the Native Gentlemen of Lucknow and promote good feeling," but Sleeman said this was not so; on the other hand "there was a good deal of talk about . . . all Officers being familiar on the Race Course with the Singers and Eunuchs whom the Resident had so often had occasion to denounce to the King as reptiles who were ruining his reputation and his Country."[29] Moreover, one of the eunuchs called Busheer was "building large stables for his racing horses close by the Cantonment road." Sleeman had written to the nawab complaining about the stables and the races in general but had received an assurance from the nawab saying only that the building of the stables would be halted but nothing about the races being stopped. Sleeman told Bird that he did not consider the latter could "conduct his duties properly" from the Cantonment and that he should work from the city Residency, and also complained again about the nawab "fitting up and keeping up that Residence . . . at a very great cost" for the Captain.[30] The next year (1852) Captain Bird still persisted in his involvement with horse racing at the nearby racecourse, in defiance of Sleeman, and the latter in a letter to the Secretary to the Gov-

[28] Ibid., no. 53.

[29] Bengal Pol. Con., 13 June 1851, no. 145.

[30] Ibid.

ernment in Calcutta hinted darkly that he suspected the Captain of conspiring with the Residency Surgeon, Dr Adam Bell, to have Sleeman "unseated" from his position as Resident. (Both Captain Bird and Dr Bell were close friends of the nawab and social occasions like the race-course meetings gave them the opportunity to mix with the Court nobles and officials.) Sleeman continued his letter saying that during the thirty years he had been in service, he had never faced such obstacles as he now "experienced in secret intrigues about this the most corrupt, the most profligate, and I believe the most incompetent of Indian Courts."[31]

It is interesting to find such a clear-cut example of how contention over a building often concealed the much deeper political intrigues that were going on at the same time. It is also clear that on the question of ownership of property decisions tended to be made on an ad hoc basis, and that the British were pursuing a laissez-faire policy which allowed all kinds of irregularities to creep into what had seemed in 1807 a clear-cut situation.

An important statement on the ownership of Cantonment land was made in answer to a query by the Governor General in 1844 as to whether Brevet Captain Cecil of the 12th Regiment, Native Infantry, stationed in Lucknow was allowed to sell his estate in the Cantonment. An Indian woman, Mohumdee Begum, wanted to buy the Captain's property and the nawab Amjad Ali Shah ruled that "The case is this, that if the Bungalow be the property of that Officer, and be in his possession, he is at liberty to sell the House but not the Ground, as that is the property of the State. He has my permission."[32] The interesting thing about this response is the date. It cannot be imagined that the question of an officer selling his property to someone else, Indian or British, had never arisen before. Different regiments had been stationed in the Cantonment and the high death rate alone ensured a rapid turnover of men, and therefore property. Yet for thirty-seven years it had apparently never

[31] Bengal Pol. Con., 28 May 1852, no. 116.
[32] India Pol. Con., 16 March 1844, no. 114.

been queried whether houses could or could not be sold to officers or civilians, and when a query did arise it could only be solved by a direct appeal to the nawab, not by consulting a book of regulations or by examining precedents, of which there must have been many.

But the most confusing aspect of all this is the way in which British officials in Lucknow positively encouraged successive nawabs to buy up their houses and bungalows in the Cantonment, when it is this very factor of nawabi ownership that was so galling to the British in the city Residency. Here the British in the Cantonment are to be found selling houses to the nawabs and then occupying them by the "personal favour" of the new owners. Moreover the same system for repairs prevailed in the Cantonment as it did in the city Residency, i.e. the nawabs' vakils paid the cost of repairs to the Cantonment bungalows and for the upkeep of the gardens from the royal treasury, and in 1853 this figure was estimated at Rs 5222 for the year.[33]

The picture of ownership of land and property in the Cantonment at the time of annexation is thus most confused and vastly different from the one envisaged by Saadat Ali Khan when he endeavoured to separate the British and the Indians, and to "contain" the former in well-defined limits. Obviously there is no one explanation of the British acquiescence in nawabi infiltration in the Cantonment. Many factors were doubtless at work about which no information survives or maybe never existed. On general considerations, however, it seems likely that the change came about not as the result of deliberate treaty-embodied policy but rather of a relaxation of the rules by the British. The purpose of the Cantonment changed radically between 1775 and 1856 and during this period the British became uncertain about the function of the Cantonment, and therefore careless in their management, so that by 1856 there were more civilians, European and Indian, in the Cantonment than soldiers. By the end of Saadat Ali Khan's rule the polite fiction that the British were in Awadh solely to defend

[33] Foreign Con., 10 June 1853, no. 128.

the country against attack by unfriendly neighbours had long since been demolished, and the nawab's determined efforts to restrict British influence in his capital had proved fruitless.

The shift in the political spectrum naturally meant that the role of the British troops stationed in the capital came to be seen in a different light. Why were they there at all? On the death of Saadat Ali Khan the customary guard of British troops at the Daulat Khana and other prominent buildings in the city was discontinued. By 1817 it was the new nawab's own troops which were on guard duty in Lucknow, including a company at the Daulat Khana.[34]

The nawab's personal bodyguard of European troops also ceased on Saadat Ali Khan's death. Although later nawabs had European bodyguards, ADCs and escorts, these were now employed directly by the court and not provided by the Company. So if the British troops in Lucknow were not to provide men for the nawab's use, were they then expected to maintain sufficient numbers to quell disturbances in the town on their own account? Apparently not, for an account of a riot in 1840 between Hindus and Muslims specifically stated that it was the duty of the *kotwal* (the magistrate or chief of police) to act to restore peace in such cases without reference to British troops.[35] The only time the British troops appeared to have entered the city specifically to restore peace was in 1837 when, on the death of Nasir-ud-din Haider, an attempt was made by his putative son to occupy the musnud. Col. Low, the Resident at that time, anticipating trouble brought a number of troops from the Cantonment to the throne room in the Chattar Manzil complex to drive out the prince and Queen Mother and proclaim Nasir-ud-din Haider's uncle as the next nawab. About thirty or forty people were killed by the troops. although the dispute was contained in the palace, and the troops were not dispersed throughout the city to maintain order.[36]

[34] Bengal Pol. Con., 4 Feb. 1817, no. 10

[35] India Pol. Con., 21 Dec. 1840, no. 57.

[36] Sharar, p. 92.

It is significant that the troops and guns Col. Low brought with him to the palace in 1837 were more for the Resident's protection and the coercion of the pretender than the maintenance of law and order in the city as a whole. Of course had the Resident been imprudent enough to arrive on this occasion without sufficient troops, and had the insurgents been intent on his destruction, he would have been dead long before help could have reached him from the Cantonment. Bishop Heber was only the first of many writers to comment on the surprising distance between the Cantonment and the city.[37] The opening of the Iron Bridge reduced the journey to some extent, but there was no form of communication between the city Residency and Mariaon except by horse. There was no system of telegraphing or semaphoring messages in the city until 1856,[38] and had a sudden and determined attack been mounted upon the city Residency, no immediate help could have been expected from the Cantonment.

Ironically it was a sudden and determined attack that neither the Resident nor the nawabs could have anticipated that put an end to the Mariaon Cantonment on the night of 30 May 1857 when the bungalows there were set on fire by rebellious sepoys, and several Europeans murdered in their own houses. Only Polehampton's house, which had a flat plaster roof instead of thatch, seems to have escaped the conflagration. Loyal British troops who were encamped beyond the Cantonment to the north repulsed the sepoys, but no attempt at all was made to defend the area and it was shortly afterwards abandoned for good. Although many of the clauses in the 1807 treaty were later disregarded, no "work like a Fort" was ever built, as Saadat Ali Khan had stipulated, and there was no building in the Cantonment which was defensible or which could have been used as shelter for European refugees in the event of an uprising in the city.

[37] Heber, i, p. 383

[38] In July 1855 Wajid Ali Shah had requested the construction of an electric telegraph line from Cawnpore, but Dalhousie had vetoed this firmly. Foreign Con., 13 July 1855, nos 55–8.

So what was the purpose of the Mariaon Cantonment? Perversely isolated by British request from the city, totally indefensible to accord with the nawab's orders and housing troops who after 1814 appeared to play no significant part in the life and order of the city, it is not surprising that the British themselves became careless or confused over the role of the Cantonment and came to see no reason why the later nawabs should not buy property in the Cantonment limits – or pay for repairs there either. Mariaon was regarded as an adjunct to the city Residency, where the "real work" was carried out, or as a retreat from the city for people like Sleeman who used it "occasionally for a few days" – but even then only as a place for sleeping and eating, while he returned to the city Residency for "the transactions of business".[39] The awkward distance from Lucknow meant that Mariaon was too near a big city to develop independently but not far enough to form the nucleus of a separate town, as happened for example in Ambala. It was also not near enough to become a residential suburb like the post-1857 Cantonment of Dilkusha to the south-east of Lucknow. It is not surprising therefore that the site of the Cantonment has since reverted to its pre-1807 state and is once again covered by wheat fields.

Even before the sacking in May 1857 the Cantonment was probably destined to disappear. When the Rev. Henry Polehampton arrived in May 1856 after the annexation of Oudh he found about two hundred British citizens there (mostly civilians) and about a thousand native soldiers, but the bulk of the vicar's congregation was already housed in the city of Lucknow where the 52nd Regiment was installed in buildings which had been seized after Wajid Ali Shah's deposition.[40] It is more than likely that the Macchi Bhavan would have been the focal point of future military dispositions in Lucknow had not the Mutiny intervened.

The clergyman's diary conveys well that curious dream-like atmosphere of pre-1857 India when the British paused complacently to consolidate their rapid territorial gains of the last fifty years.

[39] Foreign Con., 24 March 1853, no. 46.

[40] Polehampton, p. 87.

"I don't know that anything has happened since I last wrote, worthy of record," he wrote to his mother in April 1857, and even at the end of April was still writing with easy expectancy: "there will be a bit of a row, but I don't think much harm will come of it."[41] Certainly life in the Cantonment during the last year seems in his account to have been quite uneventful, except for the perpetually high mortality among Europeans, and especially children. Every evening the British officers and their families would congregate to listen to the Cantonment band which played in the Company Bagh (garden) from six to seven, or the British would stroll along the Grand Parade. "There is always a crowd of carriages and buggies there," reported Polehampton.[42] During the heat of the day people would entertain themselves at home with books from the local book-club, which was kept up-to-date and supplied by an agent from the Calcutta firm of Thacker & Co. During the colder months there were cricket matches on the local ground, meetings at the nearby racecourse (which had caused Sleeman so much anguish before annexation) and entertainments in the ballroom and theatre housed in the Cantonment Residency. Those who wished could potter round their gardens supervising the Indian *malis*, and Polehampton boasted that his bungalow had "the best garden in cantonments" with plenty of strawberries, a delicacy that went well with the ice which residents could obtain from the local ice-club for a small subscription. Every British family had an ample supply of servants who lived in the compounds of their masters' bungalows. Polehampton and his wife had a total of twenty-three servants just for the two of them. On Sundays there was morning service at the small local church which had been built in 1839 at a cost of £540 raised by grants from the Company in Calcutta and by private subscriptions. There was even a harmonium in the church.

Metalled roads throughout the Cantonment meant that travelling was quick and easy, and for the last eleven years there had been a well-metalled road to Lucknow across the new Iron Bridge. At

[41] Ibid., pp. 217 and 230.

[42] Ibid., p. 144.

least two "Europe" shops existed, dealing in goods brought in from Calcutta, which in turn were imported from further afield.

After 1857 the British built a new Cantonment in Lucknow near the Dilkusha, an area that was easily accessible from the city, the old Cantonment being left to disintegrate. By 1913 when A.T. Anderson, a writer, visited the site, all the roads had disappeared and only the Polehampton bungalow was standing.[43] A small mound was said to cover the site of the church. When I visited the area in September 1977 even less was left. I had difficulty in locating the Cantonment site and was eventually directed to a tiny village, no more than a handful of cottages, which was called Beligarad (a corruption of the Bailey Guard, the name of the main entrance to the Cantonment). A dirt track led through fields of sugar cane to a walled enclosure beyond Beligarad where I found the Cantonment graveyard. This was the most tangible evidence of the large British community which had once lived there. An impressive pair of brick and stucco gate posts marked the entrance which was now blocked up, and there were the usual once handsome tombs and funerary monuments, though as with the Lucknow cemetery, Lat Kalan-ki-Lat, all the inscribed marble and stucco inscriptions had vanished: hence none of the graves could be positively identified. An informant who knew the area well as a child recalled the names of some of the fields which marked various sites in the Cantonment – the *gend ghar* (the cricket field) the *gol ghar* (the dance hall) and the *kamasariyat* (the commissariat where provisions for the troops were stored). Another small village nearby is called Chaoni (the Cantonment) and I was told that the sepoy tank near the barracks was still in existence, although I did not see it myself.[44]

[43] Anderson, p. 16.

[44] Much valuable information on the Cantonment site has come from Akilendra Singh who kindly walked over the site, interviewed villagers and made out a sketch plan.

7

Claude Martin's Buildings

IN THE PRECEDING chapters the origins of the Residency buildings and the Cantonment have been examined in detail. In neither case has it been possible to say much about the architectural styles employed in these two settlements, and the reasons for this are twofold. In the Cantonment no visible traces of buildings remain while in the Residency complex, although there are substantial remains of houses and offices, most of them are in a mutilated state. There are two buildings in the Residency area which can be considered as having definite architectural merit: the Begum Kothi and the Banqueting Hall.

All the detailed written descriptions of the Residency buildings were made after the 1857 siege when the site assumed great symbolic importance and there was a revulsion against the nawabi buildings, which were labelled "decadent". The notable lack of enthusiasm by pre-1857 European visitors over buildings built for British occupation would seem, however, to a large extent justified, and while it is regrettable from the historian's point of view that there is so little pre-1857 information, it is quite understandable that visitors whose time was often limited should neglect such buildings in favour of the more obviously striking features of the city.

Apart from the two Residency buildings it cannot be said on the evidence of existing remains, or of pictorial or written material, that the British were much concerned with fine architecture or with projecting a definite architectural style in Lucknow. This statement must of course be qualified by saying that it will probably never be known what some of the early British building in the city was like. For example Mr Orr's house in Lucknow is only known because Asaf-ud-daula had another built in imitation of it in 1799,[1] and there are several references to houses built by the British which have vanished completely. Henry J. Clark who arrived in India in 1793 and was engaged in various capacities by Asaf-ud-daula and Saadat Ali Khan built his house near the site of Claude Martin's powder magazine and wrote, "the house is really a good one, and the situation delightful." But it was later demolished when Ghazi-ud-din Haider had his canal built in this area and there are no descriptions or pictures of the house.[2]

Claude Martin's flamboyant buildings are also being left aside for the moment, both those that he erected for himself and those which he was commissioned to build. Nevertheless with these reservations it can still be argued that the British in Lucknow, especially those in an official capacity – the Residents, surgeons, writers, and other officers of the Company – did not evolve a distinctive colonial style of architecture for themselves; nor did they borrow the styles evolved by their countrymen in Calcutta and other cities where their power and rule was undisputed. There are three reasons for the architectural reticence of the British in Lucknow. In the first place a distinction should be made between the adventurers of the late eighteenth century and the Company officials of the early nineteenth. For a fairly brief period during the time of Asaf-ud-daula there was a spate of building by Europeans, and especially by the British, which were relatively unsupervised. This was when Martin's buildings were erected and when huge sums of money earned by speculation was invested in property by adventurers. But the death of Asaf-ud-daula generally marked the end of unrestricted building by Europeans in the city and a decline in the number of freelance adventurers like Martin, Polier, and Colonel Mordaunt. Their demise

[1] *Asiatic Annual Register* (London 1799), p. 29.

[2] Foreign Pol. Con., 3 Feb. 1816, no. 22.

was partly due to repeated Company requests from Calcutta that their presence should be controlled, and partly because men of this stamp found it more lucrative to work directly for the nawabs – as for example the Derussett brothers – than to remain as free agents with no specific loyalties.

Because such employees of the nawabs generally lived in apartments in the palaces where they were "on call" when their masters needed them, it meant an end to the building of grandiose houses in the city and an end to the great measure of independence that the early adventurers had enjoyed. Their livelihood now depended to a large extent on the whims and caprices of their royal employers, and it was obviously more prudent to accumulate wealth in the form of easily portable valuables like jewels and fine shawls than to invest in house building when one might face instant dismissal from the city for no good reason.[3]

As for the British officials of the Company, they too were circumscribed after the death of Asaf-ud-daula and both nawabi restrictions and their own prejudices kept them confined in or near the Residency complex or the Cantonment. Saadat Ali Khan's restrictions on the Mariaon Cantonment meant that at first only serviceable military buildings and bungalows for officers were erected and even though this later broke down and civilians began building houses here, there do not seem to have been any wild flights of architectural fancy, nor even a conscious attempt to "plan" the Cantonment after the parade ground had been marked out. Lack of space also meant that buildings tended to be modest and serviceable for there was little point in designing an impressive façade if it was to be crammed up against a neighbour's back wall, and houses and offices in the Residency complex were often contiguous, with only narrow walls and path ways separating them from each other. The typical

[3] See for example the case of Pelegrine Treves, an old friend of Saadat Ali Khan, who, having spent several years in Lucknow, entered the service of Ghazi-ud-din Haider in June 1823 as Chamberlain, only to be dismissed six months later. Treves died suddenly later the same year. Bengal Pol. Con., 5 Dec. 1823, no. 30.

appearance of the majority of British houses in Lucknow was quite standardised, consisting normally of a one-storeyed, flat-roofed house, with at least two verandahs, thatched or tiled, and wooden "venetians" at every window. Houses were painted in the ubiquitous yellow wash picked out in white which is still common in northern India today. Such houses stood in a compound if room allowed, and had detached out-offices and servants quarters. It is not therefore surprising that visitors to Lucknow dazzled by nawabi extravaganzas should neglect these rather prosaic buildings.

The last reason for the decline of grandiose European buildings here was undoubtedly the fact that houses erected by Europeans, or by Indians in the European style, were very apt to be confiscated by the nawabs for no other reason than that the nawabs liked them. In 1797, for example, the nawab Wazir Ali, who ruled for only six months,[4] attempted to buy a house occupied by Mr Reid, the Residency surgeon. It is not known exactly where this house was, but it probably stood in the Residency complex. "His Excellency's applications are so urgent and his temper under Indisposition so whimsical and fractious that a resistance to his will may expose me to his displeasure," wrote Reid. "My house is situated betwixt and very near two Houses lately purchased by His Excellency which makes him extremely desirous to possess it."[5]

A revealing sentence about Asaf-ud-daula stated that "His Highness could never bear to hear that any person possessed anything

[4] Wazir Ali, or Vizier Ali, nawab from June 1797 to January 1798, was reputedly a son of Asaf-ud-daula, but was deposed by the East India Company after only six months as ruler. After the murder by Wazir Ali of the one-time British Resident in Lucknow, Cherry, the deposed nawab was confined by the British to prison in Calcutta, where he died. There was also a hint of Wazir Ali's connection with the Afghan Zaman Shah who had invaded the Punjab twice in the 1790s. This tenuous connection made him dangerous both for the British and for his nawabi family. Wazir Ali's last act on leaving Lucknow before his pursuit of Cherry was to raid the Aina Khana, the treasure house of the late Asaf-ud-daula. Much treasure was taken, and only a few items were ever recovered. See *The Oxford History of India* (Oxford 1958), p. 554, and *The Asiatic Annual Register* (1807), pp. 204–5.

[5] Foreign Pol. Con., 9 Oct. 1797, no number given.

superior to his own,"[6] and this attitude carried to its logical conclusion meant that to build anything of an interesting or unusual nature was to invite confiscation or run the risk of displeasing the nawab by refusing to sell. Beecher's complaint that the nawab confiscated his fine house has already been noted and there is good evidence to believe that Asaf-ud-daula was extremely anxious to possess Constantia, and that only the terms of Martin's Will and his decision to be buried there prevented the building falling into nawabi hands.[7] Certainly there was a dispute over Martin's town house, the Château (Farhad Baksh), for on Martin's death his Spanish agent Joseph Quieros, bidding against Saadat Ali Khan at an auction, bought the house from Martin's estate for Rs 40,000 (£4000).[8] But Valentia, who was in Lucknow when this happened, reported that Quieros "was persecuted by him [Saadat Ali Khan] since – so now sells it to him." The nawab was so delighted at his eventual ownership of the house that he celebrated by feasting all the Europeans in Lucknow and treating them to a firework display opposite the Château.[9] It was this nawab too, who by 1803 had "bought all the English houses [in Lucknow] except Paul's and two others," and no doubt the amount of pressure that could be put on Europeans, especially those not in the Company's service, was considerable. It became prudent not to build in a style that would attract the attention of the nawabs and this restriction, together with changing fortunes of the freelance

[6] Daniel Johnson, p. 163.

[7] Sharar, A.H., *Lucknow – The Last Phase of an Oriental Culture*, trans. by Fakir Hussein (London 1975), p. 49.

[8] Valentia, i, p. 166.

[9] There are no details on where Martin lived between 1776 when he first settled in Lucknow and 1781 when the Château was finished. The sole clue is in Martin's Will, when he refers several times to "old Luckparra" and "old Luckeypara", which appears to lie in a easterly direction from the Château. Constantia was occasionally known as *lakh pere*, which means a lakh of trees, but there is no doubt that this was an entirely separate building, and in any case was not completed on Martin's death. Martin also had another house built at Najafgarh on the river Ganges, downriver from Cawnpore, and refers in his Will to the house at Najafgarh or "Martin Ghur", recalling's Polier Ganj near Lucknow.

adventurers, meant that post-1800 buildings tended to be less flamboyant than those of the previous twenty-five years.

So where did the nawabs and their nobles learn to build their exuberant European-style houses and palaces if not from the British officials in the Residency complex or the Europeans employed in nawabi service? The answer seems to be that the palaces of Claude Martin, more than anything else, influenced European-inspired building in Lucknow and that an examination of Martin's buildings will reveal both the genius behind his creations and the origins of much of the later architecture in the city.

The Château de Lyon (later renamed Farhad Baksh) is the first identifiable building erected by Martin in Lucknow and was finished by 1781 according to an inscription over one of the basement arches. (The chronology of the other buildings as far as can be determined is Bibiapur built between 1782 and 1789, Constantia between 1795 and completed after Martin's death in 1800, and Barowen also completed after 1800.) The Château was such a unique and singular building even for Lucknow that there is no shortage of description, the earliest being in 1784,[10] only three years after its completion. A visitor during Martin's lifetime would have approached the house from the south side through a lofty arched gateway and have walked through a shrubbery with winding paths interspersed with indigenous and foreign plants and trees. To one side of the main building was a large zenana and to the other a garden "not laid out with taste, but well filled with a variety of fine trees, shrubs, and flowers, together with all sorts of vegetables."[11] To enter the main house it was necessary to cross a drawbridge, because three sides of the building were surrounded by a moat, the fourth side being built out onto the river. The drawbridge led up a few steps to "an elegant piazza"[12] which led into an octagon room.[13] From this room

[10] "An Account of Colonel Martin's Villa, near Lucknow", *The European Magazine* (London 1790), vol. xvii, Jan.–June pp. 86–7.

[11] *The Asiatic Annual Register* (1801), p. 37.

[12] See *The European Magazine*.

[13] Compare the suggested plan of the Château with the known plan of Constantia. In both cases there are polygonal rooms in the centre of the buildings,

other smaller apartments led off and the apartment nearest the river led in turn to the great hall overlooking the river and the north bank of the Gomti. This was all on the ground floor, but the most curious feature were the two lower storeys built in the river:

> The basement storey comprises two caves or recesses within the banks of the river and level with its surface when at the lowest decrease. In these caves [Martin] generally lived in the hot season, when the increase of the river obliged him to remove. He then ascended another storey, to an apartment fitted up in the manner of a grotto; and when the further [*sic*] rise of the river brought its surface on a level with these, he proceeded up to the third storey or ground floor, which overlooked the river when at its greatest height.

During the rainy season the river was estimated to rise about sixteen feet but after the monsoon it fell and remained at a fairly constant level for about eight months. The grand hall on the first floor was built out over the river and supported by arches in turn resting on piers in the river sunk at a point about one-fifth across the width of the river.[14]

Within the basement apartments were baths and fountains which sprayed water against the windows "which, when the hot winds prevail during the spring months, are kept covered in the day time with frames filled with green brambles; these being kept constantly

---

though the space has been better utilized in Constantia. The two octagonal towers in the Château probably fulfilled the same function as the four Constantia towers, i.e. providing ventilation and drainage, but the octagonal tower on the south side appears to be purely decorative and does not seem to occur on the ground floor.

[14] See *Bengal Past and Present*, Calcutta 1918, vol. 16, p. 115. There seems to have been some confusion, originating in S.C. Hill's book *Claude Martin* (Calcutta 1912), which says: "It is now evident that the Farhad Baksh was once far larger and very different from what it is at the present moment . . ." Of the "exterior wall resting on pillars placed nearly in the middle of the Goomty," the massive piers on which the pillars were built "are still in existence almost in the middle of the Gumti and are always distinctly visible to low water." These massive piers, however, I believe to be the remains of the kiosks attached to the Dilaram.

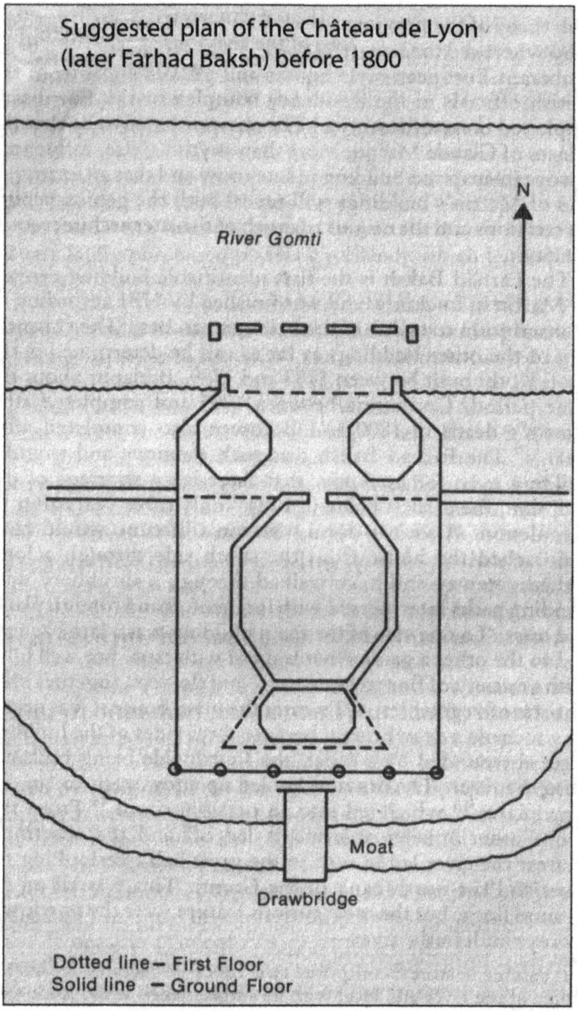

wet by the fountains, cool the wind in its passage into the apartments, and thereby procure a constant temperature within, proportioned to the strength of the wind abroad, and capacity of the frames to retain the water dripping."[15] When the river fell at the end of the monsoon the mud which had accumulated in the base-

[15] *European Magazine.*

ment rooms was removed and the rooms were annually repainted and decorated, and "by this ingenious contrivance he preserved a moderate and equal temperature in his house at all seasons."[16]

"The upper apartments, with their terraces and turrets, are principally disposed for the purpose of sleeping in the open air, and recreation during the nights of the season."[17] There was also "in the attic storey . . . a musaeum, well supplied with various curiosities, and over the whole he erected an observatory, which he furnished with the best astronomical instruments."[18] After Martin's death, when the house and zenana had been bought by Saadat Ali Khan and renamed the Farhad Baksh, it became the northern portion of a large palace complex. This complex was partially demolished and greatly altered after 1857, except for one portion, so by a strange quirk one can today see the Farhad Baksh stripped of most later additions and more or less as it appeared during Martin's life. The drawbridge, moat, arched gateway and zenana were all swept away in later improvements, and the interior was divided up when the building became part of the Central Drug Research Institute in post-independence India, but the octagon room is still identifiable and the arches of the basement storey are plainly exposed on the river side. A survey carried out by the Council of Scientific and Industrial Research in New Delhi in the early 1970s found that any attempt to pump out the water from the two basement storeys would lead to unacceptable disturbances to the structure of the building, and it is for this reason that the water level is maintained by pumps in the lower rooms, for the building of a *bund* (an earth wall for flood prevention) along the Gomti bank means that the building no longer stands in the river. The basement rooms can be glimpsed through arches, but no apparent decoration is visible and only a thorough exploration by boat would reveal the nature of this storey.

Alterations have stripped off most of the internal decoration, but externally there are important features left which were eagerly seized

[16] *Asiatic Annual Register* (1801), p. 37.
[17] *European Magazine.*
[18] *Asiatic Annual Register* (1801).

upon by those who wished to "europeanise" their buildings without radically altering the structure or nature of indigenous buildings. The festoon swags around the octagonal towers, for example, are repeated around the dome of the Shah Najaf, a large tomb further east along the Gomti bank, and in the Qaisarbagh courtyard; while the triangular pediment on the first floor recurs repeatedly, notably in the gateways of the Husainabad Imambara. The Composite Order pilasters and the mock venetian blinds in octagonal cartouches and windows are of course quite ubiquitous, occurring in practically any existing nawabi building, and these false windows in stucco were particularly useful as decoration for the high blank walls of zenana apartments. While it is not being posited that the architects of these later buildings visited the Château and then deliberately copied these ornamentations on their own buildings, Martin's buildings, the first of their kind not only in Lucknow but also it would seem in northern India, provided the initial inspiration for much of the europeanisation of later Indian buildings in the city, even if such buildings received their embellishments at second or third remove from the original instigator. The same pattern of copying non-essential features will be apparent again when Constantia is examined. The most important aspect of Martin's town house was, however, not copied by other architects (with the exception of the builder of the Khurshid Manzil) and was ignored or unappreciated by local architects and later writers. The defensive appearance of the building is not something which readily occurs to sightseers looking at the Château today. One sees only the light and airy pavilions and regrets the loss of the "elegant piazza" on the south side, while appreciating the ingenuity of the water-cooled lower storeys. But the feature that struck pre-1800 commentators most forcibly was the fortified look of the building, and to neglect this would be to lose the essential nature of the building. It would be more appropriate to regard this building as a palace fortress rather than a town house. Consider the contemporary descriptions of the Château. After noting the drawbridge entrance to the house the anonymous writer of 1784 says the moat could be filled

1. The Rumi Darwaza. Lithograph *c.* 1835 by John Luard. Mud and thatch hut dwellings erected in front of the Bara Imambara, emphasising the contrast between rich and poor in the city.

2. John Wombwell's bungalow in the Residency complex. Pen and ink drawing by Ozias Humphry, 1786. British Library.

3. Château de Lyon (later Farhad Baksh). Photograph *c.* 1862. Main entrance on the south side; the river lies behind the building.

4. Asafi Kothi, part of the Daulat Khana palace. Photograph 1976.

5A. Barowen (Musa Bagh) after its recapture by British troops in 1858.

5B. Barowen in ruins. Photograph 1976.

6. The Macchi Bhawan fort from the river Gomti. Pencil and watercolour 1789 by Thomas Daniell and William Daniell.

7. The Panch Mahalla Gateway to the Macchi Bhawan fort. Aquatint 1789 by Thomas Daniell.

8. A hunting procession near the Stone Bridge. Pencil and watercolour, *c.* 1820. Lucknow School.

9A. The British Residency. Watercolour 1814/15 by Sita Ram.

9B. Dilkusha. Watercolour 1814/15 by Sita Ram.

10. King Nasir-ud-din Haider walking through the Chattar Manzil palace grounds, escorted by the British Resident Colonel John Low and the Assistant Resident Captain James Paton. Watercolour *c.* 1830 by Mussowar Khan, after a lost oil painting, possibly by de Casanova.

11. Constantia (known later as La Martinière). Watercolour 1814/15 by Sita Ram.

12A. Constantia sphinx. Photograph 1976.

12B. Constantia statues. Photograph 1976.

13A. Well-house at Husainabad. Photograph 1976.
Note the defaced erotic statues on the pediment.

13B. The Gol Kothi (Round House). Photograph 1976.

14A. "The Nawab's New House" (Khurshid Manzil).
Pencil drawing by Robert Smith, 1814.

14B. Khurshid Manzil after the Uprising.
Photograph 1858.

15. The Mermaid Gate (Jal Pari) in Qaisarbagh Palace. Photograph 1864–5.

16. The Iron Bridge over the Gomti. Photograph *c.* 1870.

> at pleasure, either for the purpose of cooling the lower apartments or that of defence from the sudden attacks of banditti or rebels. This latter purpose of its construction will not appear very consistent with European notions of modern buildings . . . it is here, however, a most useful precaution, for the want of which Colonel Martin was near suffering severely in a neighbouring habitation during Cheit Sing's rebellion, when a body of rebels drew up in front of it to attack it, and had he not placed two small field-pieces at his doors, loaded with grape-shot, and himself at the head of his servants armed, which obliged the former to retreat.

It should not be forgotten that although Martin seemed to be skilled in whatever he turned his hand to, from casting cannon to experimenting with air-balloons, he was primarily a military man, with a deep interest in working out methods of defending buildings. When asked for example what he thought of a new silk factory built at Rungpur, he commended it saying "it is a work fit to withstand a Bombardment" – not perhaps the first criterion one would think of for a silk factory even in the 1770s.[19] He was undoubtedly acutely aware of the dangers of sudden attack, especially to houses outside the city, as the Château originally was, and this building as well as Constantia should be seen in this light rather than just as architectural follies.

The town house then "had the appearance of a fortified castle, and was indeed constructed with a view to defence, with the drawbridges, loop-holes, and turrets, and water, when desired, all round."[20] A further description comments that "The caprice of iron doors, massive walls, and narrow winding staircases, with drawbridges and battlements, give this house much the appearance of the castle in Blue Beard."[21] Interior alterations completely changed the nature of the building, putting in wide staircases more in keeping with its later role as a nawabi palace. But it is more than likely that there

[19] Home Dept, 9 May 1774. No number given. National Archives, New Delhi.

[20] Twining, p. 309.

[21] Valentia, i, p. 166.

was originally only one spiral staircase to the upper storeys in one of the octagonal towers, as was the case in Constantia, so that the house could be defended in the last resort by a few people retreating to the top of the building. It would not be surprising either if the observatory telescope in the roof kiosks was occasionally trained on the surrounding countryside as well as the heavens.

Towards the end of his life Martin began the construction of another large building to the east of the city called Constantia, from the Freemasonry motto "Labore et Constantia", and this building came to be considered as his crowning achievement, or the height of folly, according to some critics. It may not give so much aesthetic pleasure as other buildings by Martin, but Constantia is undeniably one of the most spectacular buildings erected by Europeans in India.

If it is approached, stressing again the defensive aspect, one can begin to appreciate the priorities in the architect's mind. It is described just after Martin's death as

> a Gothic castle, which he did not live to finish. Beneath the ramparts of this castle he built casements, secured by iron doors and grating thickly wrought. The lodgements within the walls are arched and barred, and their roofs completely bomb proof. The castle is surrounded by a side and deep ditch, fortified on the outer side by stockades, and a regular covered way, so that the place is sufficiently protected to resist the attacks of any Asiatic power. Within the castle, he built a splendid mausoleum, in which he was interred.[22]

The last sentence is a reminder that Constantia was not simply a fortress, and indeed the difficulty of defining exactly what it was baffled many writers, a confusion not helped by the many architectural styles employed. Valentia saw it shortly after Martin's death and found it a strange fantastical building of every species of architecture, and adorned with minute stucco fret-work, enormous red lions with lamps instead of eyes, Chinese mandarins, and ladies

[22] *Asiatic Annual Register* (1801), p. 38.

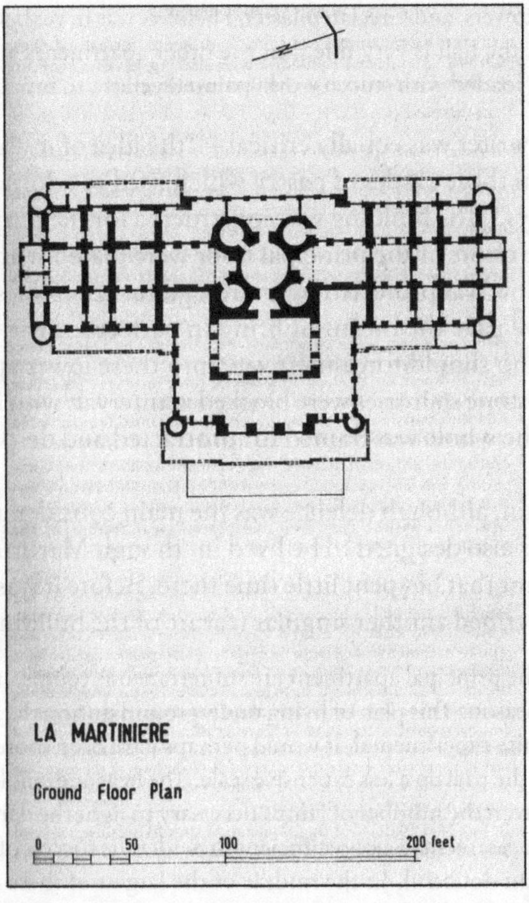

with shaking heads and all the gods and goddesses of the heathen mythology.[23]

It has a handsome effect at a distance, from a lofty tower in the centre with four turrets, but on a nearer approach, the wretched taste of the ornaments only excites contempt. A more extraordinary combination of

[23] Valentia, i, p. 163, where he writes: "Many of these [the statues] have been demolished, and most of them injured, by the earthquake of the 1st September", i.e. 1803. The earlier statuary would seem from Valentia's description to have been far more varied than the Graeco-Roman models now seen on the parapets.

> Gothic towers, and Grecian pilaster, I believe, was never before devised. Within, the hall is very fine, but the other apartments are small and gloomy, loaded with stucco work, painted yellow, to imitate gilding.[24]

A later writer was equally critical – "the idea of it was probably taken from those castles of pastry which used to adorn desserts in former days." The building was constructed for the purpose of defence. The doors of the principal floor were plated with iron, and each window was protected by an iron grate. Loopholes from passages above gave the means of firing in perfect security upon any persons who should force their way into these lower apartments. The spiral stone staircases were blocked at intervals with iron doors; in short, the whole was framed for protracted and desperate resistance."[25]

But again, although defence was the main consideration, Constantia was also designed to be lived in, though Martin's untimely death meant that he spent little time there. Before it was finished a visitor described another singular feature of the building:

> Under the principal apartment are subterraneous rooms, intended for the hot season. This plan of living underground during the hot months being quite experimental, it would perhaps have been more reasonable to make the trial on a less expensive scale. The heat and smoke and smell arising from the number of lamps necessary to light the dark chambers and passages, seemed alone sufficient to render the success of the scheme more than doubtful. In the middle of the largest of these dark rooms the Colonel had already raised his tomb, and the number of lights to be burned there, night and day, *for ever* and the sum allotted for this purpose, were already mentioned, but it was not said what was to be the state and distinction of the immense structure above when its eccentric founder should have taken possession of his narrow chamber below.[26]

In fact Martin decided that Constantia should become a school and left a large sum of money to provide scholarships for boys of

[24] Valentia, i, p. 162.
[25] *Hastings*, i, p. 196.
[26] Twining, p. 310.

all religions. Because of immense legal wrangles in the Calcutta High Court, Martin's Will was not finally proved until 1840 and the house was used before then as a guesthouse for Europeans visiting Lucknow. It had no connections either with the Residency (although Lord Moira, a Governor General, had stayed there in 1814) or with the nawabi court, and it was managed by superintendents appointed by the Supreme Court of Jurisdiction in Calcutta.[27] These superintendents included Joseph Quieros the steward of Constantia, Martin's adopted son James, and two members of the Deverinne family who had known Martin well. The superintendence of the building was still in the hands of Mutchoo and Choda (Chota) Kadir and their sons, Martin's servants.

In 1840 additional building began, supervised by Lieutenant Cunningham and later Lieutenant Fraser, engineers working for the East India Company. Martin had left explicit if confusing directions for two semi-circular wings to be added to the original buildings. Directions were also left by Martin for the building of the zenana which was to provide shelter for his two mistresses, the "faithful girl Lize" (Boola-un-nissa) and Girl Sally, as long as they cared to remain there. The zenana building was to be a good pukka house with a compound and an enclosure and was to be built on the same plan as the zenana attached to the town house.[28]

The central portion of Constantia consists of four circular "wells" sunk to a depth of twenty feet below the water level, and these wells continue to the top of the building as octagonal towers containing rooms and one spiral staircase. This staircase, barred at intervals by iron doors, was a defensive measure, so that the inhabitants, if attacked, could retreat to the top of the building, firing from the parapets and arrow slits or loopholes as they went. The four wells were constructed for the dual purpose of cooling the air by a series of pottery ducts (which are set into the walls of the wells and allow cool air to be drawn up through the walls – the air would disperse, on

[27] India Pol. Con., 22 May 1839, no. 64.
[28] Claude Martin's Will.

becoming heated, through eight funnels on the roof) and to provide drainage especially during the monsoon season when the nearby Gomti overflowed its banks. On the ground floor are the chapel and library, originally reception rooms, which are elaborately decorated with Wedgwood-type plaques and medallions. The sixteen-sided room, which has a slightly domed ceiling, is repeated between the octagonal towers; originally eight doorways led off from this room but five were later blocked up. The word "doorway" hardly conveys the idea of these communicating passages between the hall and the outer rooms. The passage leading into the long room on the north side, for example, measures five foot eight inches in width and retains the original iron hinges at both ends of this passage, so it could be doubly barred by the iron doors.

Ascending to the terrace of the first floor, the most striking features are undoubtedly the twelve lions guarding the circular staircases terminating on this terrace.[29] A closer examination shows the niches in the rear of the lions in which lamps were formerly placed, and the wall steps leading to the battlemented towers. Traces of the red paint Valentia remarked on can still be seen in places. The rooms on the first floor are decorated in a rather more chaste style than the reception rooms on the ground floor. The passageways between these rooms were also intended to be barred with heavy iron doors and the hinges on which the doors were hung are still visible. The image of massive iron doors contrasts badly with the delicate stucco tracery of the walls and ceiling.

The second floor terrace has a less defensive appearance, being softened by the open pillared cupolas, while the upper two storeys are confined to the four octagonal towers ascending from the core of the building. At the very summit, which was once crowned by statues, two arches springing from the octagonal towers bisect each other at their highest points, topped today by a flagstaff.

Practically every portion of Constantia was copied by architects and builders with varying degrees of faithfulness. On the ground

[29] The lions are a visual pun on Lyon, Martin's home town, and they appear again on his crest of arms in the chapel of La Martinière.

floor, for example, one finds that the one-storey octagonal towers surmounted by battlements may well have inspired the builder of the Khurshid Manzil, Captain MacLeod, to erect a miniature castle surrounded by a moat and drawbridge like Martin's town house.[30] A pale imitation of the lions at the battlements is still to be found on the gateway of the Shah Najaf, finished before 1827, while the Sher Darwaza (lion gate) a part of the Qaisarbagh complex, supported two marble lions which were later moved to Government House but subsequently lost.

One feature that was certainly solely attributable to Martin and indeed acknowledged to be so was the frequent and sometimes inappropriate use of statues. Honoria Lawrence who visited Lucknow in December 1842 wrote –

> a very strange accompaniment to a Musulman city,[31] to wit, statues innumerable of every imaginable design, from a gigantic soldier, painted to the life and presenting his arms with a most valiant air, to Jupiter, Venus and all other personages entitled by prescriptive right to stand up in every material from Parian marble to plaster of Paris. On one side Hercules flourished his club at you – on the other stands a shepherd in a tie-wig and three cornered hat, making love to a shepherdess in hoop and ruffles. The material is stucco, and these figures must be a sore abomination to "true believers". They were introduced about half a century ago by a certain General Martine.[32]

P.C. Mookherji adds, "Martin taught some of the local artificiers of his day how to carve out figures from stone. Not a few learnt the art and practised it in plaster, the want of the former material com-

[30] Diskalker, p. 14.

[31] "A strange accompaniment" because orthodox Islam frowns on any representation of the human or animal form, fearing that it might lead to idolatry. See Surah IV:76 of the Qu'ran. The Lucknow nawabs, who were Shi'as, never attempted to reconcile this stricture with their obvious love of statues, and in fact their religious ceremonies became more and more unorthodox, especially during the time of Wajid Ali Shah.

[32] Honoria Lawrence's manuscript journal for 1841–8. Extract dated 20 Dec. 1843, Mss. Eur., £. 85, no. 94, f. 34. I.O.L. Hereafter Honoria Lawrence.

pelling them to have recourse to the latter."[33] These statues came in for an enormous amount of invective from European travellers. Valentia's criticism on "the wretched taste of the ornaments" was only the first of many. Apart from Constantia there are now no buildings embellished with such works, but they were certainly as frequent as Honoria Lawrence describes, and at least two post-1857 photographs show statues. Wajid Ali Shah was especially fond of such works and an early photograph of one of the Qaisarbagh gateways, before it was trimmed down to its present form, clearly shows figures supporting two "crowns" at the top of the gate. Another photograph shows the Mermaid Gate, also in Qaisarbagh, and the bizarre spiral staircase to one side, the columns of which were topped by stucco women in pleated dresses, their hair in classical chignons, and holding hoops. The Dilkusha too, built about 1805, has female statues on the rear balustrades of the building. Not all of Lucknow's statues were made to embellish buildings, however, and during the 1830s and the 1840s they were used to decorate gardens, often with results that seemed ludicrous to critical European eyes.

The final feature of Constantia, the quadrant arches, appear again on the two remaining gateways to the Qaisarbagh, built between 1848 and 1850, and it must be said that in this case the later arches are more satisfactory than the rather abrupt features of Martin's building.

But again it will be clear that all the features of Constantia and the Château that were copied or adapted for Lucknow buildings not designed by Europeans are still "non-essential" features, i.e. they are for embellishment only and do not involve any structural modifications to indigenous buildings. It is easy, on first acquaintance with Lucknow architecture to be confused by the eclectic features of the buildings, but one must look beyond the idea that all the buildings were "European" or degenerate European and ask how much the europeanisation changed the essential nature of such buildings. In many cases the europeanisation was very superficial, especially in

[33] Mookherji, p. 176.

religious buildings which tend to follow traditional patterns more than dwelling places do. Nothing is lost by adding Corinthian pilasters and Adam-style fanlights to the outer wall of a kerbala. They do not alter the arrangement of the rooms and the shrines inside the building and no one's taste is offended, except perhaps that of the European purist.

Again, in private houses of a traditional pattern there was no harm in employing a stuccador to embellish the doors with broken pediments and swags and it was easy to mould Corinthian or Tuscan features around columns supporting the usual verandah of the inner courtyards. A vast amount of such decoration has been lost as the stucco falls away from such buildings revealing the bricks underneath, exhibiting the truly ephemeral and superficial nature of these embellishments. They were no more than skin deep. The use of statues too was another easy way to europeanise a building with minimal disruption to the inhabitants' life-style within. There is an interesting description which was written in 1845 of a building now lost:

> we passed an edifice of extraordinary size, where the rules of art would have required a great number of tall windows in front. The spaces for them indeed were there but, as no Mahometan likes to have any toward the street, they were all, on both stories completely walled up. Something however being necessary to break the dismal monotony of the solid masonry, each niche intended for a window was, with truly Oriental bad taste, filled up with figures as large as life, representing men of every age and every rank, painted *al fresco* in the most gaudy colours. Picture to yourself a house with sixty large windows ornamented in this manner! The one above described is a "Mehalla" or harem.[34]

Thus a traditional building like the zenana, though decorated with blank window niches filled with statues, remained essentially untouched in its true function by the addition of these embellishments, which could not of course be appreciated by the inhabitants.

[34] Hoffmeister, p. 250.

The mention of the zenana leads one on to consider the problem of how this traditional feature was maintained when buildings were europeanised, or when buildings based on European models were erected. Some builders dealt with the problem by keeping the lay-out of traditional houses unchanged and merely adding decorative features in stucco. Other builders adopted a different approach and constructed the public or "masculine" part of the house in the European style but kept the zenana in the traditional style of a distinct, though attached building, with very high, windowless walls, sometimes decorated with European features in stucco. The siting of the zenana was another problem and one finds Claude Martin involved here in what would seem to be a purely Muslim matter. It is obvious that a zenana with its essential high blank walls cannot easily be incorporated into a European building without seriously impairing the symmetry of such a building. Even if placed at the rear of such a building it then detracts from the rear approach to the house, and the European buildings discussed here were designed to be equally impressive from all angles. So Martin's mistresses, who lived in partial purdah, were housed in a separate building near enough the main public building and probably connected by some form of covered way, but their zenana was not an integral part of the Château or Constantia and did not therefore detract from the symmetry of these buildings. In some European-style buildings for Indians the zenana was attached, despite the different architectural styles. The Asafi Kothi, for example, built originally as a free-standing building, had a zenana added to the right-hand wing, which is nearly but not quite contemporary, implying that it was found inconvenient by Asaf-ud-daula not to have his zenana attached to the main building.

The best example of a European-style house with attached zenana is that of a house built in the once important town of Kakori, about ten miles south-west of Lucknow. The history of the house is unfortunately obscure but the building appears to be fairly late, i.e. after 1840 and was originally surrounded by high walls, of which only one doorway remains. The main section, the men's portion, is purely European and very handsome too, while the attached zenana to the left has its own inner courtyard, invisible of course to curious eyes, even from the main building. This zenana is still occupied by the widowed descendant of the original owner, and her daughter (1975). Though neither are in purdah there is no question of them living in the men's section of the building, even when it was habitable. They cling firmly to the traditional and familiar part of the building, the zenana, while the European section crumbles poignantly about them.

Thus only a comparatively small number of European buildings exerted any influence over native buildings in the city and the reasons for the rapid decline in grand European buildings after about 1800 have been examined. Elements from Martin's buildings have been traced in a wide variety of later native buildings, and there is no doubt that the impact of non-essential features, copied from the Château and Constantia, was massive. Despite the great destruction of pre-1856 buildings, such features appear over and over again in all kinds of buildings, great and small, religious and secular. But it should be stressed again that the majority of these elements which gave Lucknow's buildings a European air did not produce many radical changes in the life-styles of the inhabitants of such buildings. The europeanisation of Lucknow remained superficial, in most cases no more than the stucco decoration on an Indian wall. Native life continued to revolve around the inner courtyards and the zenana apartments of traditional houses, whether these houses were embellished with European features or not. Even those houses built for or by Indians entirely in the European style, like Bibiapur or the Dilkusha, were usually modified by the addition of a zenana, private imambaras and a huddle of servants' quarters; or they were neglected by the owners after a short time because they were not convenient for the Indian way of life.

8

Information on Architecture from Europe

THE EIGHTY YEARS that witnessed the rise and decline of nawabi power in Awadh was one of the most exciting periods of British architecture and saw in quick succession the remnants of strict Palladian modes, the rise of Neo-Classicism which drifted into the Greek revival, and the growing importance of the Neo-Gothic style as well as flirtations with Etruscan interpretations, Chinoiserie and Indian Gothic.

By the 1770s the influence of Palladio in Britain had become somewhat less important, and although his shadow still fell over the remainder of the eighteenth century a new interest was provided by the Adam brothers who published their first influential volume, *Works in Architecture*, in 1773. In this they explained what they were trying to do: "We flatter ourselves, we have been able to seize, with some degree of success, the beautiful spirit of antiquity and to transpose it, with novelty and variety, through all our numerous works." In the place of the "massive entablature, the ponderous compartment ceiling, the tabernacle frame" they adopted a "beautiful variety of light mouldings, gracefully formed, delicately enriched and arranged with propriety and skill."[1] The brothers, Robert and James, could not have known the enthusiasm with which their

[1] Kidson, Murray & Thompson, *A History of English Architecture* (London 1965), p. 238. Hereafter Kidson *et al.*

ideas on delicate mouldings would be received in Lucknow, where even as late as 1850 their arabesques and swags were still being translated in stucco on the Qaisarbagh palace complex. Robert Adam was one of the leading exponents of the Neo-Classical movement spreading from France and Italy in the middle of the eighteenth century. This pleasing style received tremendous impetus from archaeological discoveries made at Herculaneum and Pompeii in the mid-eighteenth century and led to a series of "Etruscan" rooms in the dull red, black and yellow colours of vases being found in Italy.[2] Several books in Claude Martin's Lucknow library reflect this interest.

While Robert Adam was stamping his unique imprint on houses in Britain, the first traces of Gothic were to be found at Strawberry Hill and Fonthill Abbey, although eighteenth-century Gothic has a frivolousness about it far removed from the earnestness of Victorian Gothic and should be seen in conjunction with other exotic styles like the Chinoiserie of Kew or the Indian Gothic of Brighton Pavilion. The first years of the nineteenth century saw the ascendance of the Regency style, exemplified by Sir John Soane and especially John Nash, and seen at its best in the terraces of Cheltenham and Bath, and in Nash's work in Regent's Park.

The beginning of the Victorian period saw at first a confusion of styles and a profusion of new techniques (notably the greatly increased use of iron and glass, which took some time to be fully exploited), and while the Gothic forces were gathering strength there were still plenty of buildings erected which would not have been out of place twenty or thirty years earlier, for example the British Museum, built 1842–7. By the end of our period, i.e. 1856, the high Victorian style was in full flower, with many striking examples of polychromatic tiling, stained glass windows, and the iron and glass fantasy of the Crystal Palace – not to mention the utilitarian build-

[2] Another reflection of this antiquarian interest is shown by a note recording that "a work on the antiquities of Herculaneum was presented to the Nawab Ghazi-ud-din Haider by His Neapolitan Majesty" in 1826. Foreign Pol. Index, 23 June 1826, no. 16.

ings like Brunel's Royal Albert Bridge and the functional King's Cross Station in London.

It will be obvious from this brief survey of architectural trends that during less than a century all manner of changes took place and several distinct styles were employed consecutively and concurrently in Britain and Europe. One might therefore reasonably expect these changes to be reflected in the buildings in Lucknow of this period, knowing something of the Awadh court's obsession with novelties from the West. The nawabs would certainly have seen much of Western architecture, with its rapid transitions of style, as novelties, compared to the unchanging nature of much indigenous architecture. But the curious thing is that the Europeanised architecture of Lucknow is strangely static and that after a brief flurry between 1780 and 1800 it does not evolve or progress in the same manner as buildings did in the West. This cannot obviously be blamed on a cessation of architectural information from the West, for by 1856 there were many more Europeans in Lucknow than there had been during the late eighteenth century, and communications between Europe and inland towns like Lucknow had greatly improved.[3] It is true, as shown earlier, that the majority of Europeans in Lucknow were not in a position to indulge in architectural flights of fancy in their own homes after about 1800, but there was certainly no dearth of visual and written information about new developments in the West that the nawabs and their nobles could have exploited for their buildings.

And yet there is a definite *lack* of development in nawabi buildings when compared to the rapid evolution taking place in Europe. It is as though the European buildings of Lucknow were "set" in some curious way about 1800 and were then incapable of further change, as one understands it. The Qaisarbagh, the last great project of the nawabs, is not, for example, a mid-Victorian building in any sense. It is, if one wishes to describe it in European architec-

[3] In May the Rev. Henry Polehampton, on taking up his brief appointment in Lucknow, was able to travel 130 miles from Calcutta by rail, although the rest of the journey had to be made in palanquins. Polehampton, p. 79.

tural terms, a series of early-nineteenth-century terraces with eighteenth-century Baroque overtones, complete with Adam garlands and swags. There is no reflection in Lucknow (apart from the Residency church) of the important nineteenth-century Gothic style or of the Victorian experiments with new materials. The Iron Bridge, by a strange quirk of fate, was undoubtedly the most advanced structure to appear in India when it was first conceived in 1812, but by the time it was erected in 1846/7 time had caught up with it and it was no longer remarkable.

If then Lucknow's European buildings did not progress along lines parallel to those in the West, did they in fact develop at all? The answer must it seems be "to a limited extent", but the very way in which this minimal development took place is in itself interesting. There are two facets of this "development" which must be looked at, both hitherto unrecorded, or at least not considered significant previously.

A close acquaintanceship with Lucknow's remaining nawabi building, and with photographs and drawings, makes apparent the involuted nature of a good proportion of these buildings and the way in which they fed upon each other to produce similar buildings, which in turn provided more material for other buildings. The word "involuted" is not used here in a pejorative sense because it is something more than the mere copying of details which was examined in the previous chapter. It is as if the builders of European houses, or of houses with a European bias, became reluctant to look outside the city for new models and ideas shortly after the beginning of the nineteenth century and this reluctance caused them to turn in upon themselves and concentrate on producing variations of buildings already existing in Lucknow. One can see here something of a parallel with the way in which Muslim poets (of whom there were and are many in Lucknow) were reworking traditional themes in Persian poetry, where the poet was judged not so much by his originality in choosing new themes but by the way in which he brought fresh interpretations to bear on old and well-tried stories. The beauty of so much Urdu poetry of the nawabi period lies in the associations the poet makes with things familiar to the listener, and the skill of the poet is in urging his audience to re-examine, and more importantly to reinterpret, the well-known images which may have become mundane by frequent usage. It does not seem fanciful to assert that this is what some of Lucknow's unknown architects were trying to do – they were reinterpreting the buildings laid down by the early European adventurers, and this important aspect should be considered distinct from the simple copying which was also taking place.

The two examples of this reinterpretation which come most easily to mind are the Darshan Bilas, built probably during the time of Ghazi-ud-din Haider and forming part of the Chattar Manzil palace complex, and the Khurshid Manzil. Another name for the Darshan Bilas (roughly translated as "Delightful Sight") is the Chaurukhi Kothi, or "House of four faces (or aspects)" because each side of this building represents the façade of another of Lucknow's European buildings. The rear of the building is based on the riverside façade of the Farhad Baksh while the front is the main façade of the Dilkusha. The two wings are both based on the rear façade of Barowen (so strictly speaking there are only three façades reutilised here) and though the interpretation of the wings is not quite so strict as the Dilkusha façade, the characteristics of Barowen are clear – the arched entrances with groups of four columns, the elaborate double arches of the fanlights, the neat ovals on the first floor terrace with ornamental urns, and the round towers on the roof. The four façades are blended together in the Darshan Bilas in an admirable way. They are not slavish copies of the three buildings represented here, but they are not so different that they cannot be immediately identified by someone who has seen Barowen, the Dilkusha, and the Farhad Baksh.

The Khurshid Manzil, which was finished by Ghazi-ud-din Haider in 1818, has been identified as the "New House of the Nawab" drawn by Smith in 1814,[4] which shows a two-storeyed building with a large central dome, and eight very distinctive towers

[4] Robert Smith's sketchbooks, no. 312/1–29, no. 17, f. 20. I.O.L.

running the whole height of the building and topped by battlements. It is these towers, isolated without a connecting first floor, that are the most striking feature of the Khurshid Manzil. Other similarities become evident as soon as one's attention is drawn to the two buildings, notably the wide bow front with three doorways, the rustication of the ground floor, and the decorative frieze dividing the two storeys. The distinctive towers are of course familiar from Constantia, where they appear at the eight corners of the ground floor, and the last appearance of these battlemented towers, after the various translations of the "New House" and the Khurshid Manzil, is at Alambagh (a country palace built by Wajid Ali Shah) where they are employed at the four corners of a two-storeyed house. So one can see that the idea of a building with towers at each corner has been interpreted in various ways, all of them different, and all of them interesting and successful buildings in their own right.

The element of copying from existing buildings, as opposed to a reinterpretation, one sees most clearly in the Dilkusha. This is almost an exact replica of Seaton Delaval, an English building by Sir John Vanbrugh in Northumberland, which appears in *Vitruvius Britannicus* in 1721. This, incidentally, is another building with octagonal towers at each corner, which may well have made it especially attractive to Saadat Ali Khan, during whose time it was built. But again the native facility for adaptation has been at work, for although the main building of the Dilkusha has been fairly closely imitated, the stables to the left of it are not based on the stables at Seaton Delaval. They represent an original idea, whereby the central element of the rear façade of the Dilkusha, i.e. the semicircular arch over the central doorway and the rusticated double pillars with their rectangular pediments, is incorporated and used as the centrepiece for the long low row of stables which complement the main building so aptly.

The idea of copying existing building in Lucknow was established at an early stage of the nawabi period, for one of the first references to a European house is to that of Asaf-ud-daula who had a house built "in imitation of one belonging to Mr. Orr, on the northern bank of the Gumti, nearly opposite the palace."[5] Doubtless there were many more examples of both imitations and interpretations of earlier building in Lucknow which have subsequently been demolished, though enough has been said to show that if one concentrates on the early nawabi period from about 1775 to 1800 and examines the kind of architectural information available in the city at that time, one will in fact be looking at most of the material needed for the whole period up to 1856. It is not of course claimed that there were no innovations at all after 1800; there were enough minor variations, especially in the quality of the workmanship, to enable one to date European-style buildings with some degree of accuracy, but the foundations, and the word is used advisedly, were laid down in this early period for later works.

To build European houses in India it was not enough merely to be a European or an Indian with Westernised tastes. Memories and impressions of buildings in Europe had to be reinforced by books, prints, and drawings, and sometimes an apprenticeship in building, though lack of this attribute was seldom thought the handicap one would today consider it to be. It is necessary to look at the two main sources of architectural information present in northern India, the written and illustrated material, which provided inspiration for the amateur and the engineers of the East India Company who adapted their European training to local conditions and materials.

It is appropriate to learn what kind of architectural information Claude Martin had access to, since his buildings exerted such influence in Lucknow. One starts with an enormous disadvantage, for on Martin's death the entire contents of his houses and his vast library containing four thousand books and manuscripts were sold by auction and there was no attempt to keep the collection together. A few odd volumes with Martin's library imprint have since come to light,[6] but it must be considered that the bulk of the collection, to-

[5] *Asiatic Annual Register* (London 1799), p. 29.

[6] There are, for example, in the Oriental Room of the British Library two books with Martin's library imprint – *Letters* written by Shaikh Abdul Fazl and a copy of the Christian gospels translated into Persian.

gether with numerous prints, drawings, and paintings, not to mention the ground plans of his buildings, are irretrievably lost. Nevertheless, one can reconstruct Martin's library to some extent by examining the inventories drawn up when his possessions were catalogued prior to an auction of his estate on 10 March 1801 in Calcutta.[7] Although the cataloguer has curtailed the book titles and authors drastically, the following titles provide an idea of the wide range of books about the fine arts and topics related to architecture and gardening which were present in Martin's library, and which were presumably made available to his friends in Lucknow.

(The titles of the books, as they are given in the inventory, are in italics. Where it has been possible to trace the book the correct title is given in inverted commas.)

D'Ankervilles Recherches sur les Arts. Recherches sur l'origine, l'esprit et les progrès des arts de la Grece . . . (London 1785).

Dictionnaire de Jardinier.

Lumsden's Antiquities of Rome.

Builders Magazine (two volumes). "The Builder's Magazine" (London 1774).

Architecture de Blondele. Francoise Blondel wrote several books on architecture, including *Nouvelle manier de fortifier les places* (Paris 1689), *Resolution des quatre principaux problems d'architecture* (Paris 1673), and *Cours d'architecture,* in two volumes (Paris 1688).

Copper Plate Magazine, one volume. "The Copper Plate Magazine or Monthly Cabinet of Picturesque Prints consisting of Sublime and Interesting Views in Great Britain and Ireland": in five volumes (London 1792–1802).

Bucks Antiquities. "Bucks Antiquities: or Venerable Remains of above 400 Castles, Monasteries, Palaces etc. in England and Wales. With near 100 views of Cities and Chief Towns", in three volumes (Messrs. Samuel and Nathaniel Buck, London 1774).

In addition to the engravings in these books Martin also had a large collection of paintings and drawings, many uncatalogued save

[7] Bengal Inventories, 1801. Range 1, vol. 24, no. 75. I.O.L.

as "a selection of prints" but which included an oil painting of the Rialto, Venice, and numerous views near Naples and Rome, as well as forty-four views by William and Thomas Daniell. Although these views were mainly of Indian buildings they were also useful for recording contemporary architectural developments in Calcutta and other centres where Europeans had settled and begun building. The inventory of items at the Château (Farhad Baksh) also mentions "One Magical Lanthorn" and boxes of "Glass Pictures with Cards for the Lanthorn", although it is not clear what the pictures portrayed. Martin's library certainly contained the largest collection of books in European languages in Lucknow, and judging by similar inventories from 1780 to 1800, was probably one of the finest collections in northern India.

In many cases the various cataloguers were at fault in drawing up inventories and frequently list items simply as "16 old books" or "odd books", but a study of inventories shows that there were a few standard architectural books widely bought by Europeans, especially the popular *A New and Complete Dictionary of Arts and Sciences* by "A Society of Gentlemen", published in London in 1754, in four volumes. A Mr Hemonseau of Calcutta whose estate was sold in 1800 owned two volumes of "Palladio's Architecture" (*sic*) and "One Book of Architecture" by Jacques Barrozzio, but generally views and illustrated books like *The Copper-Plate Magazine* were the most popular. To read these eighteenth-century architectural books is to appreciate that the building of houses, large or small, had not at that time become the exact science it is today. Naturally there were at that period celebrated architects in Europe, often working under royal patronage, but for many "country gentlemen" architecture was not so much a strict profession as a serious hobby in which they engaged for a time, rather as they pursued archaeological excavations – with the enthusiasm and dedication of the amateur paving the way for a later generation of professionals. The title page of *The Builder's Magazine* illustrates this intelligent interest excellently:

> The Builder's Magazine: or Monthly Companion For Architects, Carpenters, Masons, Bricklayers etc. as well as for Every Gentleman who

would wish to be a competent Judge of the elegant and necessary Art of Building. Consisting of Designs in Architecture, In Every Stile and Taste, from the most magnificent and superb Structures, down to the most simple and unadorned; together with the Plans and Sections, serving as an unerring Assistant in the Construction of any Building, from a Palace to a Cottage. In which will be introduced Grand and Elegant Designs for Chimney-Pieces, Ceiling, Doors, Windows, etc. Proper for Halls, Saloons, Vestibules, State Rooms, Dining Rooms, Parlours, Drawing Rooms, Anti-Rooms, [*sic*] Dressing Rooms, Bed Rooms etc. together with Designs for Churches, Hospitals, and other Public Buildings. Also Plans, Elevations and Sections, in the Greek, Roman and Gothic Taste, calculated to embellish Parks, Gardens, Forests, Woods, Canals, Mounts, Vistos [*sic*] Islands, extensive views etc. The Whole Forming a Complete System of Architecture, in all its Branches and so disposed, as to render the Surveyor, Carpenter, Mason etc. equally capable to erect a Cathedral, a Mansion, a Temple, or a Rural Cot.

The work was in two parts, the first theoretical, with "such instructions as are necessary to form the complete Architect", and the second practical, with "Plans, Elevations, Sections, etc. with their Explanations, as models for the practical Builder."

The book lives up to its promise of the title page (though one might hesitate to embark on a cathedral without some practical experience), and it defines architectural terms in great detail, including instructions on how to take moulds in plaster of paris and how to make cement. There are a lot of detailed notes about various types of bricks which are most suitable for different types of building. The handsome plates in the second half of the book show many designs for mansions and villas as well as internal decorations for ceilings and wall panels, and detailed instructions on the construction of proper brick and stone arches. Although this book was intended for carpenters, masons, bricklayers, etc. as well as "gentlemen", the price of such a work would surely have placed it far above the reach of the ordinary manual worker, even supposing the worker to be literate, so it was presumably bought by the gentlemen who intended having a house built and wished to supervise the people engaged in the actual construction. The very detailed illustrations would show the illiterate worker the effect that the architect was aiming at.

Two other books which were known in northern India in the 1780s define the role of the architect at that time – he is "a person skilled in architecture, who not only draws the plans of edifices, but superintends and directs the artificiers" while "architecture or the art of Building, includes a multitude of subordinate arts, such as masonry, Carpentry, and those of Bricklayers, Tylers, Slaters, Glaziers, Smiths, Plasterers etc. As to Architecture, properly so called, it considers the Solidity, Conveniency, Beauty, and Proportion of all manner of Buildings" (*A New and Complete Dictionary of Arts and Sciences*). *The Builder's Magazine* says it is the architect's business to consider the whole manner and method of the building and to calculate the expense, "In the management of which, he ought to have regard to its situation, contrivance, strength, beauty, form and materials. The term Architect is also used for the surveyor or superintendent of an edifice, the management being wholly committed to his circumspection."[8]

The architect, then, was to be a man of many parts, actively concerned in the erection of the building he had drawn up and placed in a suitable spot, but he was not always a professional who made his living solely by designing and supervising building. One would not, for example, describe Claude Martin as an architect in any professional sense, although he fulfilled precisely the conditions laid down in the extracts quoted above. The idea of the gifted amateur or gentleman builder persisted for much longer in India than it did in England and Europe, doubtless often more from necessity than inclination. As late as 1843 George Johnson was complaining about European architecture in Calcutta, saying there was "not one architect of sufficient taste to furnish a decent design."[9]

[8] *A New and Complete Dictionary of Arts and Sciences* (London 1754), published by "A Society of Gentlemen", and *The Builder's Magazine* (London 1774).

[9] Johnson, George, *The Stranger in India or Three Years in Calcutta* (London 1843), ii, p. 173. Hereafter George Johnson.

The British in India, when they wanted anything built, had to use engineers of the military service and "the edifices erected from designs furnished by private gentlemen, who fancy they are lighted by Palladio's lamp are often dreadful abortions."[10] Johnson's criticisms are rather unjust for there were certainly professional Indian architects in Calcutta in 1790 who were quite competent at building in the European style. William Hickey who lived in Calcutta had a native architect, a Bengali, from whom he procured "a plan and estimate for one verandah from the bottom to the top of the house," and Hickey was obviously pleased with this man's work for he had the same architect draw up plans for his new house at Chinsurah. "He . . . gave me three different drawings: I adopted the one that most resembled my town residence though upon a much smaller scale." The building was executed "in a very masterly and capital style."[11]

But there is no evidence to show whether these native architects from Calcutta travelled upcountry to Lucknow, and one must therefore postulate that European buildings in the city were erected by three different groups of people. Firstly, the gifted amateurs of the late eighteenth century, like Martin and Polier, who were fulfilling that century's definition of architect as men concerned with every aspect of planning and construction who organised and taught their own workforces with the help of written and illustrated material. Secondly, the unknown local builders who became adept at copying and reinterpreting the buildings that men like Martin and Polier had erected, and who may well have employed people who had worked for the Europeans. And lastly, the engineers of the East India Company, employed both by the nawabs and the Company in Lucknow.

Two things should be said here about these engineers. Firstly, only in a very few cases is it known exactly what they were working on in the city. Not until the 1840s does one begin to get engineers' reports, and then only in a few cases. Their work and influence in

[10] George Johnson, ii, p. 174.

[11] Memoirs of William Hickey, iv, p. 132.

the city is therefore an unknown factor and possibly the most serious gap that exists in the history of Lucknow's architecture. The second point is the extremely casual nature of training given to the early engineers, some of whom seem considerably less competent than gifted amateurs like Martin. "There was no expert or unified control of engineering in the eighteenth century," wrote Edward Sandes, author of *The Military Engineer in India*,[12] and it was not until the 1750s that engineers were sent to India with some training in building, albeit the building of fortifications rather than dwelling places. The Chief Engineer of the Western Settlement (Bombay), who was said to be a very skilful engineer, received £40 a year as an engineer but £200 a year as the Captain of Artillery, showing the relative importance given to the two professions at that time.

It was not until 1812 that the Institution for Royal Engineers was founded at Chatham and 1826 before C.W. Pasley, principal of the institution, published his handbook *Outline of a Course of Practical Architecture, Compiled for the Use of the Junior Officers of Royal Engineers*. In his preface Pasley wrote about junior officers "who are often sent to the British colonies soon after they enter His Majesty's Service and are there required to perform duties, analogous to those of Architects or Civil Engineers, without having had any previous opportunity of acquiring a Practical Knowledge of the details of those duties,"[13] and Sten Nilsson has shown from the library of Fort William College in Calcutta that it was not only gentlemen builders who relied on *The Builder's Magazine* and *Vitruvius Britannicus* but these early engineers as well.[14]

As might be expected, the engineers' chief concern in India was with military buildings, forts, cantonments, bridges, and roads, and it is through this military connection that the first European engineers arrived at theAwadh court. In 1773 Antoine-Louis Polier (1741–1794) "fut nommé à la Cour de Shuja ud daulah en

[12] Sandes, E.W.C., *The Military Engineer in India* (Chatham 1933), p. 39.

[13] Pasley, C.W., *Outline of a Course of Practical Architecture* (Chatham 1826), preface.

[14] Nilsson, p. 157.

qualite d'architecte,"[15] and the career of this important man should be briefly noted. Polier's work in India has unfortunately been greatly overshadowed by that of Claude Martin, to which there are of course, obvious similarities. Because Polier left no buildings in Awadh which can be positively identified he has been rather neglected, although he was in a position to exert as much if not more architectural influence as Martin since he, Polier, was the official architect and engineer at the nawabi court. The most likely reason for his neglect is that he never appeared to become embroiled in court affairs as Martin and others did, and he is one of the few important Europeans who was not a creditor of Asaf-ud-daula, although he did die owing money to Martin.[16] The first mention of Polier in his capacity as engineer is about 1765, when he was the Chief Engineer in the East India Company working on Fort William in Calcutta.[17] He then moved to Faizabad (where the Awadh court was situated at that time), became a close friend of Shuja-ud-daula and was probably responsible for much of the work on the Faizabad Fort, which was a far less onerous undertaking than the larger and more complex Fort William. It is not known if Polier accompanied Asaf-ud-daula to Lucknow on the latter's removal to the new capital, but in 1780 a request was made to the Board of Directors of the East India Company that they "confirm his appointment of Architect and Engineer in the Nabob's Service."[18] The Company sanctioned this appointment and Polier settled in Lucknow, but only two years later he wrote to the Company asking if they would reinstate him as his appointment as Court Architect and Engineer "had been annulled".[19] No reason was given for the annulment, but Polier received permission to remain in Lucknow as Company surveyor for Awadh.[20] He lived there until January 1788 and further exemplifies

[15] Modave, p. 442.

[16] Bengal Inventories, 1801, Range 1, vol. 24, no. 75. I.O.L.

[17] Home Miscellaneous Series 195/1, p. 177. I.O.L.

[18] Bengal Pub. Con., 22 May 1780, no number given.

[19] Bengal Pub. Con., 15 April 1782, no number given.

[20] Ibid.

the existence of Europeans employed and paid by the nawabs while nominally attached to the Company.[21] There is no information about what Polier did while in Lucknow except that he became a close friend of Martin's and was engaged in producing the perfume known as attar of roses,[22] presumably as a hobby. He returned to Europe in 1788 and was killed in a brawl in 1794–5. During his residence in Lucknow an important painting was executed by Zoffany sometime between 1784 and 1786 which is described thus – "The interior of an apartment, probably in Colonel Polier's House at Lucknow, with a group of nine figures. The artist [Zoffany] seated at an easel, painting. Colonel Martin holding dividers in his right hand, is explaining to Major Wombwell [the Company accountant] the plans held by a native servant of a house he is about to build near Lucknow."[23] Polier also appears in the painting dressed in military uniform.

Five years before Polier's second appointment to the court, Asaf-ud-daula had requested another European officer as architect:

> The Nabob . . . requested me to procure him the plan of a house after the European taste, and Captain Marsack being at that time at Lucknow, I troubled him for one which His Excellency [the Nawab] desired of Captain Marsack to execute for him, but he declined to do it without being properly authorised. His Excellency has since desired of me to apply to the Honourable Board for their permission for Captain Charles Marsack to superintend the Building.[24]

This interesting letter shows not only the nawab's liking for European houses at the beginning of his rule (thus refuting several

[21] Letter from Claude Martin to Ozias Humphry, dated 11 March 1789. Ozias Humphry Collection. Royal Academy Library, London.

[22] *Asiatick Researches* (London 1801), i, p. 161.

[23] A reproduction in La Martinière, Lucknow, of the painting by Zoffany in the Victoria Memorial Hall, Calcutta. This written description is attached to the reproduction.

[24] Secret Index, 18 Sept. 1775, John Bristow to the Court of Directors in Calcutta. No number given.

critics, notably Maulana Sharar and Dr Führer who claimed Saadat Ali Khan was responsible for "degenerate" European buildings) but also the extremely casual nature of these first designs. The letter above gives the impression that Marsack could have produced anything that looked sufficiently "European" and it would have satisfied the nawab. It is not even clear whether Captain Marsack was among the Company's engineers at the time, for two years later he was claiming expenses incurred while raising a regiment for Asaf-ud-daula.[25]

It must be stressed that neither Captain Marsack nor Lieut. Bellas (another builder working for Asaf-ud-daula) were considered architects per se. Marsack was primarily a soldier, and even Bellas, who was obviously competent, was called merely an engineer who "is well acquainted with the art of building." To what extent the professions of "engineer" and "architect" were interchangeable in pre-1857 India is something which has never been fully examined: indeed the first time the question was raised would seem to be in 1968 in Sten Nilsson's pioneer work.[26] Without greater research all one can say at present is that Europeans in Lucknow are found classed as "engineers", as "architects", and as "engineers and architects", and that while one does not find architects engaged to erect a bridge or to build a road one certainly finds engineers engaged in domestic buildings and palaces. Of all the Europeans known to have been in the city during the nawabi period, only three gave their profession as "architect" and two of these, Antoine-Louis Polier and William Trickett (who worked in Lucknow from 1815 to 1836), also called themselves engineers. The remaining Europeans who were known to have been actively connected with building in Lucknow were all engineers and the meagre details that exist about their work will be examined now.

After the request for Lieutenant Bellas in 1793 there are no resident engineers recorded at the court until 1811 when Captain Duncan MacLeod arrived, having been "lent to Saadat Ali Khan

[25] Home Miscellaneous Series, 220/1, p. 389. I.O.L.

[26] Nilsson.

to superintend the construction of some buildings,"[27] and to survey the Gomti for the erection of the Iron Bridge.[28] During 1812 the Captain was engaged in "'submitting information and guidance" for the artist who was to design the Iron Bridge. MacLeod had carried out a survey of the proposed site and "his talents and ingenuity displayed . . . in preparing an elegant Model of a Bridge, as well as from other professional sketches and designs, for the satisfaction and gratification of the Vizier, have been so highly agreeable to His Excellency that he wants him to superintend the execution of some other works of importance which are at present in His Excellency's contemplation."[29]

It was at this point that MacLeod's salary was raised to £150 per month although he was still considered as working for the Company – for in June 1813 he resumed his duties as "superintendent of the Military Road" while continuing in the nawab's service. But only a month later MacLeod decided to resign his job as Superintendent of the road, "preferring to remain in the Nabob Vizier's employ."[30] He was given a house by Saadat Ali Khan and Rs 5000 for its repair and the building of seven "out offices for kitchens and sculleries."[31] On the nawab's death Ghazi-ud-din Haider raised MacLeod's salary further to £200 per month and noted that "the Superintendence of several other Buildings has been recently entrusted to him."[32] A dispute arose between the new nawab and several Europeans, including MacLeod, and he was dismissed from the nawab's service at the end of 1814 and left Lucknow.[33] But the next year found him reinstated in the city in his old job (neither the reason for his dismissal nor his reinstatement are recorded) and in November 1815 he was working with "Hukim Mehndee

[27] Hastings, i, p. 178.

[28] Bengal Pol. Con., 11 Oct. 1811, nos 21 & 22.

[29] Foreign Pol. Con., 29 Feb. 1812, nos 70, 73 and 74

[30] For. Pol. Index, 18 June 1813, no. 31, and 9 July 1813, no. 20.

[31] Bengal Pol. Con., 6 Dec. 1814, no. 37.

[32] Bengal Pol. Con., 30 Aug. 1814, no. 22.

[33] Bengal Pol. Con., 6 Dec. 1814, no. 37.

[Hakim Mehndi, the chief minister] and meeting daily at the Old Palace of Dowlut Khana which they were jointly employed in repairing, the one as Engineer and the other as superintendent of the Works."[34] During his time in Lucknow MacLeod built the Khurshid Manzil, the castle-like building to the north of Hazratganj, though no details are recorded about its construction. This is, however, the only named nawabi building attributed to a British engineer, and as such should be noted.[35] MacLeod is last mentioned in 1834 when he was working for Nasir-ud-din Haider, still as superintendent of the construction of buildings.[36]

A little more information is available on J. Munro Sinclair who was appointed civil engineer to the nawab in 1822 but who is also described as being a "general mechanic".[37] Sinclair had tried for several years to get himself appointed at court and had been introduced to Ghazi-ud-din Haider, to whom he had sold a "grinding mill" and other goods. At that time he had been supplying timbers for boat building at Cawnpore but sought work at court through the intervention of a Muslim noble and by addressing the nawab direct in an *arzee* or petition. The nawab refused both pleas but three years later, after the persistent Sinclair approached the Governor General (the Marquess of Hastings) who in turn approached the Lucknow Resident, Major Roper, he was appointed civil engineer to the court at a salary of £100 per month. Sinclair, apart from obtaining timbers for boats, had been a civil architect and a soldier in the Company. He described himself as being "perfectly acquainted with the Mechanism of the Steam Engine, having lately erected Several with Machines of all kinds attached."[38] He also spoke Hindustani and could build ships, boats, roads, and bridges,

[34] For. Pol. Con., 3 Nov. 1815, no. 5.

[35] Diskalker, p. 14.

[36] Correspondence between the India Board and the Court of Directors of the East India Company. Appendix D (Calcutta n.d.), Mahmudabad Library, Mahmudabad, Uttar Pradesh, p. 113.

[37] Bengal Pol. Con., 17 Jan. 1827, nos 56 and 61.

[38] Bengal Pol. Con., 12 Jan. 1827, nos 59–60.

and was in correspondence with "the most eminent Engineers of the day."

But Sinclair was not to be employed solely as a civil engineer – like other Europeans employed at court his duties were eclectic. In 1825 he was commended by the nawab for making some "artificial Fire Works" and the workmen delegated to him by the nawab were rewarded with a bonus of Rs 100, while Sinclair got a *khelat* (ceremonial robe) as well as Christmas presents. Two years later he was obtaining sundry articles including horse-drawn carriages, silver spectacles and china tubs "for Bathing" from Calcutta, and his salary was increased to £150 per month. But Sinclair was also dismissed abruptly in 1827, the reason given being that he had slighted the nawab by not appearing at the durbar daily, as was compulsory for Europeans in the nawab's service.[39]

Before Sinclair left Lucknow he compiled a list of work done for the nawabs with the cost of each item. None of the items was strictly connected with building, except perhaps a model of a house made in 1826. The majority of Sinclair's time was expended in making steam engines and pleasure boats but he also made "a stand for a Gold Hookah" and repaired "hydraulic bellows".[40] After Ghazi-ud-din Haider's death Sinclair was reappointed by the next nawab, though at a much reduced salary of £80 per month, and he remained in Lucknow, occupying a house in the Cantonment until his death in 1845.

For engineers working for the nawabs there was not only a lack of distinction between the terms "engineer" and "architect", but such people employed in either category were often given completely different commissions to execute at the same time. People like Sinclair were not only jack-of-all-trades but were treated as such by their employers. Unfortunately, there is little information about native architects employed by the nawabi court, whether they were working in traditional styles or in European modes. Only two architects

[39] Bengal Pol. Con., 19 Oct. 1827, no. 134.
[40] India Pol. Con., 9 Dec. 1848, no. 36.

concerned with specific buildings are named, Kifayut Ali, architect of the Great Imambara, and Chota Mian, architect of Qaisarbagh. A nawabi building department did exist, and Sleeman reports that it was corrupt. Yet even this meagre fact is contradicted by G.D. Bhatnagar who claims there was no special department of the court in charge of building during Wajid Ali Shah's time, and that the current chief minister was in charge of all such works.[41] Bhatnagar believes that when the nawab ordered a new palace or other buildings the general procedure was to give the contract to an influential person at the court who would appoint an officer to supervise the works. An estimate would be passed by this officer and money advanced to the contractor with, it seems, minimal supervision from the nawab. The Sikandar Bagh, for example, a handsome building erected in a walled garden, was supervised by Husain Ali Khan who was a Commander of the Suleimani platoon, while an illiterate but favourite barber, Azimullah Khan, was the Superintendent of the Ordnance and Building Department during the time of Muhammed Ali Shah. A few names are recorded in Company records of Indians working for the nawabs as architects, though again their area of responsibility is left vague.

Munu Khan was noted in 1815 as "Architect, or Master builder in the Vizier's Service" superintending repairs to a tomb in that year[42] and he may have been the *daroga* of building mentioned in the same year in another report.[43]

Raja Darshan Singh had in 1821 the "superintendence of the Repairs of the Palace [the Farhad Baksh complex] and other Establishments,"[44] and was involved in requisitioning building materials from luckless inhabitants of the city.[45] But the most frequently recurring name was that of Raja Bukhtawar Singh who was originally

[41] Bhatnagar, G.D., *Awadh under Wajid Ali Shah* (Banares n.d.), p. 208.

[42] Bengal Pol. Con., 26 July 1815, no. 70.

[43] Bengal Pol. Con., 7 March 1815, no. 25.

[44] Bengal Pol. Con., 10 Nov. 1821, no. 23.

[45] See ibid. for an account of Darshan Singh removing new timbers and *chunam* from a house in Lucknow.

a trooper in the East India Company cavalry and became a building superintendent in 1807. He worked for thirty years and was "often entrusted with the construction of houses, Bridges, public roads, and other Government works at Lucknow, most of which works he executed well."[46] In 1831, when Captain Herbert was appointed astronomer to the Lucknow Observatory and given the Khurshid Manzil to live in, it was Raja Bukhtawar Singh who completed repairs to Herbert's house and the Raja was also appointed by the nawab to begin work on the Observatory in 1832, under Herbert's guidance. Simultaneous with this work the Raja was pressing ahead with a military career, having been transferred to the nawab's army, and it would be interesting to know how he apportioned his time between two differing, but seemingly full-time occupations.[47] There are no recorded attempts by European engineers to train Indians to build in the European manner, but one can accept that working for a European like MacLeod entailed a reasonable amount of knowledge of European designs, if not method, and that these work-people with their specialized knowledge would then be employed by native superintendents. As for the "influential person at the capital" or even the illiterate barber and the commander of the platoon, one does not feel that their involvement amounted to much more than an occasional visit to the site, a considerable rake-off from the difference between the estimated prices and the actual prices, and great credit for the finished project.

[46] India Pol. Con., 27 Feb. 1837, no. 32.

[47] Fisher, Michael, "The Imperial Court and the Province" (thesis presented to the University of Chicago 1978), pp. 148–9.

9

The Four Palace Complexes

DURING THE EIGHTY years of nawabi rule in Lucknow three new palace complexes were built – the Daulat Khana, the Chattar Manzil, and the Qaisarbagh. The old fort on the south bank of the Gomti, the Macchi Bhavan, was also greatly extended and improved. The palaces of the nawabs, like those of the Mughals and other contemporary Indian rulers, were expected to fulfil a wide range of functions and it is worth repeating the brief description of the nawabi palace at Faizabad to emphasise this point. "It is a large building without taste, and without proportion, with courtyards, gardens, and workshops of all kinds, which form *a separate city within the city.*"[1]

Such a complex was also expected to accommodate the Court officials (the darbari) during their working day, including the judicial officials; to provide the Divan-i-Am and the Divan-i-Khas (the Halls of Public and Private Audience of the ruler), the mosques, barahdaries, and associated religious buildings with attached schools for boys; the zenanas and enclosed gardens for the female relatives of the ruler; kitchens and food storage areas; wells; quarters for the rulers' bodyguards; stables for their animals; dungeons for selected prisoners; rooms for artists who were under patronage, *hammams* or bath-houses for both sexes; storehouses for records; and workshops where artisans would be employed in all kinds of utilitarian and luxury crafts, from gilding palanquins to

[1] Modave, p. 143.

making palace furniture. In addition there would also be formal walled gardens within the palace complexes, usually with fountains and small canals; pavilions where the ruler would entertain by giving banquets, holding *nautches* (exhibitions by dancing girls) and other diversions; and the rulers' private apartments, although one should remember about this last item that in Muslim court life (as in European court life) "the most important thing . . . is the extent to which medieval life was lived in public, at least, by the kind of people who could afford to build themselves fine homes . . . they lived the greater part of their lives before a constant audience of their dependants and retainers."[2]

In appearance such a palace complex was a series of courtyards, large and small, and usually surrounded by walls of differing heights, where the various separate buildings were subjugated to form an integral part of the whole complex. No one building normally assumed undue prominence over another and there were in any case, linking passageways, corridors, and garden walks so it was not always easy to see where one building began and another ended. In the Chattar Manzil complex, for example, at least thirteen separate "houses" were noted,[3] including the jewel house, the tea house, the looking-glass house, and the palanquin house,[4] although such buildings were fused together by "a perfect labyrinth of courtyards, inner gardens, balconies, gateways, passages, verandahs, rotundas, outhouses and pavilions,"[5] as one confused observer wrote. It is important to bear this picture in mind, especially as the palaces in Lucknow have suffered a drastic kind of pruning. Today one sees a single building, such as the Chattar Manzil, or the Begum Kothi (now demolished), and is told it was the palace of such and such nawab, when in fact it represents only one building among a great number

[2] Kidson, *et al.*, p. 144.

[3] Foreign Pol. Con., 13 Feb. 1857, nos 157–9.

[4] The word *kothi* means a house that is built from baked brick or stone (as opposed to a hut of unbaked brick or a bungalow), see for example the Begum Kothi, but it can also mean a room or separate chamber within a house.

[5] Ruutz Rees, p. 252.

of others that went to make up that particular palace complex. If one visualises palace life as it is depicted in many Mughal paintings, full of activity and bustle, where people are employed in various sections of the palace or in gardens or pavilions within the main walls, one will have a better idea of the picture that greeted the traveller in nawabi days, rather than the lonely and often deserted buildings one sees in present-day Lucknow.

A further point should be made here, and this is that although the palace complexes did contain such a multitude of people and offices they were not self-sufficient and did not have the kind of resources that would allow them to exist independently from their surrounding towns. No evidence appears to exist, for example, that animals were slaughtered for consumption within the palace complexes (unlike the British Residency, where there was a slaughterhouse within the grounds) nor is there any reference to gardens producing fruit and vegetables inside the palace walls, although it is known that Asaf-ud-daula did have market gardens somewhere in the city producing food for the court.[6] The traditional functions of the Islamic city were never usurped or threatened by the palace complexes, the bazaars continued to flourish in the old city, moneylending, money-changing, and the minting of Lucknow rupees were quite unaffected, as were the weavers of materials, the embroiderers, lace-makers, *bidri* workers, people engaged in the tobacco and sugar industries, perfume makers, prostitutes, and many other workers. On the contrary, because the palace complexes were not self-sufficient, the building of a new complex in a hitherto sparsely populated area like the Daulat Khana gave a tremendous impetus to open up new bazaars and ganjes to provide necessities and luxuries to the court. There still exists near the Daulat Khana an area known as the Milkman's Quarter which, local people told me, used to provide milk and dairy products to the palace, and by a nice turn of fate, this area is flourishing while the Daulat Khana is in ruins.

[6] Blane, William, *An Account of the Hunting Excursions of Asoph ul Doulah* (London 1788), p. 7.

In addition to such people who were providing services to the court, there were also the petitioners who would visit the court seeking redress and advice on criminal and civil matters, artists and entertainers who hoped for patronage from the nawab and his ministers, and people simply hoping for employment. All these visitors to the palaces generated yet another category of people who provided services for the travellers, including serais or lodging houses, food and drink, and scribes who would write out petitions and advise on etiquette and form. Faiz Bakhsh, a traveller to Faizabad while the nawabi court was still there, described his astonishment at the great number of food and drink vendors on the outskirts of the city and the many different kinds of food available to travellers. There was such a concourse of people, he reported, that he believed he had reached the centre of the town, when in fact he was still four miles away from the city gate.[7]

This last category of people providing services to travellers can be seen as the last circle in a series radiating outwards from the palace complex. The more celebrated and famous the court the wider would the circles spread, drawing in all kinds of people who would find it convenient to live near the centre. So the building of a new complex was equivalent to developing quite a large area of land by the time the resulting settlements were taken into account.

By 1766 the first palace complex, the Macchi Bhavan, had become the most prominent feature in a sizeable town: "constructed in the form of a chateau, surrounded with walls and high towers. There is a lofty gateway, and a great fore-court, that stands before a tall building with arcades, designed for sounding the tambour."[8] The main complex within the battlemented walls was called the Panch Mahalla or Five Palaces, an arcaded building which stood just inside the north wall of the fort and was visible from the river banks. The building appears quite untouched by European influence and had small *chattris* (pavilions) at each corner, and merlons

[7] Sharar, p. 49.
[8] Tieffenthaler, i, pp. 256–7.

along the parapets. It was probably fairly similar to the more celebrated Panch Mahalla at Fatehpur Sikri built by Akbar about 1570. The Lucknow building was either demolished or severely altered during Asaf-ud-daula's period and does not feature as a major building in the Macchi Bhavan complex after his move to the Daulat Khana.

Early pictures of this area, including a view by the Daniells from the north Gomti bank looking south, show that the chief characteristic of this complex was that of defence, emphasised by the massive brick buttresses rising from the not inconsiderable hill on which the complex developed. William Hodges, who was one of the first European visitors to the palace in 1782, said: "the exterior of the building is not to be commended: it reminded me of what I had imagined might be the style of a Baron's castle in Europe, about the twelfth century."[9] The fact that the British Chief Commissioner during 1857, Sir Henry Lawrence, paid Rs 50,000 (£5000) to the owner of the area, Yah Ally Khan,[10] and later proceeded to blow up the structure for fear that it might become an impregnable stronghold for the mutineers, shows that the site and its subsequent development were entirely apt for defensive purposes. None of the latter palace complexes appear to have paid more than lip service to the notion of defence, which reflects perhaps more strongly than anything the early realisation by the nawabs that it was impossible to attempt to stem foreign invasion by mere bricks and mortar, even had they wanted to.

Apart from its important defensive position, the Macchi Bhavan commanded three essential points of communication in Lucknow. Two roads from the south and the west converged in front of the palace, the south approach to the Stone Bridge – the major crossing point over the Gomti – was controlled by the complex and the Gomti itself ran beneath the walls of the building. There are no records of quays or landing stages here although there was a consi-

[9] Hodges, p. 101.
[10] Ruutz Rees, p. 30.

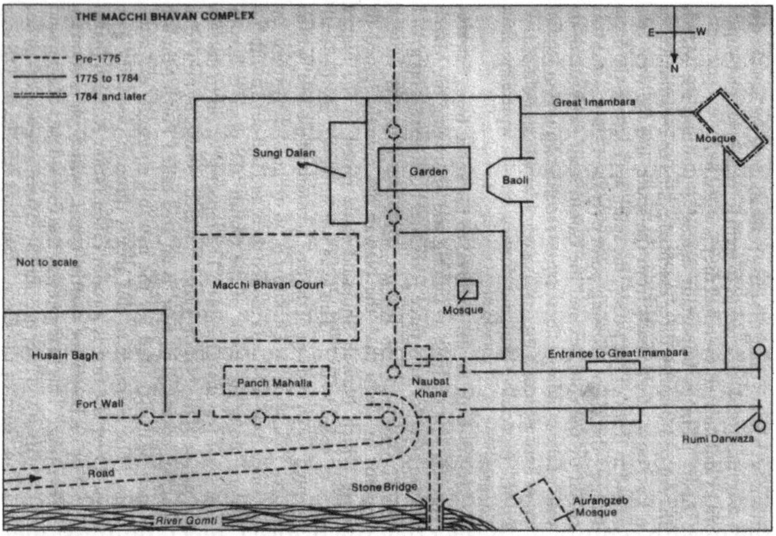

derable amount of river traffic, especially bringing luxury goods upstream from Calcutta.[11]

Asaf-ud-daula on his removal to Lucknow from Faizabad evidently lost no time in altering and improving the Macchi Bhavan area, for only three years after his accession his grandmother Sadrun Nisa Begum complained to the Mughal emperor in Delhi that "the Nawab has entirely ruined the house which Nawab Shuja-ud-daula raised to the highest pitch of splendour."[12] This was not, however, the generally accepted view, and one of the first accounts of the area, written before 1785, says that Lucknow is "an irregular dirty town" but that since Asaf-ud-daula moved there and laid out a number of gardens along the bank of the Gomti "the place is become somewhat less disagreeable." The report goes on to describe the "palace of the Nabob Vizier"[13] which consists by now of six principal courts. The first "is an area called Putch Mhullah" (Panch

[11] The Orme Collection No. 334, maps, nos 9, 10, and 13. I.O.L.

[12] *Persian Correspondence*, v, p. 189.

[13] *Asiatic Annual Register* (London 1800), p. 97. First published in Calcutta in 1785, this article called an "Account of Lucknow" by F. Gladwin appeared in London for the first time in 1800.

Mahalla) used for the nawab's equipage and attendants. "The entrance to this area is through two lofty gateways. Over the first is a room called Nobit Konnah [*naubat khana*] or orchestra for martial music, which plays morning and evening." This first gateway had formed part of Shuja-ud-daula's palace and later became the eastern gateway of the new square in front of the Great Imambara (the Rumi Darwaza formed the western gateway). Unfortunately this early gateway was demolished after 1857 so that the great square is now three-sided. The second courtyard consisted of the state apartments "encompassing a square garden, together with an external enclosure for smaller rooms . . . called Bowly [*baoli*] from the large well within it, which includes a staircase and smaller recesses, with openings in the well from top to bottom." Opposite the baoli was an "arcaded chamber with a piazza, for sleeping in during the summer heat."[14] This baoli is still standing, though in a mutilated condition, and was probably saved from destruction by the fact of being hollowed out of the mound that formed the Macchi Bhavan area.

The sad and dilapidated state of the baoli today can give no hint of its former splendour. Viscount Valentia stayed in the "Bolee Palace" in 1803 when his apartments consisted of

> two rooms at the back of a very beautiful garden pavilion, with, as usual, a basin of water in front. They are heated by flues under the floor. The first room is about twenty feet square, with three fountains for either hot or cold water, in oblong niches on three sides of the room. On the fourth side is the entrance into the inner room. At each corner is a pillar, from which arches spring that sustain the roof, which gradually narrows into a cupola. The whole is covered with fine white chunam, ornamented with black, to correspond with the floor, which is entirely of white marble, inlaid with a mosaic work of black and red.[15]

The second room was similar, with two basins filled with warm water and here were "fountains playing into the middle of the room

[14] *Asiatic Annual Register* (1800), p. 97.
[15] Valentia, i, p. 140.

the whole was built of red porphyry to the height of a few feet from the ground, the rest of a red stone."[16]

Parallel to the Baoli Palace was the Sangi Dalan or Stone Hall, comprising a grand hall surrounded by a double arcade and crowned by four cupolas at each corner, each copper dome covered with gilding. To the north of the Sangi Dalan lay another garden court containing public offices, which is probably where the durbar was held, described by William Hodges, the English artist, as

> a range of three arcades, parallel to each other and supported by columns in the Moorish style; the ceiling and the whole of this is beautifully gilt, and painted with ornaments, and flowers. It is ascended by steps from a flower garden, laid out in the same manner as we see in Indian paintings, which are all square plats, in which are planted flowers of the strongest scent.[17]

In contrast to the splendour of the buildings here was the zenana of Asaf-ud-daula, described as three heavy piles of unshapely houses, the Shish Mahal (glass palace), Khord Mahal (the general term for a zenana) and the Rang Mahal (coloured palace) with high walls and a few small latticed windows.[18]

The sixth and last court of the Macchi Bhavan complex was an area to the east called Husain Bagh which was described as a flower garden at the river's edge, enclosed with a brick wall covered with vines. These six courts formed the palace complex proper, but attached to it was a building that attracted great interest, the Aina Khana or mirror house. The external appearance of this building was unremarkable but inside was an absolute confusion of treasures collected by Asaf-ud-daula so that it was variously described as a museum and something approaching a large pawnbroker's shop stuffed full of "the whimsical curiosities purchased by the Nawab consisting of several thousand English prints framed and glazed, Chinese drawings and ornaments, mirrors of all shapes and

[16] Ibid.

[17] Hodges, p. 101.

[18] *Asiatic Annual Register* (1800), p. 98.

sizes, lustres, and innumerable other articles of European manufacture."[19] There were also "watches, pistols, guns, furniture, philosophical [scientific] machines etc. all crowded together with the confusion of a lumber room."[20] The indiscriminate profusion of this mirror house and the contrast between the extravagance displayed here and the poverty of many of the citizens of Lucknow outside the palace walls led to bitter comments by European travellers, but the adjoining aviary with its "uncommon collection of birds," the menagerie which included "several serpents of extraordinary dimensions,"[21] and the fine armoury seem to have escaped criticism.

None of these early descriptions tell one very much about the people that inhabited these buildings in the complex. One should not imagine that the European travellers who were shown round the palace buildings found them quite deserted, rather that their interest was directed towards the structures than the various occupations in which the palace servants and officials were engaged. A record exists of some of the people engaged in servicing Asaf-ud-daula's complex, before reductions in staff were ordered by the East India Company. Compiled in great detail it lists both the "common labourers" (1107) and the gardeners (129) as well as the more highly skilled craftspeople like seal-cutters, artificial-flower makers, musicians, trumpeters, coffee makers, and those in charge of tents and camp equipage. There were also 278 workers in the elephant, camel, and horse stables, and indoor domestic servants. Not only working animals were stabled in the complex but leopards, cats, antelopes, pigeons, and a number of other birds, making this a small private zoo.[22] No female staff are listed, though of course there were female servants within the zenana. Various female dancers and singers would also have been employed, though not necessarily on a full-

[19] Valentia, i, p. 155.

[20] Twining, p. 311.

[21] *Asiatic Annual Register* (1800), p. 100.

[22] The Nawab's Household Accounts, 1780–1783, Mss. Add. 29093, ff. 14–90, B.L.

time basis. In addition to the people listed above were various other craftspeople including goldsmiths and armourers, who may not have been permanently attached to the complex, as well as the nawab's personal attendants who included one ear-picker and two candle-snuffers.

Even if the families of all these workers lived outside the complex a large number of people were still actively engaged within the area itself and required workshops and special equipment with which to pursue their occupations. Reading descriptions of the Macchi Bhavan complex one must therefore people them with these numerous workers and endeavour to see "the city within the city" that existed.

After Asaf-ud-daula's removal to the Daulat Khana a significant change took place, both in nawabi and European attitudes towards the palaces. European descriptions of the late eighteenth century were still to a very large extent influenced by the "Age of Reason" with the enquiring open-mindedness which characterises this period – unlike the prejudiced attitudes of many Victorians. Gladwin's 1785 description of the Macchi Bhavan area should be regarded as a near perfect example of objective writing and can be paralleled in art by the sketches and painting of the Daniells, where the purpose of description and delineation was to convey information to the curious mind (a "curious" person being seen in the context of the time as someone receptive to new ideas and impressions rather than someone merely inquisitive). But this attitude was to change dramatically at the turn of the century.

How much the nawabs themselves realised and reacted to the change is problematic, although there is certainly a marked difference in the behaviour of Asaf-ud-daula and Wajid Ali Shah towards European visitors to their palaces. There were few restrictions placed on visitors to the Macchi Bhavan area, they were allowed to wander more or less where they pleased, and to draw and sketch the buildings as they wished. Valentia and Salt were even allowed into part of Asaf-ud-daula's harem, and although this was after the nawab's death it is inconceivable that Wajid Ali Shah would have permitted European men into his late father's harem. On the contrary a newspaper report of 1855 recorded Wajid Ali Shah driving in an English carriage with his "amazonian troops" in the Qaisarbagh, "a mysterious retreat into whose intricate labyrinths only the eunuchs are allowed to enter."[23] Only one contemporary description of the Qaisarbagh exists while the nawab was still in residence, and even then it only describes the garden of the main courtyard which was opened annually for the Joghi performance.[24] The reporter of 1855 who was allowed in dismisses the vast complex in one sentence as "stupendous piles of buildings surmounted by glittering domes that constitute the palace, which have not the slightest pretensions to architectural beauty."[25] There are no contemporary sketches or photographs of the Qaisarbagh by Europeans and all information on the complex comes from post-1857 photographs, written descriptions, and present-day observations. It is ironic that one knows more about the Macchi Bhavan than the Qaisarbagh, though the former was at its zenith between 1775 and 1782 and was entirely destroyed apart from the baoli, while the main Qaisarbagh square still stands, albeit in a sadly depleted state.

The reason for the nawabi withdrawal behind the palace walls was twofold. It was partly a response to the change in European attitudes and the difference between late-eighteenth-century ideas and mid-nineteenth-century prejudices, and also because the British and thus other Europeans no longer regarded the court of the nawabs as a political force of any weight, and the nawabs knew this. Because the British assumed virtual control of Awadh in deed if not in name they no longer looked towards the court as the final arbiter on events in the province. By 1856 the true political power lay with the British Resident, who had successfully usurped most of the functions of the earlier nawabs.

[23] *The Englishman*, a Calcutta newspaper: this item dated 16 Feb. 1855.

[24] This was a great fair called the Joghi Mela, held every August, to which the public were admitted. Wajid Ali Shah, dressed in the saffron robes of a sadhu or fakir, would sit under a mulberry tree and the public were not admitted unless they were also dressed in yellow.

[25] *The Englishman*, this item dated 14 Aug. 1855.

But though the British had by their actions divested the court of the importance it possessed before their interference in the late eighteenth century, they were quite happy to indulge the nawabs in other ways so long as these ways did not impinge upon British designs on Awadh. Thus one finds that the 112 workmen employed in Asaf-ud-daula's arsenal were dismissed because this could obviously pose a danger to the British who were at that time comparatively few in number in Awadh, although the 129 gardeners were retained, as were the 200 people working in the nawab's stables.[26] After Saadat Ali Khan had ceded part of Awadh to the Company in 1801 and had been relieved of much of his army by the British, Gore Ouseley, the former aide-de-camp to the nawab, was able to justify this by claiming "the nabob is now happy and contented, eased of a burden of a part of the country continually open to the Seiks and Mahrattas; his splendour, furniture and houses, in a state infinitely more magnificent than they were before; for he has more opportunity of knowing what funds he can bestow on these things."[27] What the nawab had "saved" by the enforced disbandment of his army and by ceding some of his kingdom he was now encouraged to spend on luxuries including the building of palaces and houses. As a kind of consolation for losing real power the nawabs were allowed to indulge in making Lucknow one of the most visually splendid cities in northern India. Although there was some British criticism of extravagance and corruption when Wajid Ali Shah built the Qaisarbagh there was never any attempt to curb him: in fact as has been shown in some matters, notably the Observatory, the nawabs were actively encouraged by the British to beautify the city.

So one should not wonder too much at nawabi reticence on the one hand and extravagance on the other. While the Macchi Bhavan was at the beginning of Asaf-ud-daula's reign an important and symbolic focus of nawabi power and a defensive area too, by 1856

[26] See The Nawab's Household Accounts, ff. 14–26.

[27] *Asiatic Annual Register* (1807), p. 176.

the Qaisarbagh was nothing more than a beautiful, expensive home for the last nawab and his dependants, a place which had little more import than any of the other garden palaces that this nawab built. As for defence, the Qaisarbagh fell like a shot bird into the hands of the British on their recapture of Lucknow in 1858 when they raced from room to room in a perfect orgy of destruction.[28] All three palace complexes built after the Macchi Bhavan reflect the feeling that the real power of the nawabs had somehow been spirited away but that it was necessary to maintain the belief that all was well; and this was done by building a succession of palaces each more splendid and extravagant than the last, the Qaisarbagh being the natural conclusion of this belief.

Before the Qaisarbagh, two more palace complexes were developed – the Daulat Khana and the Chattar Manzil. It is not known what prompted Asaf-ud-daula's move in the 1780s to the Daulat Khana after he had been at such pains to beautify the Macchi Bhavan and build the Great Imambara adjoining it, but by 1789 European visitors to the city were being shown both the "Old and New Palaces".[29] Much of the Daulat Khana area has suffered almost complete demolition, and a large village of two-storeyed houses to the west of the site is built mainly of reused *lakhori* bricks which came from the Daulat Khana area. It is likely that this was the largest palace complex in Lucknow because the only natural barrier to expansion is the river and marshy ground to the north-east of the site.

Despite the demolition some notable buildings still stand, the most important being the Asafi Kothi which, as the name implies, belonged to Asaf-ud-daula. This building is supposed to have been designed by Claude Martin and is nearer in architectural terms to Bibiapur than to Constantia, being neither a defensive nor a highly fanciful building. It certainly seems likely that the designer of the Asafi Kothi and of Barowen were one and the same person. There

[28] Russell, W.H., *My Indian Mutiny Diary* (London 1970), pp. 100–5. Hereafter Russell.

[29] Hardie & Clayton, p. 64.

are obvious similarities, not only in the working of the arches and the Composite columns but in the intelligent adaptation of a European building to suit the needs of an Indian court. The Asafi Kothi was originally approached through a garden and the great arcaded verandah provided a suitably impressive entrance into the central grand hall, a terrace wide enough for seats during the winter months, and shade for inner rooms against the summer heats. The five central doorways led straight into a grand hall, two storeys high, and eminently suitable for the durbar, with smaller more intimate rooms on each side. The rear of the house has been much added to, so that the fine curve of the bow front is now an inner wall, but the building appears to be intact and is in reasonable condition.

The Daulat Khana complex followed the same pattern as the Macchi Bhavan in that it was a series of buildings interspersed with gardens and tanks. The "inner tank" (so called to distinguish it from the better-known tank in front of the Picture Gallery) still exists with its foundations of pavilions built into the water at the southern end, and was connected to the nearby river Gomti. Few structures can now be distinguished and those that remain, apart from a small marble mosque, are in a ruined condition like the enormous Gol Kothi, a handsome European-style building with its great curved front recalling that of Barowen. Two curiosities are worth noting, however, since the first is still extant. This is a huge structure, pitted today with bullet holes, which was in Nawabi days a racket court known as the Gend Khana. Two stout octagonal fluted pillars stand at the entrance to this massive building, and there were attached buildings on either side, now marked only by indents in the stucco. The story of how the Gend Khana was sold twice to people who tried to demolish it and how it withstood both attempts is told in this area with great amusement, but a similar Gend Khana which stood exactly where the Husainabad Clock Tower stands today was not so lucky and is only known from a photograph of 1858 taken from the top of the Rumi Darwaza. In the same photograph is a six-storeyed slender building, towering over the rest of the complex,

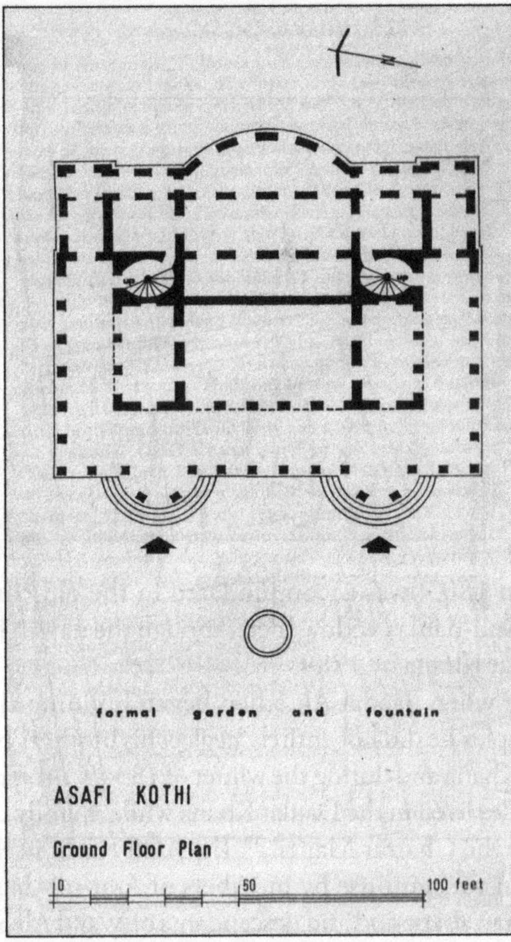

ASAFI KOTHI

Ground Floor Plan

which is probably the "pagoda in the Dowlut Channah" recorded in 1816.[30] It is remarkable that this structure, now lost, which stood two storeys higher than the well-known Sat Khande, has never been recorded.

Although the removal of the nawab to the Daulat Khana necessarily meant that his great train of attendants moved too, the old Macchi Bhavan complex was not left deserted. Viscount Valentia, visiting

[30] *The Asiatic Journal* (1816), ii, p. 579.

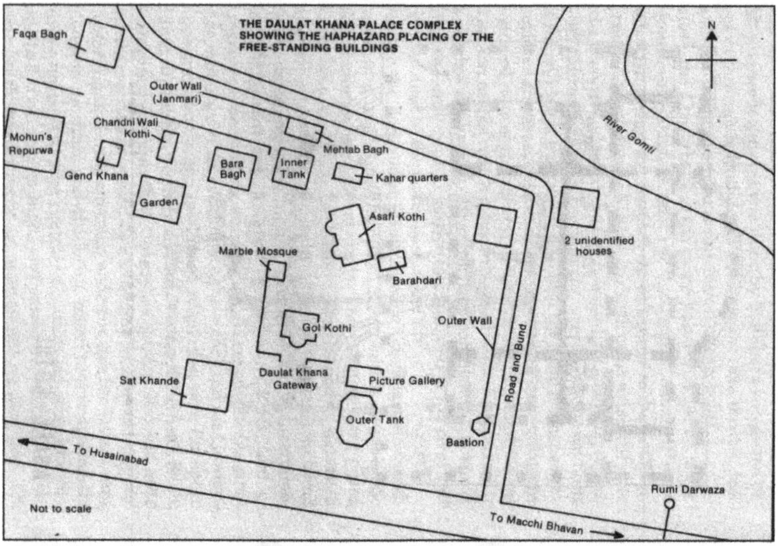

Lucknow in 1803, was accommodated in the old complex and visited Asaf-ud-daula's widow there, though the nawab had moved to the Daulat Khana by 1789.

Similarly when Saadat Ali Khan began building the Chattar Manzil complex he did not entirely neglect his brother's buildings in the Daulat Khana and during the winter of 1834/5 the nawab Nasir-ud-din Haider lived in the Daulat Khana while a family dispute was going on in the Chattar Manzil.[31] The Asafi Kothi itself seems to have been in constant use by members of Asaf-ud-daula's family during the nawabi period and descendants of Wajid Ali Shah[32] have since been reinstated in this building after an interlude when it was used by an American Methodist organisation. There was never any shortage of dependent relatives who expected to be accommodated, and some of the bitterest disputes recorded among Lucknow inhabitants are those where relatives feel they have been unjustly denied accommodation which should be theirs simply by right of relationship to the owner of the house. It is known that building work

[31] India Pol. Con., 18 May 1835, no. 69.

[32] Rasmara Kufida Begum to R.M. Llewellyn-Jones, 30 Jan. 1975.

continued in this area and that Captain MacLeod and Hakim Mehndi were "jointly employed in repairing [the] Old Palace of Dowlut Khana" in 1815 at Saadat Ali Khan's instigation.[33]

It was at the end of June 1803 that Saadat Ali Khan purchased Claude Martin's town house, the Château, from Joseph Quieros, Martin's Spanish agent, and so great was the nawab's joy that he celebrated by entertaining all the Europeans in Lucknow to a banquet and firework display.[34] It was around Martin's house that the third great palace complex was developed, becoming the longest inhabited palace in Lucknow and the chief nawabi residence from 1803 to 1852 when the Qaisarbagh was completed.

The name by which this area is known today, Chattar Manzil, appears to be a post-1857 designation, for the usual term before annexation was the Farhad Baksh Palace, and this is what it was called by the majority of visitors, by the nawabs living there, and by the British Residents. The term Farhad Baksh refers today only to the remaining portion of Claude Martin's house and it was two later buildings, the Greater and Lesser Chattar Manzils, that give their name to the area today. Saadat Ali Khan was particularly pleased with his purchase of Martin's house because he had already built one large house called "The New Palace" in the Daulat Khana area but had "taken a disgust" to it.[35] Though he was reputed to have spent eight lakhs of rupees on this house he subsequently used it only as a storehouse because he considered that area of Lucknow to be very

[33] Foreign Pol. Con., 3 Nov. 1815, no. 5.

[34] Valentia, i, p. 166. Although there was friction over Martin's house between Joseph Quieros and Saadat Ali Khan it was not so serious as to sever relations between the two, for Quieros entered the service of the nawab in the early 1800s and remained working for the next nawab until his death in January 1822. The descendants of Joseph Quieros lived in Lucknow well into the twentieth century, some are buried in the Residency graveyard and a Quieros was until recently a pupil at La Martinière school. Refs. Foreign Pol., Index 26 Jan. 1822, no. 32, and an interview with Mr Frank d'Souza, Vice Principal of La Martinière, 10 Jan. 1975.

[35] *Asiatic Annual Register* (London 1807), pp. 176–83. Major Gore Ouseley's statement. The Major was at one point aide-de-camp to Saadat Ali Khan.

unhealthy,[36] whereas Martin's house further downstream "was a more desirable situation" altogether.[37] There were other reasons too why Martin's house was considered so suitable for Saadat Ali Khan, for as Valentia explained it had "a very commodious zenana annexed . . . at all his [the nawab's] numerous garden houses he has no separate habitation for his women."[38] Moreover, and perhaps most importantly, the house was one of the finest and earliest examples of the European style which had become so popular during the last twenty-five years and which had been encouraged by Saadat Ali Khan's half-brother Asaf-ud-daula. Although by 1803 the immediate land around Martin's house was no longer the empty wooded area it had been when the Frenchman built his house in 1782, there was still sufficient room to the east and south of the house for a substantial new palace complex to develop, and over the next forty-seven years numerous buildings were erected here, ultimately dwarfing Martin's house.

But the influence of the original house was immense, and although European visitors were to describe the Farhad Baksh palace as "truly eastern",[39] the oriental flavour was achieved more by gardens, pavilions, marble tanks, and velvet drapes than by the majority of the buildings which were firmly rooted in the European architectural tradition. Unlike the Daulat Khana complex which must be seen as transitional with its rather haphazard placing of semi-European free-standing buildings among gardens, tanks, and traditional structures like zenanas, the Farhad Baksh palace was a planned sequence of European houses with a central garden separating the river bank houses from those built along the Khas Bazaar street to the south. It was only the addition of innumerable small buildings like barahdaries, pavilions, covered passageways, verandahs, gateways, and walled areas that gave this complex its labyrinthine char-

[36] Nugent, Lady Maria, *A Journal from the Year 1811 till the Year 1815* (London 1839), ii, p. 329. Hereafter Nugent.

[37] *Asiatic Annual Register* (1807), p. 177.

[38] Valentia, i, p. 166.

[39] Nugent, i, p. 303.

acter, and the demolition of these subsidiary structures, though greatly to be regretted, does enable one to see as it were the skeleton of this complex. Saadat Ali Khan's original intention was, it appears, that the Farhad Baksh buildings should be seen as separate entities, European buildings complementing each other across a carefully planned central garden. But later nawabs could not reconcile these self-contained buildings with the needs of an Indian court, hence the jumble of subsidiary structures that grew up around the earlier buildings.

It is necessary to return to the previous reign of Asaf-ud-daula in order to appreciate the substantial contribution that Saadat Ali Khan made towards the beautification of the eastern half of Lucknow and his conscious attempts towards town planning, both of which have been little appreciated by later writers. One of the earliest criticisms made by European travellers visiting the city at the end of the eighteenth century was the appalling state of the road along which they had to travel to reach the area around the Macchi Bhavan, the Daulat Khana, and the Residency complexes. Thus when Thomas Twining wrote of the Lucknow which he knew between 1792 and 1795, he said:

> the length of the city in this direction [i.e. from the south-west of Lucknow up through the Chauk to the Gomti] was about five miles. The streets all this way were narrow and dirty, and crowded with bazaars and poor people, presenting, upon the whole, an air of wretchedness that much disappointed the expectations I had formed of the splendour of this celebrated capital. It was evident that this splendour was confined to the palace, while misery pervaded the streets: the true image of despotism"[40] [and again] on passing and repassing through the streets, I observed the same wretchedness as before.

In 1798, the year in which Saadat Ali Khan ascended the musnud, things were no better and another visitor wrote –

> Happening to enter the town at the west end, and which contains the poor mechanics, and labourers of every sort, I never witnessed so many

[40] Twining, pp. 308 and 313.

> varied forms of wretchedness, filth and vice. The street which leads to the palace is upwards of five miles, more than one half of which you wade through mire and filth. During the lapse of time, the streets sink from cleaning, or by the blowing away of dust while dry, so that they are fallen in the middle to the depth of ten or twelve feet.[41]

Obviously there had been little improvement since Joseph Tieffenthaler's complaint that the streets were narrow and stinking in 1766. But in 1819, five years after Saadat Ali Khan's death, a visitor was full of praise for the handsome street that led from the Dilkusha to the Farhad Baksh palace and the Residency. "The Cheni ki Bazar, which is of considerable length, with neat ranges of shops on each side, all of the same height and having piazzas along their whole front" was much admired by the writer who added "the streets in this part of the city are regular and handsome."[42]

Another traveller whose account of Lucknow was published in 1828 wrote –

> the second quarter of Lucknow was built mostly by the late nabob Saadat Ali. It stands near the Goomty, towards the south-east, and consists of one very handsome street, after the European fashion, above a mile in length, with bazars striking out at right angles, and a well-built new chowk in the centre, with a lofty gateway at each extremity, which presents a Grecian front on one side and a Moorish one on the other. The houses that compose the remainder of this street belong to the king, and are occupied by members of his family or officers of his household. These are for the most part in the English style, but with a strange occasional mixture of Eastern architecture. The same remark applies to the palaces and gardens that occupy the space between the street, and the river, and reserved by his Majesty for his own use. All these palaces are filled with European furniture and pictures, and may rank with comfortable English houses.[43]

Along this "very handsome street" were Saadat Ali Khan's Chaupar Stables, a large building in the form of a cross, "so that standing in the centre, a person may see the horses in any of the arms of

[41] Tennant, ii, p. 104.

[42] Lumsden, p. 9.

[43] Hamilton, ii, p. 131.

the cross. This building has a large space in the centre, stables on each side for the horses, and beyond them, on both sides, piazzas to shelter the horses completely from the sun and rain."[44] To the west of these stables was the Kankar Wali Kothi, one of several European-style houses erected by the nawab. The eastern end of the street began from the Dilkusha, another European house built about 1800 and surrounded by a fine park. The whole street was well over two miles long and formed something of a triumphal way along which visitors were obliged to travel in order to reach the Farhad Baksh palace and the British Residency. There are no further reports of the wretched state of the old road through the Chauk after 1798, not because it had improved dramatically but because European visitors were diverted from it to the new road which still exists today as Hazratganj, an impressively wide road.

This digression about roads demonstrates that the Farhad Baksh complex was intended to provide a palace worthy of the builder and a fitting climax to the triumphal way, the southern line of palace buildings, the Lal Barahdari, the smaller Chattar Manzil, the Gulistan-i-Iram and the Darshan Bilas forming an impressive frontage or closure at the end of the great road. Because the southern and eastern areas of land around the Farhad Baksh were relatively undeveloped, Saadat Ali Khan was able to extend the city in these directions and impose a measure of town planning which has hitherto been unappreciated. Not only was his long and broad road with its bazaars at right angles an unusual concept,[45] but the type of houses fronting the route were also foreign in appearance – like the Kankar Wali Kothi and the Nur Baksh Kothi, an Italianate looking building thought to have been built by Saadat Ali Khan for one of his sons.[46]

[44] Lumsden, p. 10. A very small portion of these stables, part of the north/south wing, still exist at the end of Lawrence Terrace, just north of Hazratganj.

[45] Unusual because although most Indian cities have at least one broad street, the Chauk, the idea of streets developing from it on a grid pattern is only found, as far as I know, at Jaipur, which was laid out by the Maharaj Jai Singh in the eighteenth century, near the old medieval city.

[46] Nugent, i, p. 303.

It is known that Saadat Ali Khan's taste inclined almost exclusively towards European buildings and that he took an active interest in designing his own palaces.[47] It is possible that some buildings normally attributed to European architects may in fact have been planned by the nawab, though as yet there is no documentary evidence of this. In 1803 Valentia had noticed that the nawab's "chief gratification seems to be building palaces of an architecture that resembles Grecian, but as he never employs an architect the faults are numerous," and ten years later the British Resident found him "exhibiting designs for new palaces and decorations of rooms, the execution of which had commenced, and the completion of which, if intended must occupy and serve to amuse him for a period of several years."[48] The nawab's sudden death in 1814 concluded his architectural ambitions and the attitude expressed by the British Resident that anything the nawabs built was an "amusement" (unlike the serious British buildings) has played no small part in diminishing the considerable achievements of Saadat Ali Khan who, while incorporating many elements suggested by Claude Martin's buildings, was able to impose a choate form on the eastern portion of Lucknow which is still visible today.

The condescending attitude displayed by Europeans and especially the British towards Saadat Ali Khan's buildings may also have accounted for the confusion and lack of precise description about the Farhad Baksh complex by such visitors. As though it was almost beneath their authors to enquire too closely about the palaces, thus displaying a notable change from the attitudes of late-eighteenth-century visitors, the nineteenth-century descriptions of Lucknow and the palaces are far from satisfactory. Some visitors found it difficult to distinguish one palace complex from another, and Von Orlich[49] has amalgamated his own description of the Farhad Baksh, which he saw in 1845, with Gladwin's description of the Macchi

[47] Valentia, i, p. 173.

[48] The Oudh Papers (1808–15). John Baillie's statement of 2 July 1813. National Archives, New Delhi.

[49] Von Orlich, ii, pp. 106–7.

Bhavan written in 1785.[50] The result is a composite palace which he calls the "Furrahbaksh" but which has many of the features of the old palace of Asaf-ud-daula, none of which of course existed within the Farhad Baksh complex.[51]

Even the date when Saadat Ali Khan began building can only be deduced from an oblique reference by the nawab, who wrote: "I began to build the Houses and Parks of my present residence during the time of Colonel Scott and Colonel Collins"[52] (i.e. from about 1802 to 1807) and there appears to be only one description of the palace during the nawab's lifetime, written just before his death, when Maria (Lady Nugent) viewing the palace from the roof of the British Residency wrote that "it is certainly very pretty and truly eastern – its various courts and colonnades, the variety of birds, the style of the gardens, etc. put me very much in mind of those we see on old China cups and jars."[53] Lady Nugent went to the palace on several occasions and one night the entertainments included a firework display, a walk through an impromptu garden of pavilions, temples, bowers, and fountains, all constructed and built the previous day, and interestingly a look at some "transparencies and a model of the iron bridge,"[54] the erection of which was cut short by the nawab's death.

In 1818 Ghazi-ud-din Haider who succeeded Saadat Ali Khan was granted a pass by the East India Company which allowed him to employ James Lock, who entered the nawab's service "to superintend certain improvements to be made in the neighbourhood of

[50] See pp. 172 and 174, and F. Gladwin, *The Asiatick Miscellany* (Calcutta 1785), pp. 97–9.

[51] This confusion is unfortunately still present today, for a recent (1976) guide-book *History of Chattar Manzil* confidently repeats this muddled description, although a little thought would have shown that the Sangi Dalan, the Baoli and the three palaces could not conveniently be accommodated in the guide-book's plan of the Chattar Manzil. See *History of Chattar Manzil*, ed. J.K. Shukla, etc. (Lucknow 1976).

[52] Foreign Pol. Con., 4 March 1814, nos 102–4.

[53] Nugent, i, p. 303.

[54] Ibid., p. 323.

the Palace of Farrah Buksh."[55] It is not known what these improvements were but they may have been the refurbishing of the Lal Barahdari (so called from the dark red paint employed over the stucco to imitate red sandstone) which had been the grand durbar hall of Saadat Ali Khan, but which became the Throne Room and Coronation Hall of Ghazi-ud-din Haider. This does represent a significant change in the use of a building from traditional Islamic court functions to one designed to reflect the "honour" bestowed by the British on the new nawab. Few people even at the time believed that the title of "King of Oud" was more than an empty gesture on the part of the British,[56] but the nawab, having accepted the title, thought it only fitting that his coronation should be carried out with due pomp in suitable surroundings.

An English visitor described "the immense hall" where the throne was placed and "the view of the interior of the palace garden, which is very pretty, having a fine sheet of water through the centre, with fountains, beautiful walks, flower borders, and many statues."[57] This central garden was one of the most splendid features of the palace and another visitor in 1827 who dined with Ghazi-ud-din Haider described how they sat

> in a large veranda, looking into a capacious quadrangle surrounded with elegantly columned cloisters. In the centre was a spacious tank of water, with sparkling jets d'eau, ornamented with marble statues, and illuminated by many coloured lamps. The prospect bore a pleasing and fairy-like effect: the faint manner in which the distant colonnades and statues were lighted up reminding me in some degree of the effect produced in the background of Martin's famous picture of Belshazzar's Feast.[58]

In the centre of this tank was "a neat pavilion, brilliantly painted externally, but of a picturesque form with its painted minarets and

[55] Foreign Pol. Con., 9 Jan. 1818, no. 2.
[56] Mundy, i, p. 13.
[57] Lumsden, pp. 15–16.
[58] Mundy, i, p. 32.

miniature domes."[59] This small pavilion was reached by boat, and Knighton considered it to be the "most elegant structure in Lucknow." Inside the little pavilion "were two rooms of moderate size, both luxuriously fitted up, with divans running round the walls. A perfect model of the entire palace stood on a table inside. This particular pavilion was no bigger than a walnut."

On the north bank of the Gomti directly opposite the Farhad Baksh palaces stood the Dilaram Kothi which, had Saadat Ali Khan lived longer, might well have been incorporated into a larger complex spanning the river and linked by the proposed Iron Bridge. As it stood it was used by the nawab as a "sleeping house"[60] and was a three-storey building in the European tradition. Demolished in 1917, it formed the backdrop for three water temples which stood in the river. It was from the centre temple that Saadat Ali Khan "used to sit . . . in the cool of the evening and fish with rod and line: the whole three have been described as elegantly ornamental structures."[61] The house itself was set in a square enclosure with four small pavilions at each corner, and the tiled roofs of these pavilions are worth noting both because they provide one of the very few examples of chinoiserie in Lucknow, and are an interesting example of the continuity of foreign motifs in the city's buildings. These distinctively ridged tiles first appear in the pavilions of the great wall at Barowen, here in the Dilaram, on an unnamed building near Husainabad, and finally are still to be seen on the restored gateway of Sikandar Bagh – one of the last nawabi buildings of Wajid Ali Shah.

So the whole Farhad Baksh complex was different from its predecessors, the Macchi Bhavan with its distinct courtyards and the Daulat Khana with its irregularly placed buildings. If one looks forward at the Qaisarbagh and asks whether the Farhad Baksh complex anticipated it in any way the answer is that any similarities between the two are of a very superficial nature, often no more than

[59] Knighton, p. 27.

[60] Nugent, i, p. 323.

[61] Darogah, Haji Abbas Ali, *The Lucknow Album* (Lucknow 1874), plate 47.

architectural detailing which could well be attributable to buildings other than the earlier palace complexes. The Qaisarbagh, lying to the south-east of the Farhad Baksh, was built between 1848 and 1852 for Wajid Ali Shah and has been undergoing demolition in a piecemeal fashion ever since. It is undoubtedly one of the most remarkable palace complexes ever erected and had it not been especially singled out for destruction by the vengeful British and later neglected by the people of Lucknow it would have become one of the most celebrated structures in India. Post-1857 photographs show something of the virtuosity of the architect, the panache and fantastic vision translated into buildings that have a truly surreal quality.

The complex consisted of three main squares, the largest to the east incorporating the two tombs of Saadat Ali Khan and his wife,[62] while the Roshan-ud-daula Kothi or Kacheri at the south-west corner was complemented by the Chaulakhi palace at the south-east angle. Both these separate palaces, the Roshan-ud-daula Kothi and the Chaulakhi, were built before the Qaisarbagh palace was conceived and Wajid Ali Shah is supposed to have confiscated Roshan-ud-daula's house while he bought the Chaulakhi palace from his barber, Azimullah Khan.[63] Two main gateways led into the largest courtyard and there were a number of free-standing buildings within, including the Chandniwali Barahdari, the Naginawali Barahdari, two tanks, three small marble kiosks, four wells, and the Lanka, a building that seems to have no parallel anywhere.

There were also somewhere in the Qaisarbagh complex a series of gateways decorated with large stucco mermaids and fish, and while the fish was an ancient symbol of sovereignty and had been associated with the nawabs for a least a century (e.g. the Macchi Bhavan "Fish House") the use of mermaids for decoration was a new motif developed out of the usual stucco fish found on Lucknow's gate-

[62] Wajid Ali Shah also wanted his own tomb to be built in the complex, but it was not incorporated in the original design and he apparently did not start it during his brief reign. India Pol. Con., 29 July 1853, no. 53.

[63] Sharar, pp. 89 and 103.

ways.[64] In the Mermaid Gateway of Qaisarbagh one sees not only how the architect incorporated four mermaids into the arched gateway and the pediment on top but how he has reinforced the image of the ocean by the wavy lines of the parapet, and this image is repeated again in the low wall to the right by the clever use of tiles. It is touches of humour like this and a meticulous attention to detail which makes one realise how much has been lost by indiscriminate demolition.

Just to the left of the Mermaid Gateway was another fantastic structure, a double spiral staircase where each turn of the steps was crowned by a stucco woman in Grecian dress, each woman holding hoops which were linked up to each other. This staircase, being a double spiral, did not of course lead anywhere except back to where one started from, and was purely decorative. It was demolished shortly after the Mutiny and the only photograph of it shows that it was already in a dilapidated condition before its removal.

But if one disregards for the moment the details of the individual Qaisarbagh buildings and looks at the overall layout of the complex, I think one is struck by the way in which the architect has been able to simulate the great tent cities of the Mughals and the earlier nawabs by using the terraces and walls to divide the gardens up and encircle these and their buildings from the plain outside. Whether this was a deliberate idea on the part of the architect or whether it was simply a subconscious attempt to return to the "encampment" pattern using masonry instead of canvas is not known, but the whole theme is carried through with such assurance that one suspects the former. Of course the notion that the Mughals, especially Babur and Humayan with their Central Asian backgrounds, were trying to recreate in stone something of the tent cities they had formerly inhabited is not a new idea – Fatehpur Sikri has been seen as a series of "petrified tents" – but this analogy has not so far been extended

[64] The ornamental bridge over the small canal at the north of the largest Qaisarbagh square was decorated with mermen, thus complementing the mermaids on the gateways. A rather worn column base on the western Qaisarbagh gateway shows two small boys playing or wrestling with a giant fish.

to Qaisarbagh which, close observation suggests, must come into the same category. If one studies the Qaisarbagh series of photographs, all taken in March 1858, with the idea of free-standing buildings encircled by a regular wall, as tents were encircled by surrounding canvas walls, one finds that the architect has been able to convey this idea while at the same time maintaining the feeling of a European palace with a series of terraces. This seems to have been accomplished by imitating the doors and windows of such a terrace in stucco, on a wall which is no more than a few feet thick. The buildings within these courtyards or "enclosures" reinforce the impression of light and airy tent-like structures, especially the Lanka, pegged to the ground by eight towers and flanked on either side by two square colonnades supporting nothing but ornamental ironwork. A description of the Macchi Bhavan (the first palace complex) noted that the garden houses were "constructed of brick and beautifully stuccoed with chunam; they are raised on chaupoutres [platforms] with steps to ascend from the garden to the first storey. They are spacious having broad terraced roofs, and at each angle a small cupola covered with the same delicate stucco. Some of them are surmounted by an elegant square canopy with curtains depending from the four sides. These canopies are supported upon small pointed arches."[65]

What could be more like a tent than these small pavilions with their curtained sides which reappeared in Qaisarbagh eighty years later? In some ways then the Qaisarbagh with its references to earlier, even Mughal, structures is more traditional than the Chattar Manzil, where a more European layout was attempted, though the designs and decorations based on European features had become highly stylized in the Qaisarbagh and only served to confuse the uninformed visitor. Confusion was compounded by recognising certain elements of European architecture (like the stucco women on the spiral staircase) but being unable to trace the gradual interweaving of such elements as Corinthian columns, Adam-style

[65] Caunter, Rev. Hobart, *Oriental Annual* (London 1835), p. 128.

swags, and the statuary of Claude Martin's buildings through the previous fifty years of Lucknow's architectural history. Such visitors assumed that the architect of Qaisarbagh had plucked these European elements at random out of the air and thrown them all together in complete confusion.

Typical European comments described Qaisarbagh as "an immense courtyard with fantastic buildings on all four sides, a stucco Louvre, in which Italian and Moorish styles blend in a manner that is more grotesque than graceful, and where gilding and ochre and whitewash tend to give a strange appearance of the theatre to the residence of this Oriental Gerolstein."[66] The Roshan-ud-daula Kothi was described by the same author as "a still more fantastic structure than the great palace itself with which, however, it tallies well. Ionic columns, balustrades with globe-like finials, Moorish minarets, Hindu umbrellas, arches, pediments, lanterns, are all blended in a confusion which the eye may long seek vainly to disentangle, and surmounted with an unmeaning gilt band."[67] By 1934 the whole complex was dismissed in a few words – "judged from an architectural view-point the result is a gigantic failure, it could hardly be otherwise considering the indolent and flabby nature of its parent Wajid Ali Shah."[68] This common confusion between imagined architectural decadence, if such a thing even exists, and political decadence is more fully examined later, but it is necessary to mention it here in order to conclude the story of Qaisarbagh which fell a victim to British revenge after 1857.

From the time that the British effectively lost control of Lucknow at the beginning of May 1857 to the recapture of the city in March 1858, Qaisarbagh was the headquarters of the rebel forces and during this period the Secretary to the Chief Commissioner of Oudh, writing in 1859, claimed that there was "serious damage done by the Rebels themselves who showed no desire to spare the edifices

[66] Keene, H.G., *Handbook for Allahabad, Cawnpore and Lucknow* (Calcutta 1896), p. 58. Hereafter Keene.

[67] Keene, p. 59.

[68] Hilton, p. 73.

or statues."[69] Admitting that some damage had also been caused by British shot during the recapture of the palace he added that "The Chief Commissioner has issued stringent orders for the preservation of all marble statuary and the Buildings generally," but this statement needs to be seen in the context of other contemporary reports, including a long list of claims of property made by the courtiers and retainers of Wajid Ali Shah, from which one learns something of the immense destruction of the city. Thirty-five houses in the Khas Bazaar belonging to Begum Khas Mahal, a wife of Wajid Ali Shah, were demolished, the Khas Manzil in Qaisarbagh which she also owned was declared *nuzal* (i.e. Government property) and her houses adjoining the Chaulakhi were also demolished. More significantly a courtier called Musa-ud-daula who claimed property near Qaisarbagh was told that one house "appears accidentally to have escaped demolition" which certainly implies a policy of systematic destruction.[70]

W.H. Russell's graphic description of the recapture of Qaisarbagh shows that British soldiers ran amok, smashing down doors and breaking into rooms in a search for portable loot. Those things they could not carry, like marble statues, furniture, heavy draperies, and massive jade bowls, they smashed in a frenzy of destruction. No attempt was made to restrain the soldiers, and indeed the British officials present would have found it difficult to do so since they were equally busy collecting together some of the vast quantities of jewellery seized from the nawab and his relatives which was despatched to British safekeeping at Allahabad.

Because so much loot was taken in March 1858 by the British it seems clear that the rebels occupying the buildings had left the bulk of the nawab's treasure and furnishing intact, no doubt against his expected return. But the most telling statement of British attitudes was in a letter from the Secretary to the Commissioner of Oudh, who wrote –

[69] Foreign Con., 30 Dec. 1859, nos 860–73.
[70] Ibid.

> It is not by an indiscriminate massacre of the wretched sepoys that we should avenge our kindred. Had Delhi been levelled it would have been well. A stroke like that would have been a beacon and a warning to the whole of India, and a very heavy blow to the Mahomedan religion. It is now too late however. But the Chief Commissioner sees no reason why that fate should not befall Lucknow. There ought to be some place which the mutineers may recognise and point to as the monument of their own crime and of our retribution: and now that the time for Delhi has passed away the Chief Commissioner would sacrifice Lucknow in which sepoy and Mahomedan atrocity has not fallen short of that perpetrated at the capital of the House of Timour. At all events, only such buildings should be preserved as may be requisite for our own military or other purposes. No mosque – no temple should be spared. The Chief Commissioner would not desecrate them but he would destroy them or at least declare them to be the absolute property of Government to be dealt with hereafter as we may deem proper.[71]

In reply to this proposal the Secretary to the Governor of India wrote – "As to Buildings in Lucknow, the only one that I think it might be well to level to the Ground is the 'Kaiser Baug' as that is the Palace where our chief enemies have resided during the rebellion and whence they have issued their proclamations and orders against us."[72] Caution is advised over the demolition of mosques and temples as this could be "interpreted as the commencement of a war against religion," but what the British did do was take over the larger religious monuments, often for storage purposes, for photographs exist showing both the Great Imambara and the Hazratganj Imambara with rows of gun carriages drawn up in the courtyards, piles of cannonballs, and British soldiers lounging round the buildings.

The statement that "the Buildings generally" were to be preserved is also contradicted by a report made in July 1859 when the Secretary to the Chief Commissioner declared:

> it is necessary on military grounds to pull down the greater part of the Chutter Munzil, and the Farhad Buksh palaces and eventually it may

[71] Secret Con., 29 Jan. 1858 nos 361 and 362.
[72] Ibid.

> be necessary to open out the Kaiserbagh also. Mr Wingfield does not think the southern portion of the Kaiserbagh could be properly repaired for less than one lakh rupees and the Military authorities would also probably object to allowing so large, intricate and defensible a mass of buildings to remain so near our fortifications.[73]

The Governor General had "stated that a road would be made through the Kyser Bagh," and by 1862/3 this main road is clearly marked on a map prepared by British surveyors.[74] This effective British method of breaking up the palace complexes by re-routing the roads had been used in the Chattar Manzil, and later in Sikander Bagh, a handsome two-storeyed Grecian-style building set in a large walled garden.

In addition to the road cutting through the largest Qaisarbagh courtyard, by 1877 the whole of the southern wall had been demolished together with the Chaulakhi palace, and the other sides of the great courtyard were said to be in a ruinous condition. Gradually the free-standing buildings were demolished, one of the black and white marble kiosks and several statues being re-erected in the Zoological Gardens of Lucknow and the Lanka, with its adjoining colonnades disappeared, to be replaced by the present Amir-ud-daula Public Library. The northern wall of the main courtyard also vanished, possibly weakened by the partial demolition when the new road was cut through this terrace, and the courtyards and passageways that stood between the Qaisarbagh and the Chattar Manzil disappeared, with the exception of the Sher Darwaza, or Lion Gate, which had an emotive significance for the British because an officer of the relieving force in September 1857 died under the gateway. The two tombs of Saadat Ali Khan and his wife, which had been incorporated into the northern terrace of the largest Qaisarbagh courtyard, were stripped of the surrounding enclosures and stood starkly by themselves again, as they were before the building of Qaisarbagh. But the gradual silting up of the ground floor chambers means that only the first floor and upper storeys are visible today.

[73] Foreign Con., 29 July 1859, nos 366–70.

[74] See Vanrenan.

The Roshan-ud-daula Kothi, which became a British Court House, was denuded of its two upper storeys, and the whole building is now awaiting demolition, while the smaller courtyards with their painted walls have long since vanished.

When P.C. Mookherji wrote *Pictorial Lucknow* in 1883 he reported: "As the spirit of vandalism is not yet extinct, the edifices, which have historical association or otherwise any architectural pretension, are gradually transformed into debris and ruins." Mookherji was especially critical of British demolitions in the Qaisarbagh and he refuted the commonly held idea that the nawabi brick and stucco buildings were unstable. The "stone" bridge, for example, which was completed by Asaf-ud-daula, stood until it was demolished and replaced by the Hardinge Bridge in 1911, and Claude Martin's town house, later the Farhad Baksh, has been standing partially submerged in the river Gomti for nearly two hundred years. Mookherji claimed that nawabi buildings demolished by the British after 1857 had to be mined and blown up by sappers, so resistant were they to pickaxes.[75] Constant assertions that the buildings of Lucknow always hovered on the brink of collapse and that the material from which the buildings were constructed is "so disappointing and so pregnant with premature decay"[76] are disproved by the great amount of nawabi building still standing, albeit usually in a condition far removed from what the original builders anticipated. The remaining buildings of the Qaisarbagh courtyard appear in no danger of collapse, and one must constantly ask when finding buildings that are said to have fallen down whether they did in fact fall or whether they were pushed, and if the latter then what were the motives of the demolishers?

[75] Mookherji, p. 212.

[76] Keene, p. 59.

10

The Old City

THERE WAS NEVER a point where one could have said Lucknow was complete, for the city was in a constant state of flux. The nawabs' subjects could seldom be sure that a building or garden seen one month would not be demolished and replaced by something completely different the next. An immense amount of building activity went on during the nawabi period, not only on the outskirts of the city where a town is normally expected to expand, but also in the heart of Lucknow. In some cases land cleared for elaborate gardens would subsequently be built on again, and in more than one case encroachment blocked off major roads or seriously narrowed them.

An attachment to old buildings, merely because they are old is not, generally speaking, an Indian characteristic, and only those buildings with religious significance like tombs, shrines, temples, and mosques were relatively safe from demolition, and these could be considerably changed or even rebuilt if a donor wished to beautify such buildings to add kudos to his or her name. There was a constant feeling that innovation was desirable for its own sake and that no justification for a new building or garden was necessary other than that it was different from what had stood there earlier.

But the price that the citizens of Lucknow had to pay for this ever-changing panorama was heavy. Abu Talib, a nobleman who had been at the Lucknow court during the time of Asaf-ud-daula and who later travelled to London, remarks of the period around 1790:

> And the wrongs which God's people suffer by this building mania are many. First, wherever he [Asaf-ud-daula] lays out a building, residents of the place, who have for years lived there, are ordered by him to leave at once without getting either money, compensation or another house. It has often happened that people have not had time to carry away their furniture, the labourers have dismantled the house before it was vacated, and the occupants of a tenement have been compelled to quit, leading their wives and children by hand. Second, the Wazir's workmen, on every possible pretext, utilize the houses of the people to furnish bricks, timber, and other building materials. In this matter their tyranny is so great that where there is a house with doorways or pillars of brick, and the rest of the building of mud, and there is a family living in it, they ruin that whole family for the sake of the fifteen or twenty thousand bricks and pull down the house. Third, the dearness of building materials, caused by the hurry and the want of method on the part of the officials. Fourth, building materials and carpenters and masons are frequently interdicted to the public. When this happens, people are put to such straits and so hampered in their urgent requirements that they cannot get bricks to build masonry tombs over their relatives, not to say that they cannot repair their houses for the rains. Fifth, the servants of the Wazir, nay even all moneyed men, on the principle of "like master, like man", follow the example of the Wazir and engage in building mansions and oppressing the poor. And every one in his own muhalla turns out the residents and enlarges his own house. The Wazir and all the rest of them are so brisk about their building that they do not take time to burn bricks and lime thoroughly, so that a building is hardly completed before it begins to decay. Accordingly most buildings erected by the Wazir in his first years are now becoming dilapidated.[1]

Not only did the nawabs seize materials and land in the city, forays were made into other towns especially during the time of Asaf-ud-daula to satisfy his "building mania". Describing the palace in the Allahabad fort erected by the emperor Akbar an anonymous writer said: "The pillars are richly ornamented and the whole executed in a masterly style. In the centre of the terrace, on the top of

[1] Hoey, William (trans.), *Tafuzzil Ghafi'lin (History of Asaf-ud-daula)* (Allahabad 1885), Tagore Library, Lucknow University, p. 59.

the building stood a turret of white marble, very elegantly finished, which was taken down by order of the Nabob of Oude, and sent to Lucknow in the year 1789." Since then, the writer continued, "the Nabob of Oude has ordered the whole of the building to be taken down and carried to Lucknow, with the intention, it is said, to be again erected in that city."[2] Another report of 1798 noted that "the decay of Currah and Mannipore, has been greatly hastened by the late Nawab of Oude Azoph Dowlah, who ordered several of the most elegant buildings to be destroyed for the freestone of which they were built, that he might be supplied with materials for his new buildings at Lucknow."[3]

It was the chief minister of Ghazi-ud-din Haider, Agha Mir, who was responsible for the greatest destruction of property and seizure of land in the city and his outrageous behaviour prompted many complaints. Agha Mir, it was said, "has caused to be dug up the houses of hundreds of persons, noble and otherwise, that the materials may be employed in building a palace for himself. Also . . . under pretence of mending and making roads, he has knocked down thousands of houses and many of the muhallas of the city of Lucknow have been deserted in consequence."[4]

By 1832 Agha Mir's conduct had become indefensible and in writing to the Government at Calcutta the Lucknow Resident, John Low, stated that

[2] *Bengal Past and Present* (Calcutta Jan.–June 1923), p. 24.

[3] Tennant, i, p. 356.

[4] White, Captain W., *The Prince of Oude* (London 1838), p. 55. Hereafter White. There are two conflicting reports on the parentage of Agha Mir. The first says "his figure was coarse, his manners unpolished and his intellect generally estimated below mediocrity [and that] he was a wanderer in the streets, and attached himself at the age of fifteen to the class of labourers employed in building and repairing houses for men of substance" (White, p. 75). This, if true, would explain a lot of his subsequent behaviour and his readiness with the pickaxe. The second, more prosaic account by John Baillie, the British Resident, said that Agha Mir was "by birth a sayyid of respectable parentage and connexions – his father's name was Mir Mohammad Tukee and his own proper name is Sayyid Mohammad": Foreign Pol. Con., 3 Nov. 1815, no. 5.

> one of the modes in which Agha Mirza oppresses the people is by getting leave from the king to purchase houses in the city for himself, and his friends. He and his friends then fix on a house and offer a price for it such as he says is the proper value and desires the owners to quit – the latter decline to sell – the price being inadequate and Agha Mirza then proceeds to pull down the house by a party of men armed with pick axes etc. who attend him for the purpose.[5]

Consequently he was "dreaded and detested in no common degree" by the inhabitants of the city.[6] Agha Mir was finally arrested and confined in his grandiose house of Daulatpura, which seems to have been near the Nur Baksh Kothi, another of his houses, near Hazratganj. The Daulatpura house was "a building erected by himself in the most extravagant and splendid style"[7] and it was claimed that the "palace of Dowlutpoora has cost considerably more than a crore of rupees" while the Nur Baksh Kothi has cost "between thirty and forty lacs of Rupees."[8] It was said of Agha Mir that "all the emoluments of his office which had not been dissipated in his current expenses had been sunk in his buildings in Lucknow."[9]

After Agha Mir's arrest it was revealed that not even the nawab Nasir-ud-din Haider had been immune from his insatiable habit of demolition and requisitioning of property. The nawab claimed that his gardens had been seized by Agha Mir and that the latter's nephew had "destroyed the houses and the buildings of Charbagh," acting on his uncle's orders. Gardens belonging to the nawab had yielded revenue in the form of rent, and the seizure of property meant that the nawab was deprived not only of the actual land but the income from it too.[10] Not surprisingly when Agha Mir was banished to Cawnpore the nawab "in order to vent his spleen on his fallen servant, and to remove so obnoxious an object from his

[5] Foreign Pol. Con., 5 Nov. 1832, no. 31.

[6] Ibid.

[7] Spry, i, p. 255.

[8] Bengal Pol. Con., 24 Sept. 1830, no. 30.

[9] Ibid.

[10] Ibid.

sight, caused the magnificent palaces of Aga Meer to be razed to the ground."[11]

The amount of waste entailed in unfinished projects did not go unremarked by critics of nawabi extravagance either. In 1835 Nasir-ud-din Haidar was described as "a profligate and a sot . . . he squanders his money like a child, spending thousands in building a palace one year, and pulling it down the next . . . it is lamentable to see money so wasted which might do so much good. Steam boats, windmills, and other works are begun and partly completed, and then the fancy dies away."[12] A similar report on Wajid Ali Shah said, "the King has endless palaces, such as they are, every monarch erecting a new edifice, and robbing his predecessors' to adorn it . . . everything was dilapidated to the last degree, the plaster dropping from the walls, dirt on every corner, the magnificent furniture all destroyed . . . money is paid for the palaces. The palaces crumble."[13] There was little or no cohesion in the planning of the city from one ruler to the next, and the accession of a new nawab often meant a complete reversal or abandonment of his predecessor's ideas on building.

Lucknow was not so much a series of carefully planned avenues and groups of buildings designed to complement each other but rather a town that had grown haphazardly, and it was this picture of Oriental confusion which accorded so well with the expected ideas of European visitors and gave the city much of its undoubted charm. Honoria Lawrence who visited the city in December 1843 found it a curious and splendid place and detected resemblances to Moscow or Constantinople:

[11] Spry, i, p. 257. But not all the palaces of Agha Mir were destroyed in the purge. The present Jubilee College in the Deorhi Agha Mir area, together with a large house here, belonged to the Minister, while the Serai Agha Mir, on the Nadan Mahal road is marked as an extensive courtyard on the 1862/6 map. Agha Mir is also believed to have built the large religious complex on the present Aishbagh Road, known as the Malka Jalian Kerbala, as well as the Zahur Baksh Palace to the east of Qaisarbagh, which still exists today.

[12] Shore, p. 275.

[13] *Calcutta Review* (Calcutta 1855), July–Dec. p. 128.

> Gilded domes surmounted by the crescent – tall, slender pillars, lofty colonnades, half-grecian looking houses of several stories high with pillars, verandas and windows, iron railing and balustrades (entirely foreign in this country), cages of wild beasts and brilliant birds, gardens, fountains and cypress trees make a confused and very dazzling picture . . . Here the sight-worthiness of the place consists not in any one building but in the architectural groups, the long vistas or arches, domes and minarets, the glittering crowds, the whole bewildering mixture of Europe and Asia and the air of wealth which despite bad taste and inconsistency, altogether comes nearer to anything I have seen to realise my early ideas of the Arabian Nights and Lala Rookh.[14]

Even after the devastation of the 1857 uprising the city fascinated people like the Irish reporter W.H. Russell as he stood on the roof of the Great Imambara: "Lucknow, in its broad expanse of palaces, its groves and gardens, its courts, and squares, its mosques and temples, its wide-spreading, squalid quarters of mean, close houses, amid which are kiosks and mansions of rich citizens, surrounded by trees, all lay at our feet."[15]

Russell was not the first to comment on the somewhat promiscuous siting of the houses of the rich among the mean and squalid streets of the city. Bishop Heber, one of the few Europeans to visit the old city, wrote in 1825 of "the Minister's house – a very large pile of building, in a bad part of the town, and both in architecture and situation, a good deal resembling the house of the Mullich family in Calcutta."[16] The Minister, it is believed, was Agha Mir, and this particular house (for he had many scattered about the city) due to his aggressive habits was probably the building now known simply as Agha Mir's Palace which is situated between Yahyaganj and Nawabganj. Heber, who spent some time in the old quarter of Lucknow, also referred to the "many stately khans and some handsome mosques and pagodas scattered in different corners of these wretched alleys." But when one remembers that Lucknow was a thriving community well before the nawabi arrival it is not so

[14] Honoria Lawrence.

[15] Russell, p. 203.

[16] Heber, i, p. 385.

surprising that families who had lived around the Chauk area for generations should continue to do so. Almost certainly they regarded Saadat Ali Khan's buildings and new roads with some suspicion as foreign innovations, which indeed they were.

Rather than remove their houses to the developing eastern part of Lucknow a consciousness of the new European styles was expressed in non-essential decoration on houses which were of traditional form, built in narrow and unprepossessing streets. Throughout the older quarter of Lucknow there are numerous examples of such houses, though in some cases all trace of European decoration has crumbled away and one sees simply the bare bones of a traditional Indian house. Around these houses were the usual buildings of a pre-industrial Indian town, the bazaars with their open shops where customers step up onto a platform to avoid the open drains running down the street, the communal wells and tanks, the workshops where different occupations were pursued, the brothels housing both female and male prostitutes, the mosques and tombs of the Muslims and the temples and shrines of the Hindus, and the coffee houses for men. Those few Europeans who did go into the old quarter of Lucknow were able to compare it (always unfavourably) with the eastern part of the city, and in 1844 Henry Lawrence summarised this view when he described the city as being divided into two quarters:

> an old, and a new city adjoining each other: the former, like other native towns, is filthy, ill-drained, and ill-ventilated. The modern city, situated along the south bank of the river Goomtee, is strikingly different, consisting of broad and airy streets, and containing the Royal Palaces and gardens, the principal Mussulman religious buildings, the British Residency, and the houses of the various English officers connected with the Court. This part of Lucknow is both curious and splendid, and altogether unlike the other great towns of India, whether Hindu or Mahomedan.[17]

In some ways it could be argued that this "modern city" was the equivalent of the public and accessible part of an Indian house,

[17] *Calcutta Review* (Calcutta 1845), Jan.–June, p. 380.

while the old city with its air of secrecy mimicked the zenana, and the parallel can be extended by stressing that the new and "public" part of the city had a European flavour, a feeling of experimentation and innovation in contrast to the older traditional areas where any apparent change was of the most superficial.

One unfortunate result of the difficulties, either real or imagined, that prevented most Europeans from entering the old part of Lucknow has been the paucity of information about buildings here, both religious and secular. To say that these buildings are "unknown" is misleading for they are obviously known to the people who live in them or who worship in them even if the original names and the builders have been forgotten. The majority of surviving nawabi religious building is naturally connected with the Shi'a sect in which the procession of *taziyas* plays an important part. These portable shrines, representing the graves of Husain and Hasan, are often extremely elaborate and are housed for a year in imambaras before they are taken through the streets to be ceremoniously buried. The taziyas are invested with an immense feeling of sacredness and the fact that they must be housed in a suitably solemn and grand building led to the development of the imambara which reached its ultimate expression in Lucknow and especially in the Great Imambara built by Asaf-ud-daula in 1784 which, at one time, contained the largest vaulted hall in the world. The taziyas which are not buried at the end of the mourning period, i.e. those made with beaten silver panels, or finely carved in wood or ivory, are permanently housed in the imambara and are shown to visitors as part of the "treasure" of the imambara as a fine altar piece or lectern would be pointed out in a Western church. Also housed in the imambara are other associated items of religious significance like the *alams* or standards, which represent the banners carried by Ali and his party before the battle of Kerbala, and pictures depicting the battle and fine examples of calligraphy on sacred themes. The *mimbar* (usually translated as a pulpit) is also exhibited and this is a series of steps with decorated panels set into the side, or draped with a fine cloth. Unlike the Western pulpit the mimbar is a free-standing and moveable structure.

But the most striking feature (for Europeans at any rate) is the absolute profusion inside the imambara of chandeliers of all shapes and sizes and the huge stands for lamps or candles, often five feet or more in height, and made from highly decorated china, coloured glass or metals. The effect when all the chandeliers and stands are lit is dazzling, especially in the cool and dark halls of the imambara, and although they do not have any religious significance the presentation of elaborate chandeliers and stands was often made by wealthy people as an act of merit. Many of the best chandeliers in Lucknow were sent out from Europe and a Birmingham firm of chandelier-makers regularly exported their goods to Calcutta during the 1840s and 1850s.[18] The imambaras of Lucknow have unfortunately suffered particularly heavily from the loss of their treasures, especially moveable items like lustres, jewelled alams, and panels of gold and lace cloth. (An especially exotic item disappeared from the Great Imambara during the Mutiny, a pair of life-size green glass tigers brought, it is believed, from Siam or China, and there is no reason to think that the religious buildings of Lucknow lost any fewer treasures through looting than did the palaces.)

Not only were imambaras repositories for the taziyas and other treasures but some also became the burial place for their builders and other relatives. Asaf-ud-daula is interred in the Great Imambara while Muhammad Ali Shah and his mother are buried in the Husainabad Imambara. These burials are marked in the ground-floor rooms[19] of the imambaras often by nothing more than a shallow rectangle covered by a piece of embroidered cloth, or occasionally by a small silver railing. Such burials do not, however, affect the primary function of the imambara as the repository of the taziyas and although an imambara can also be referred to as a *maqbara* (a tomb), a structure which is designed solely for the purpose of burial

[18] See the Boulton & Watt Collection, Birmingham Public Library, and the letter books of E. & C. Osler, Chandelier Manufacturers.

[19] Muslim burials are usually made below ground level because it is considered presumptuous for anyone to be buried in an elevated tomb. This is the reason for the "false" tombs on the ground floor.

can never be referred to as an imambara.[20] Thus the tombs of Saadat Ali Khan and his wife in the Qaisarbagh complex are known as maqbaras and nothing else, while the building of Malka Afaq Sahiba off the Sitapur Road on the north bank of the Gomti is known both as an imambara and a maqbara because, although this princess is buried there with some of her female relatives, the burial is of secondary importance. The distinction is also emphasised by the different buildings. Whereas an imambara is a long low structure with the main hall divided into three rooms and the burial, if any, in the central room, a maqbara is normally a square building, always with a semi-basement storey, a central dome over the main hall, and the false tomb, which is a raised structure, directly in the middle of the whole maqbara.

There are a number of imambaras in private homes where they are not found as free-standing buildings but are incorporated into the courtyards of Muslim homes, and in these imambaras burials would certainly not take place. Some private imambaras can be of considerable size and there can be more than one in a house, especially where the women in the zenana have their own imambaras. The Mahmudabad country house has four imambaras, the largest and most splendid in the public part of the building and three smaller ones in the zenana section.[21]

There are numerous examples in Lucknow today of buildings which have been secularised and are now used as private homes or offices. At least two imambaras visited have been turned into homes – the house now known as Mishra Bhavan just in front of the mosque

[20] Suleiman, the Raja of Mahmudabad, to R.M. Llewellyn-Jones, 6 Jan. 1975. The Raja (1943–2023) was head of one of the leading Shi'a families in the subcontinent and much of my information on imambaras came from him.

[21] Within one of the imambaras in the zenana section of the Mahmudabad country house is a child's imambara, a little wooden replica complete with miniature taziyas and alams. There is also a reference in an inventory of F.M. Arnott, the trader, to "Two large ivory Imambarahs" which were got expressly for Asaf-ud-daula, showing that imambaras should not always be regarded as buildings, but as small portable *objets d'art* as well. See Humphry & Paull.

and maqbara of Janab-i-Alia in Golaganj; and the imambara which is now part of the zenana section of the Khanqah Makan in the same area. The Hazratganj Imambara, a large building surrounded by an extensive courtyard, which was built by Amjad Ali Shah who is buried there, was used by a firm of carpenters and as part of the local census office, and also in Hazratganj is a *taziyagah* (a place where the taziya procession halts during its march for a short time). This taziyagah now forms part of a private house, and the small square building with a double dome (i.e. a false dome beneath the true one, to minimise the height of the room below) is much prized by its owner for its coolness during hot weather. Similarly the tomb of Husain Ali, the Akbari commandant buried east of the Chauk, now houses a family, though they are living there from expediency and not by choice as the ground-floor room round the tomb is a cramped and dark place. Families also lived in the northern gateway of the Great Imambara for years, though again probably not by choice. Both the Great Imambara and the Husainabad Imambara were widely visited by Europeans in nawabi times because both fell within the "tourist" route, though reactions to these buildings were mixed, ranging from the critical to the derisory.

But the narrowness of this European circuit is illustrated by the fact that a huge complex similar in grandeur and size to the Great Imambara but which lay to the west of this circuit has never been mentioned or visited by Europeans as far as is known, and no photographs of it appear to exist. This second complex was built by Ilmas Ali Khan, deputy governor of Awadh during Saadat Ali Khan's time, and it is certainly worthy of note, if only because of its immense size. Similarly there is another unrecorded imambara in the same area, that of Zain-ul-abdin, which is now in an extremely dilapidated condition. But the finest of these "unknown" imambaras is probably that in the area of Janab-i-Alia's maqbara and mosque in Golaganj which, as photographs show, carried the art of stucco decoration to a superb pitch.

Once a year the taziyas were taken out from their imambaras and carried through the city, resting in the taziyagah en route. The destination of the taziyas is the *kerbala*, a building which represents and commemorates the battlefield and the burial place of Hasan and Husain in Iraq. The largest kerbala at Lucknow is the Talkatora to the south-west of the city, approached through a large gateway of European pattern. But the buildings within are entirely Islamic, consisting of a large square bordered by a series of cells, and the square central building on a raised platform which is, properly speaking, the kerbala itself. This building is topped by a gilt dome and flanked by two minars or towers. The ground between the kerbala and the cells in the outer wall is filled with graves, marked by plain stones. Outside the main square is a semi-ruined barahdari in a highly decorated style.[22]

There are several other kerbalas of similar form in the city, the second largest being that of Malka Jahan in the Aishbagh Road, and there was an extensive group of buildings including a kerbala on the north bank of the Gomti named after Mariam Makam Sahiba, as well as the kerbala in the newer part of the city to the east of the present-day Sikander Bagh Road. The kerbala of the eunuch Dianutud Daula in Saadatganj is particularly noteworthy because of its original and unusual mirror work interior, which consists of small regular pieces of mirrored glass set into cement so that the light is caught and thrown back from thousands of different facets. This mirror work is frequently found in palace rooms throughout India and Pakistan, but this appears to be the only surviving example in the city and certainly the only use of mirror work in a religious building. This kerbala is also decorated along its outer walls by a series of false doors with panels of stucco imitating the slats of venetian blinds, and with Adam-style "fan-lights" over each door, a common enough feature on palaces and private houses in Lucknow but unusual on a religious building. The building was erected together with the surrounding shops and enclosure during the time of Wajid Ali Shah and after 1858 it was restored to the eunuch (one of the

[22] Anwar Askari to R.M. Llewellyn-Jones, 14 Nov. 1974, 25 Jan. 1975 and 3 Feb. 1975. Mr Askari comes from an old Lucknow family of writers.

nawab's courtiers) because he could prove undisputed ownership, and because the building had not been demolished as had happened in many other cases.[23]

Not only were the kerbalas ignored by European visitors but other important buildings associated with the Shi'as were similarly neglected. The *dargah* (shrine) of Hazrat Abbas situated in Rustum Nagar, although in appearance a small and insignificant building, was of immense importance during nawabi times and still attracts a large number of Shi'as today. It is believed that the original dargah building was a kutcha structure of unbaked bricks plastered with mud and was constructed to house the metal crest of a banner belonging to Hazrat Abbas which was brought from Iraq.[24] Saadat Ali Khan, inspired by a dream, rebuilt the dargah with pukka materials, but the flaw in this oral tradition (for there is no remaining written evidence) is that the gateway referred to above is such an unhappy compromise between an Islamic and a European entrance that remembering Saadat Ali Khan's other buildings one finds it difficult to believe that he was responsible for it. One could surmise that as in the case of the Talkatora Kerbala, where the European gateway is not contemporary with the other buildings there, the dargah gateway was also constructed later, doubtless as an act of merit by its builder. This dargah has the distinction of being the only religious building in the old part of the city mentioned in British records, although it is misleadingly referred to as a temple,[25] a word which has Hindu connotations. It was here that the coronation procession of Ghazi-ud-din Haider came in November 1819, before the nawab returned to the Lal Barahdari for the actual crowning ceremony.

The second important Shi'a building in the old city is the Kazmain, said to be an exact copy of the tomb of two imams or religious leaders from Khorasan.[26] It consists of two domes set on

[23] Foreign Con., 30 Dec. 1859, nos 851 & 882.

[24] Raza, Sikander (ed.), *Wajid Ali Shah and Monuments of Avadh* (Lucknow 1974), no pagination. Hereafter Raza.

[25] Foreign Pol. Con., 20 Nov. 1819, no. 58.

[26] Raza.

very deep drums which are covered with brass sheets. There are pointed minars at each of the four corners, and the whole enclosure is surrounded by a high wall. The building, because of its distinctive domes, cannot fail to be noticed from any high vantage point in the old city, but again it has been totally ignored both from a religious and architectural point of view in European writings.

In contrast the Shah Najaf and the Qadam Rasul north of Hazratganj have frequently been commented on, not least because they were among the buildings occupied by the British during the recapture of Lucknow in March 1858. The Qadam Rasul (the name means footprint of the Prophet because the building housed a supposed footprint of the Prophet Muhammad marked in stone) is today a semi-ruined building at the summit of a small artificial hill, and it consisted of a simple domed chamber with a small minar at each corner. The adjoining Shah Najaf is a large and impressive building erected by Ghazi-ud-din Haider between 1814 and 1827 and was "the place destined during his life-time to be the repository of his Remains."[27] Some of the nawab's wives are also buried here and the building is correctly speaking a maqbara although, because it is a copy of the mausoleum of Ali at Najaf in Arabia, it is usually referred to as the Shah Najaf or the Najaf-i-Ashraf. The main tomb, as mentioned earlier, makes only one concession to European influence, and that is in the festoons and swags around the dome, but the small mosque to the left is a highly individualistic and eclectic building full of elaborate painted stucco with Persian designs of grapes, flagons, and cypress trees: there is also a Hindu "wheel" of stucco over an iron framework; panels of work which can best be described as "Chinese Chippendale"; and festoons around the pillars which derive originally from the portico at Barowen.

The majority of nawabi mosques seem to have been quite free from the influence of European decoration, and are normally simple undecorated structures of brick and stucco whitewashed over. But the Jame Masjid[28] standing to the south-west of Husainabad, and

[27] Foreign Pol. Con., 16 Nov. 1827, nos 12–18.

[28] Nawab Mir Jafar Abdullah to R.M. Llewellyn-Jones, 30 Jan. 1975. The Nawab lives in one of the remaining houses of the Daulat Khana complex.

of traditional form, is noteworthy because it still preserves some of the best examples of painted stucco work which was extremely popular in Lucknow but which in the majority of cases has faded almost to nothing on most nawabi buildings. The painted work inside the Jame Masjid is still carefully renewed annually, using the same colours, and a close examination shows how the characteristic nawabi features, especially the double arches decorated with stylized flower buds over every cusp, were emphasized with the use of colour, and how these sinuous patterns accord with the more common geometric patterns of Islamic decoration.

The only hint in the Jame Masjid of the pervasive European influence outside is in the fluted sandstone columns seen at the central entrance to the building, which are topped by Corinthian capitals. It is possible that these columns reflect a change of styles made during the erection of this mosque because it is known that building was begun in 1839 by Muhammad Ali Shah[29] but completed by one of his wives after his death three years later. The buildings of this nawab, which are mainly in the Husainabad area, do reflect a certain uneasiness with European architectural ideas and there is none of the perfect amalgam of Indian and European influences which one finds in earlier nawabi building. The conflict between the two is seen clearly in the Sat Khande, built by Muhammad Ali Shah, where alternate façades of the tower were to be Indian and European with no attempt at a compromise between them, and it is also reflected in the gateway of the Husainabad Imambara which is possibly the most unhappy mixture of styles in Lucknow. Because no plans exist of the Jame Masjid as it was originally to be built it is fruitless to speculate on what the mosque was to be like, but the presence of these European-style columns at ground-floor level and in a different material do lead one to consider that there may well have been a change in design after the nawab's death. As it stands now the Jame Masjid, viewed in purely architectural terms, is a splendid building full of interest, reflecting the nawabi style un-

[29] Safi Ahmad, p. 158.

mixed with European ideas, harking back to the Great Imambara complex, but certainly not an unthinking imitation of it.

Among the secular public buildings of the nawabs are the barahdaries (the word means "having twelve doors or openings" although such buildings frequently have a greater number of entrances). There is occasionally some confusion, certainly among Lucknow residents, over whether certain buildings are imambaras or barahdaris and this confusion is understandable, for when an imambara is stripped of its furnishings and does not incorporate a burial it is similar in form to a barahdari which is generally a long, low building of one storey, with smaller rooms to the side. There does, however, seem to be a greater range of styles among barahdaris than imambaras and certainly a wider range of functions. Barahdaris are secular buildings, although they can be associated with religious complexes, as for example the barahdari at Talkatora Kerbala. The essential requisite for a barahdari is that it should be a light and airy building, habitually free-standing, and its chief characteristic is a series of arched openings which may be closed by glazed doors, although such doors would not detract from the appearance of the building. There are only two nawabi references to barahdaris, the first by Haider Beg Khan who wrote that Asaf-ud-duala's Divani Kacheri was held in a barahdari,[30] and the second is to the Lal Barahdari which was originally used as a durbar hall by Saadat Ali Khan. The barahdari it seems, can be used by any gathering of people as a meeting place, though it does not appear to be used as a permanent home.

Lucknow has always had a greater number of Hindu residents than Muslims; in fact it was estimated in 1829 that two-thirds of the city's population were Hindu, and of the remaining one-third there were Sunni Muslims as well as Christians.[31] But because the city was dominated by the Shi'ite nawabs there is a disproportionate emphasis on Shi'a buildings and very little information exists on Hindu buildings in the old city. Only one official British reference occurs

[30] Letters from the Resident, John Bristow, to the East India Company in Calcutta, 1782–3. Add. 29120, f. 98.

[31] Foreign Pol. Con., 23 Oct. 1829, no. 40.

which mentions Hindu buildings, and this is a report on a communal riot in which forty-seven Hindu temples were destroyed in 1829.[32] The locations of these temples are given, showing a fairly even distribution, including temples in the pre-nawabi areas of Rakabganj and Rastogi Muhalla, where one would expect to find them, but also in areas developed during the nawabi period like Tikait Rai Ganj and Nawabganj. The fact that Tikait Rai, one of Asaf-ud-daula's ministers, was a Hindu may well have encouraged fellow Hindus to settle in the ganj which he founded. Tikait Rai also built, rather surprisingly, a number of mosques, as well as Hindu temples, and some of the latter, which are dedicated to the god Siva, contain the characteristic double arch of nawabi buildings – and in one case the nawabi emblem of two fish over the doorway.[33]

A very few references exist to private houses built by Hindus, which shows that Europeanised buildings were by no means confined to the ruling Muslim classes. The house of Raja Mhera (or Mehra) Ram near the Daulat Khana seems to have been particularly handsome. A report of 1816 which says that this raja had been head-palanquin bearer to Asaf-ud-daula, in whose service he had acquired "immense wealth", described the house as having "a Frenchified look, and puts one in mind of the Louvre at Paris. It is not quite finished, but being very completely roofed in, and furnished with doors and windows, it is turned into a *godown* to lodge part of the property of the Vizier."[34] The house was still standing in 1827 when the British Resident breakfasted there,[35] but later reports are confused and it may have been demolished before 1857. Post-1857 maps show that Hindus also owned substantial tracts of land, as for example the land of the moneylender Shah Behari Lal on the north bank of the Gomti.

The term *bagh* is usually translated as garden, though this can present rather a misleading picture. There appear to be at least three

[32] Ibid.

[33] Raza.

[34] *The Asiatic Journal* (London 1816), p. 579.

[35] Foreign Pol, Con., 19 Oct. 1827, no 142.

kinds of bagh present in Lucknow, as in most other Muslim cities, and the chief distinction seems to be whether the bagh was to be used solely as a pleasure garden, which was often exclusively for the use of the nawab and his entourage and guests (or in the case of a nobleman, either Muslim or Hindu, for his immediate family), or whether it was to be a piece of land leased out by the owner where cultivation of crops like sugarcane, tobacco, roses and maize was carried out by *kisans* and *malis* (farmers and gardeners).

A European visitor in 1846[36] speaks of the barahdaris and summerhouses in such gardens, which were built "in half-French, half-Moorish style: their large and heavy roofs supported by many slender and feeble columns . . . never even in the smallest of these pavilions is the warm bath wanting, and but seldom the private mosque, which I can only compare to a child's toy in appearance. The centre of the garden is usually occupied by a marble tank, in which many fountains are playing, and cypresses alternate with roses in embellishing its margin." The writer thought that the "regular flower beds with their little canals for irrigation," and the straight paved walks, "produce a very stilted effect in the general aspect of the grounds," and he also criticised the mania for placing statues "at every turn and corner". The central tank in these gardens "usually forms the uniting link between the larger summer-house or kiosk and a small wooden pavilion, which destitute of all ornament save a neat balcony, is only intended as a point from which may be commanded, at one glance, the prospect of the whole long row of fountains playing in the reservoir."

This description certainly fits a garden like the Badshah Bagh on the north bank of the Gomti and the Wilayati Bagh[37] to the extreme south-east of the city. These were based on the Shalimar

[36] Hoffmeister, pp. 258–9.

[37] There are two explanations for this name *wilayati* (foreign). One, that the garden was specially built for a foreign wife of Ghazi-ud-din Haider, or, two, that the garden was planted with European shrubs and flowers which were sent to Lucknow, some from the Botanical Gardens in Calcutta. See Foreign Pol. Con., 17 Feb. 1826, no. 225.

Gardens of the Mughals, where the ground is landscaped to form a series of terraces with small waterfalls, though nothing so ambitious has survived in Lucknow. The gardens of Wajid Ali Shah, the Sikander Bagh, the Alambagh, and the Qaisarbagh, were different for in each case the buildings in the gardens were the main attraction, and there was not sufficient room within these walled enclosures for any very elaborate attempts at large-scale vistas or formal layouts, but such gardens should still be classed as pleasure gardens, unlike the areas for cultivation round the city which are also referred to as baghs.

These other areas, which were especially concentrated to the west and south of the old city and which were usually named after the owner, for example the Husaini Begum Bagh and the Sukhi Lal Bagh were virtually indistinguishable from the surrounding fields, except that they would have been marked by a low wall. Two gardens referred to in the nawabi period and still in existence today, the Musa Bagh or Barowen garden and the Ilmas Ali Khan Bagh on the Hardoi Road, should be seen as gardens which changed category, for the Barowen garden was at one point described as very fine by European visitors,[38] later as overgrown,[39] and later still was planted with crops, as it still is today. Similarly the Ilmas Ali Khan Bagh once contained a large house, tanks, and a handsome mosque, but is today given over to crops and the encroaching waste land. Many of the gardens to the south-west of the city merged imperceptibly into *topes* (groves or orchards) and such areas with their trees, together with better-known gardens like the Char Bagh, which was described as a wood;[40] the enormous Dilkusha Park with its "avenue of mighty trees",[41] and the mango-tree tope of Constantia, show that Lucknow has suffered severely from deforestation, the outskirts of the city having been much more wooded than they are today. Despite the devastation caused by the 1857 uprising and the greater

[38] Archer, i, p. 38.
[39] Spry, i, p. 234.
[40] Forrest, p. 164.
[41] Russell, p. 55.

havoc of British demolition when whole *muhallas* were blown up, there still remains in Lucknow even today a great number of nawabi buildings. Often in a poor state of repair, these buildings have been forgotten to the extent that their original names are lost. Unless a concerted effort is soon made to restore these fine buildings the sum of nawabi work in Lucknow will be very small indeed.

11

Bricks and Mortar

No architectural drawings remain of any of Lucknow's nawabi buildings, and it has been necessary to reconstruct the ground plans for half-a-dozen buildings by working backwards, i.e. measuring the existing structures and consulting old photographs. The pattern that has emerged is one of pleasing symmetry and an almost Palladian-like style. Even in cases where the original building has been confused by additions and alterations, like the Asafi Kothi, it has been possibly to deduce the plan of the whole by examining only a small area. Similarly at Barowen once a quarter of the site had been measured it was comparatively easy to fill in the remainder, except where interior walls had vanished completely.

Naturally in an attempt to reconstruct a building on paper one has other clues too. One carefully examines the bricks where the stucco has fallen away, one checks the remaining stucco work to see if it appears to be of the same quality and design, and one constantly asks what each room was used for (often by considering present-day usages). It would be presumptuous to say that the reconstructed ground plan of Barowen is the definitive one of that fine building; nevertheless it is as accurate a plan as one can hope for, unless the architect's original drawings should turn up, and judging by the destruction still being wreaked on Barowen by the elements, both human and natural, it is probably the only plan that will ever exist.

As for contemporary references to architects' plans, the earliest mention found is the request by Asaf-ud-daula for "the plan of a house after the European taste" which he made of Captain Marsack in 1775.[1] Three years later, when the British Resident Nathaniel Middleton proposed erecting a strong brick building as a treasury in the Residency complex, he promised to forward to Calcutta "an accurate Plan and Section of the Work" as soon as he found out the cost of building.[2] Later in the year he sent off a "Plan and elevations of a Building for a treasury" which would indicate that a proper architectural drawing to scale had been made,[3] and presumably the specifications about bricks, mortar, and timber to be used would be described in the estimate. During this same period there is also Claude Martin's remark that Constantia was to be finished "if I have time to make a Regular Plan and elevation of all what I intend Building" and after describing the various rooms, terraces and the obelisk (which was later erected in front of Constantia) Martin wrote, "for all these I will endeavour to make plan and elevation."[4] One must then ask how exact were the architects' ground plans and elevations, whether the scales were worked out precisely throughout the building, how much was left to the initiative of the masons, carpenters, and stuccadors on the site, and by how great a margin the finished building differed from the architects' original designs. Because of the lack of contemporary plans and elevations from Lucknow, these important questions cannot be answered with any great degree of confidence, and though it is known from plans of buildings erected in other parts of India in the late eighteenth and nineteenth centuries that architectural designs and plans were conscientiously drawn up and executed, one cannot assume that the same system worked quite so precisely in smaller Indian towns.[5]

[1] Secret Index, 18 Sept. 1775, no number given.

[2] Home Public Index, 20 July 1778, no number given. National Archives, New Delhi.

[3] Home Public Index, 28 Nov. 1778, no number given. National Archives, New Delhi.

[4] Claude Martin's Will.

[5] See the illustrations in Nilsson, especially plates 32A & B.

Captain Wilcox, who supervised the erection of the Lucknow observatory from his own designs, admitted later that

> it is clear that in contemplating the possibility of work of the kind being accomplished (by native artificers at least) in the short period of one or two months, I ran into that error of inexperience, which must occasionally attend on a new undertaking.[6] I had not only to provide working drawings for every part of the building but I had to engage in the perfectly novel undertaking to me of making myself sufficiently acquainted with that style of Architecture to enable me to finish a building of some pretensions, of which no plan corresponding with the fabric, as I found it, fell into my hands.[7]

This revealing sentence shows that even as late as the 1840s it was not considered strange that an astronomer should be asked to design his observatory rather than work in conjunction with an architect. Another criticism of the gap between planning and actual building was written in 1810 when Thomas Williamson wrote: "Some of the *rauz*, or bricklayers, in India, are very clever, so far as relates to mere practical operations, but they have not the smallest idea of planning from paper, or on paper." Furthermore there were differences in the allocation of jobs, because "the Hindu is both bricklayer, plasterer, tarras-maker, etc. and the blacksmith and carpenter are often the same person . . . it is true, that many of the bricklayers, employed under regular architects, may be seen to use our tools of every description, but this takes place only under such guidance."[8] No matter then how precise the architects' intentions, ultimately it was up to the supervisor on the site to ensure that the plans were carried through, or to adapt the plans to the abilities of the workforce and materials available.

From plans, or rather the lack of them, it would be appropriate to examine the materials used for building in Lucknow. The commonest materials were baked bricks and stucco, and this is what

[6] Foreign Con., 28 June 1841, nos 159–61.

[7] India Pol. Con., 27 July 1840, no. 138

[8] Williamson, i, pp. 515 and 517.

was used in the majority of the houses of the well-to-do as well as the nawabi palaces and religious buildings. A structure made of baked bricks, i.e. bricks that had been kiln-fired, was *pukka* while buildings of sun-dried bricks were considered *kutcha.* All the remaining nawabi buildings are pukka structures, and the usual kind of brick employed is called *lakhori*, a word which does not appear in Platt's *Dictionary* but which is thought by Lucknow people to mean something originating from Lahore where they believe this small kind of brick was first developed.[9] These lakhori bricks are only three-quarters of an inch thick, and normally about four by six inches, and are of a fine local clay with crystalline flecks. When baked they are a pleasing dull orange or red in colour. A larger and heavier brick of the same clay but almost two inches thick is known as *pan patta* or, according to P.C. Mookherji,[10] *ilmasi,* after Ilmas Ali Khan, Deputy Governor of Awadh during the time of Saadat Ali Khan, who reputedly used these thicker bricks in his own buildings. Claude Martin seems to have had his own bricks made for Constantia, for in addition to the lakhori bricks in the main body of the building there is a larger brick rather like the pan patta but stamped with an "F". There is also a series of curved bricks which make up the elaborate balustrade of the second floor, and triangular bricks used to build up the core of the statues.[11] The great advantage of lakhori bricks is that they can be used both with the pan patta bricks and by themselves to form remarkably fine details even before any stucco has been applied. The more skilful the bricklayers the less coarse work was there for the stuccadors, who could

[9] I think it more likely, however, that the word *lakhori* derives from *lakh*, meaning "a hundred thousand" or an immense quantity, because such a great number of small bricks were needed for a building.

[10] Mookherji, p. 213.

[11] There is a further type of curved brick used for balustrades, of a much simpler pattern than the Constantia balustrade bricks. Examples of this are found on the house of Munu Das, off the Aishbagh Road, and along the low row of shops just east of the Husainabad gateway, all that now remains of the elegant shops that once lined this road between the Rumi Darwaza and Husainabad.

concentrate on delicate work instead of covering vast areas with stucco to mimic a stonework effect.

Not only were whole bricks used in building, but they were also pulverised to form one of the constituents of the cement used. These crushed bricks were called *surkhi* and are first noted by Modave who estimated that this further use of bricks tripled (at least) the number needed for a building.[12] The other constituents of cement varied depending on whether the mixture was to be used purely for joining bricks together; for coarse plastering over walls; for the floors and roofs of buildings (when it was known as tarras) or for the final coating over the walls. The composition of *chunam* (which is often translated as "lime", but which should be rendered as "stucco"), was similar to that of cement, but the fineness of it was determined by the materials used to produce the lime. In Madras a beautiful lime was made by using pulverised sea-shells, but this was so expensive that it was seldom used in Bengal or the Upper Provinces. Lucknow workmen believe that the stucco in the Jame Masjid there was made from red lime, gum, a kind of fine pulse called *urad ki dhal, jagri*, shells, and a sticky substance called *seras*, and it seems certain that the composition of chunam could vary considerably according to the pocket and the taste of the builder. The nawabi chunam of Lucknow was especially commended and frequently commented upon, and a few examples of marble-like chunam do remain, for instance in the Residency Banqueting Hall. However, chunam in other parts of India like Udaipur, and Jaipur in Rajasthan, where marble would have been used, is consistently better preserved and of the highest quality. Lucknow has unfortunately suffered badly from ubiquitous whitewashing, so much so that in places even raised decorations in stucco have been nearly obliterated by the build-up of coats of lumpy whitewash year after year.

Stucco could be used to produce effects in quite deep relief, even when applied to a flat wall, as in the pediment on the Husainabad well where figures in the Graeco-Roman style are moulded to produce

[12] Modave, p. 79.

a two-dimensional effect without relying on a skeleton of brick or iron. Similarly the false domes which appear on the walls of the Safdar Jang tomb in Delhi, the Great Imambara, and the Residency complex Begum Kothi in Lucknow, and which are very characteristic of eighteenth-century nawabi architecture, are moulded in stucco to a smooth wall and not built up over a brick core.

The lack of stone near Lucknow has frequently been noted and buildings which did incorporate imported stone were something of a rarity, a sign of the owner's status.

Only two buildings are recorded that were constructed entirely from stone – the Sangi Dalan in the Macchi Bhavan complex and the Lal Barahdari in the Chattar Manzil. Although this latter building is now painted red outside and could easily be mistaken for a brick and stucco structure, it is in fact made from Jaipur stone of poor quality. Most stone used in Lucknow was brought from Chunar, a town to the extreme south-east of the province of Awadh which supplied the capital for at least forty years. Claude Martin's inventory for Constantia mentions "363 slabs of Chunar Stone for use in the House,"[13] and in 1841 Colonel Wilcox speaks of "the immense stones [which] were brought from Chunar" for the piers erected in his Observatory.[14] Even rarer than sandstone was the marble used in a few buildings, which was imported from as far afield as England in one case. Various uses of marble in the interiors of buildings were recorded though very few examples now remain, it being hardly surprising that such an expensive material should not be re-used perhaps more than once. Only two carved marble fountain basins are noted (although from descriptions of rich houses these were so common that they almost escape comment), the first taken from the palace of Zahur Baksh and presented to Lucknow Museum about 1888,[15] and the second of fine white marble with a black inlay in the Banqueting Hall of the Residency complex. The

[13] Bengal Inventories, Range 1, vol. 24, no. 75. I.O.L.

[14] Foreign Con., 28 June 1841, nos 159–61.

[15] Minutes of the Managing Committee from 1883 to 1888. The North-West Provinces and Oudh Provincial Museum, Lucknow, p. 47.

large tank in the centre of the Chattar Manzil complex was of marble, as were the baths in the Badshah Bagh on the north bank of the Gomti. Marble floors were found in some of the most elaborate buildings, including the white marble floor "inlaid with a mosaic work of black and red"[16] which was laid over the heated flues of the *hammam* or bathhouse in the Macchi Bhavan complex. It is probable that this was the floor referred to in a newspaper report of 1792, which says:

> The Prince of Oudh [Asaf-ud-daula] has given an order to a very eminent and ingenious artist in this country to prepare him a flooring of marble etc. for a smoking room. [*sic*] The order is completed, and is the first thing of the kind that was ever made in this country. It is 20 foot square, and is composed of upwards of 8000 pieces. In this flooring are introduced all sorts of marble, Spa petrifications, etc. which are arranged with a taste and judgement that do infinite credit to the artist.[17]

Of the many marble statues that once adorned gardens and courtyards only three appear to exist today, all in the Zoological Gardens, where they were removed from Qaisarbagh.

But one of the real strengths of nawabi architecture, like its refinement of stucco into a new art form, was the use of humble materials to create something unique and splendid. Pottery was extensively used, not only for utilitarian purposes – like the pottery ducts at Constantia and Barowen that conducted hot air away from the lower room to vents in the flat roofs – but for decorative purposes too. Potters soon learnt that they could imitate balusters in clay and many still survive, especially on roof parapets, as at the Asafi Kothi, and for garden walls at ground level. As the pottery breaks up in the course of time, one can see the iron rods often inserted to hold the balusters in place in their brick framework. A more fanciful use of pottery, and one that seems peculiar to Lucknow, was for roof finials and ornaments. These were carried out in a green glazed ware, produced by adding copper to the glaze, and when placed in position along roof parapets and towers produced a strik-

[16] Valentia, i, p. 140.

[17] Seton-Kerr, ii, p. 353.

ing effect. Of those still in existence the commonest types are the "pineapple" and the *guldusta*, a cluster of flower buds. Both types of ornament can be seen, the first at Kakori and Mahmudabad, the second at the Captain's Mosque in the Daulat Khana complex. Early pictures of the Rumi Darwaza show a whole series of guldustas around the arch which P.C. Mookherji believed were originally to have been fountains throwing jets of water up from the heart of each guldusta.[18] A further use of ornamental glazed pottery is on the dome of the maqbara of Malka Afaq Sahiba to the north of Lucknow, where glazed "flower buds" surround the base of the dome, which was itself tiled with glazed earthenware. This appears to be the only remaining example of such work in Lucknow, but a close examination of early photographs of the Dilkusha indicates that the distinctive towers above the four circular staircases were also of glazed pottery, and probably one of the most ambitious efforts in this medium.

A specialised use of pottery was made in producing small clay medallions, now found only in Constantia (La Martinière) though they were also used in Martin's other buildings in Lucknow. There has long been a debate over whether the so-called Wedgwood plaques and small medallions of Constantia are genuine or not. The Wedgwood order-books, now in Leicester in England, are inconclusive on the point; and while it cannot be said categorically that Claude Martin never ordered Wedgwood from the English factory, were every plaque in Constantia to be real Wedgwood such an enormous order would not have gone unrecorded elsewhere in the Wedgwood archives.

Martin's inventory for the Château and Constantia does provide almost positive proof that the majority of the plaques are local work. The relevant items from the inventory that he made are as follows:

4 Figures of Wedgewood Ware (an Apollo of full Length and 3 busts)
1 Drawer with Earthen Beads for Ornamenting Walls
1 Drawer with 7 imitations of Antique Medallions

[18] Mookherji, p. 239.

1 Drawer with 109 Bronze Medallions (and further drawers of similar)
22 Papers of Earthen Beads for Ornamenting Walls
150 Bronze Medallions of great men in Gilt Frames Coarse
2 Framed Wedgewood Medallions
1125 Plaister of Paris Medallions
138 Moulds for Medallions
29 Wax Medallions Europe Made
1 Box of small Medallions.[19]

From these items it can be deduced that not only were the people drawing up the inventory able to distinguish genuine Wedgwood when they saw it (even if they could not spell it correctly) but also that the medallions in Constantia today are made either of local clay or of plaster of paris. These medallions were made from moulds taken from antique patterns, from squeezes of bronze medallions, or copied freehand from a few genuine Wedgwood plaques. The quality of the work is extremely fine and detailed, and there is no reason to doubt that local workpeople were responsible not only for these small medallions, but for the other stucco work too. The fact that they had "antique medallions" from which to copy should not detract at all from their achievements.

Iron was a material so rarely used in Indian buildings of this period that its presence always excited comment. Honoria Lawrence remarked in 1843 that the "iron railings and balustrades" that she saw in Lucknow were "entirely foreign in this country,"[20] and nearly every visitor to Constantia remarked on the unusual iron doors that shut off one section of the building from the other. The Iron Bridge was the prime example of a new use for this material, and though it lay un-erected for thirty years by the side of the Gomti it would have been unnatural if the imagination of the wealthier citizens of Lucknow had not been fired by the inherent decorative possibilities of this European treasure. Apart from railings on houses there was the more practical use for the cages of wild animals. Prince Saltuikov noted during his visit in 1842 that tigers and bears were shut

[19] Bengal Inventories.
[20] Honoria Lawrence.

in iron cages both inside and outside the palace buildings,[21] and Rev. Polehampton remarked on the two tigers kept in cages at the entrance to "the rich nawab's house" along the Sitapur Road.[22]

Most of the wood remaining in nawabi buildings today came from local trees with the exception of the large teak planks used in roofs. Teak was considered effective in repelling the white ant menace, and although it was expensive it was better where possible to use it rather than to have one's staircases and roof beams eaten away unseen above one's head. Much of the teak used in northern India came from the Pegu region of Burma or "from the high parts of Bengal"[23] and that used in Lucknow was brought upriver from Calcutta. There is a mention in 1813 of "100 Teak Planks, purchased and sent to Lucknow for the use of His Excellency,"[24] and during the building of the Observatory "many large beams were procured from a great distance" for it.[25] The wooden doors of Constantia, however, which replaced Martin's iron doors in 1844 when the building was adapted for a school, came from local trees,[26] most probably the mango tope which had given the house its second name of "Lacperry" (a lakh of trees).

Wood was used in a variety of ways, not just for doors and lintels, but for "venetians" or slatted shutters for windows and doors which were normally fastened back on the outside of the building during the day; for the beams and joists between different storeys or verandah roofs; and for circular staircases as well as balconies, eaves, and porches. Many of the empty masonry arches in nawabi buildings today were originally closed by wooden shutters and glazed doors and many empty openings, especially lunettes, were latticed over with wood. The character of Bibiapur House has been quite changed by the removal of its wooden doors, and photographs

[21] Saltuikov, Prince, *Lettres sur L'Inde* (Paris 1849), p. 155.
[22] Polehampton, p. 90.
[23] Modave, p. 79.
[24] Foreign Pol. Con., 20 Aug. 1813, no. 52.
[25] Foreign Con., 28 June 1841, nos 159–61.
[26] Foreign Con.. 13 Jan. 1844, nos 8–11.

of the Husainabad Imambara gateway in 1858 show that all the arches on each side of the main gateway at first-floor level were glazed with small square panes set in wood which had been completely removed forty years later. A substantial number of joists and beams are still *in situ* in some nawabi buidings, and as the stucco and brick work falls away one can see more clearly the construction of the storeys and the roofs. Both the Asafi Kothi and Bibiapur retain a good number of their original teak beams which have been in place for nearly two hundred years.

Wood was also used for some of the "shells" of the gilded domes of Lucknow. Rather than constructing masonry domes, a curved wooden framework was erected over which panels of beaten copper were nailed, thus considerably expediting the erection of a building, but leading critics to complain that such domes were a sham, and that the effect was theatrical rather than architectural. The erection of a typical nawabi pukka building was a slow process. First, deep foundations had to be dug, not just because of the light and friable nature of the soil and the weight of the proposed building, but because the basement or semi-basement rooms embedded in the soil were valuable as retreats during the hot season. These rooms, the *tykhane*, had small downward pointing shafts near the ceiling to provide light and air, but not direct sunlight. The floors of such basement rooms were of considerable thickness, constructed of layers of brick and cement with flues inserted at regular intervals for drainage, although two rows of inverted pots were sometimes substituted, packed round with sand, then covered with a layer of tiles and cement.[27] Wooden beams were not used at all at this level because of the fear that imperfect drainage during the monsoon season would rot the wood.

All walls were made of solid masonry, sometimes of a surprising thickness. It is common to find even partition walls two feet in breadth, composed solely of lakhori bricks and cement, and some solid walls in Constantia measure five feet across. Where walls have

[27] Williamson, ii, p. 32.

been partially robbed for their bricks one can observe that they are indeed of solid masonry, with no rubble core. The only exception are the outer walls of Constantia and Barowen which incorporated pottery ducts as air-cooling devices cemented into the walls.

Beams still *in situ* show no sign of having been spliced or joined and the importance of thick masonry walls to support the ceilings is obvious. Over the beams were placed wooden joists or battens of thinner wood, and across these joists were laid flat pottery tiles, cemented in place. Normally two layers of tiles were used, each sandwiched in with cement (although Thomas Williamson recommended that only one layer of tiles should be used) then four to five inches of rubble or mortar laid on top before the final coat of mortar was laid, which would then in turn be stuccoed over and polished. Conventional wooden boarded floors were seldom used because the underside of the boards would not be visible for inspection for white ants and because of warping. Most buildings were of no more than three complete storeys, including the semi-basement, though they often incorporated a smaller fourth storey over the centre of the building, as in the Dilkusha; and Constantia has six storeys between the four "wells" sunk into the earth.

Once the masonry had been completed wooden lintels and frames were inserted where appropriate, and doors, windows and shutters were hung, "invariably painted green . . . some prefer all verdigris; others, a deep clear green for the framework, with verdigris for the several leaves or valves."[28] Windows were normally glazed for glass was cheap and readily available in Lucknow, having been sent upriver from Calcutta. Inside the building were the inevitable circular staircases, always surrounded by a masonry stairwell.

Even buildings as palatial as the Asafi Kothi continued the tradition of small and awkward staircases, which were a curiously neglected area that owed nothing to the European idea of grand entrances and exits from flights of steps. Until the 1780s most staircases were masonry, but wooden staircases then came into use,

[28] Ibid., p. 17.

"these rest on strong visible beams, all joists are painted or tarred."[29] The joists and beams were visible so they could be frequently examined for signs of white ants, and it was for this reason that ceiling cloths were stretched between the walls, giving the illusion of light at the top of the room but also providing something which could be easily removed when the ceiling was inspected. Many nawabi buildings retain iron rings near ceiling level, both inside and outside, where cloths could be attached. Punkahs were attached to the ceiling beams by iron rings, and the verandah roof at Bibiapur still retains part of the wooden punkah frame.

Inside the house, after the walls had been stuccoed and the ornamental moulding made, delicate colours like lilac and sky blue were applied, often with the moulding and beading of the mock door panels picked out in white. Many nawabi houses still retain conventional European fireplaces with wide flues, but one must conclude from the complete absence of chimneys at roof level that such fireplaces were either purely decorative or, what is more likely, that they held moveable braziers of charcoal during the winter.

That the idea of a fireplace with a chimney was not understood by nawabi builders is vividly illustrated in the diary of Captain Herbert who was living in the Khurshid Manzil in 1832. He placed a fire basket in one of the grates there and had fires lit for several weeks during the autumn. He found that the ashes from the fire which collected on the hearth were scorching the floor, and on throwing water over them they exploded, revealing

> a bed of glowing fuel. On digging up the floor and hearth it was found that an immense log or timber extended across the breadth of the chimney piece lying immediately upon the two principal beams or girders which traversed the middle of the bedroom and the room adjoining. To defend this timber . . . from the fire there was half an inch of mortar. The whole of the beam when uncovered was found as [a] mass of live coal extending even into the jambs of the chimney piece.

Thus though fireplaces were usually built into European-influenced rooms to form a focal point, the mechanics of how they

[29] Ibid., p. 30.

worked had not been appreciated.[30] Where interior doors were used they were normally panelled, and certainly in Calcutta (and therefore by implication, in the wealthy houses of Lucknow) handsome brass mountings with mortice locks were common. Those buildings, which had open archways rather than doors leading from one room to another, would close off the rooms by screens of *khus khus* in the summer and thick padded curtains in the winter.

[30] Diskalker, p. 31.

12

European Criticism

NO ONE WHO HAS read this far will have failed to notice the pejorative tone of much European writing on Lucknow. The city seemed to engage some deep vein of prejudice and sarcasm in its visitors unmatched elsewhere in India. Tedious though these nineteenth-century descriptions are, they are worth analysing for the muddled thinking they reveal and the physical effects on the buildings that arose from such prejudice.

Lucknow was not an easily accessible city for Europeans in India, because it lay off the main route between Calcutta and Delhi and travellers journeying up the Ganges had to make a diversion at Cawnpore if they wished to visit the city. For this reason the number of Europeans who visited Lucknow and who subsequently wrote about their visits is comparatively small, and travellers' accounts average out at less than one every two years during the nawabi period. Apart from official reports of the British Resident and his staff there are no satisfactory accounts by long-term residents about life in Lucknow until the Mutiny, after which the minutiae of life under siege conditions were eagerly pored over in Britain, but one cannot expect such accounts to be objective.

Even the travellers' accounts are often unsatisfactory because their visits were short and their attempts to cram as much sight-seeing as possible into a few days led to a surfeit of palaces, mosques, and imambaras from which a confused picture was drawn and later incorporated into general travel books on India. Imperfect though many of these accounts are, it is all that Britons at home had to go by (except for the few who had access to official reports) and this in turn meant that British opinion was fed on short, scrappy, and emotive reports which frequently presented a biased picture of Lucknow.

Criticism by Europeans can be divided into three main categories. There are general comments about the filthiness of the city, later channelled into a growing British awareness that cleanliness was not only aesthetically more pleasing but more hygienic too; secondly, criticisms that it was "immoral" for the nawabs and their nobles to live in obvious splendour while their subjects were condemned to a miserable existence in the same city (and it was here that the pleas for annexation came in); and lastly, the unfavourable comments on architectural grounds by purists who were affronted at buildings which challenged conventional notions.

It has already been shown how criticisms of filthy streets were a constant theme in European writing, and although the building of Hazratganj by Saadat Ali Khan provided some amelioration for travellers coming from Cawnpore there was no improvement in the condition of the streets in the rest of the city. Travellers who wished to strike out from the main tourist route could not avoid passing through dirty streets. C.R. Forrest commented in 1824 that "the town itself is as filthy a hole as I ever put foot in: the streets, narrow, the huts miserable, while a nauseous odour, arising from the piles of dirt and rubbish which frequently obstructed the passage, was in the extreme disgusting."[1] Henry Lawrence found no improvement by 1845 when the old city was described by him as "filthy, ill-drained, and ill-ventilated".[2] But between these two comments there was a considerable change in the consciousness of British attitudes, a realisation that piles of dirt and rubbish in the streets was an obstruction in the travellers' path but also a danger to health. Lawrence's remarks incorporate the two great European, and specifically British obsessions, of the mid-Victorian age – drains and ventilation. (One says

[1] Forrest, p. 164.

[2] *Calcutta Review* (Calcutta 1845), Jan.–June, p. 380.

"obsession", but this is perhaps too strong a word because mortality among the British in India was a constant preoccupation, and as late as 1856/7, 12.5 per cent of the Protestant community alone had died in Lucknow in the space of a single year, and of the 300 who died only nine were over forty years of age.[3])

Ideas on cleanliness in British towns underwent a radical change during the 1840s and 1850s as newly swollen towns like Birmingham and Bristol suffered epidemics of cholera and typhoid no less severe than those in Indian cities. It was the transposition of new ideas on hygiene to India that led to much radical town planning and building by the British there. But ironically a movement which had begun in Britain chiefly from humanitarian motives quickly provided ammunition for xenophobes abroad, for the more conscious Europeans became of the need for cleanliness the more did they begin to fear and criticise the dirty native quarters of Indian cities and, of course, their inhabitants.

In nawabi Lucknow the British were powerless to effect any change in the town except in the two areas where they lived, the Residency complex and the Mariaon Cantonment, and here the limited measures which could be adopted for the preservation of health only served to emphasize the isolation of the British, hemmed in by a kind of invisible *cordon sanitaire*. Visitors to the Residency complex before 1857 invariably noted the contrast between the neatness (and therefore cleanliness and healthiness) of this area compared with what they conceived to be the near anarchical chaos outside. W.H. Russell, the most unbiased commentator on Lucknow, compared the native quarters of Indian towns where the inhabitants "sit in their decaying temples, haunting their rotting shrines, washing in their failing tanks and drinking semi-putrid water" with the "European station which is laid out in large rectangles formed by wide roads . . . The Europeans live in detached houses, each surrounded by walls enclosing large gardens, lawns, out-offices. The natives live packed in squeezed-up tenements, kept from falling to pieces by

[3] Polehampton, p. 208.

mutual pressure."[4] Such descriptions were not of course unique to Lucknow, but whereas in Indian towns under British administration it was possible for residential British accommodation to be built well away from the existing native city, the British in Lucknow had perforce to put up with what they already had – the Residency complex surrounded by crowded Indian dwellings.

When the Residency site was first being developed in the 1780s it was on the outskirts of Lucknow and was the second highest area (the Macchi Bhavan hill was the first) in the vicinity of the city, far enough removed from the foetid atmosphere of the native city but convenient for communication with the nawabi palaces. Similarly when the Mariaon site was being debated Lieut Col. Thomas said he had selected the "only space of elevated land south of His Excellency's Hunting Lodge"[5] and in the same report complained about the soldiers in the pre-1807 Cantonment being "pent up in a small Hindustanee Building within an assembly of Native Huts and the vile effluvia of such places." It will be recalled too that the Resident William Sleeman was in the habit of occasionally spending a few days in the Cantonment residency "at the close of the hot winds and commencement of the Rains, when epidemic diseases prevail in the City from accumulated filth."[6] Sleeman's remarks show that "accumulated filth" was by this time, i.e. the 1850s, being treated seriously as a source of infection, though the exact link between flies, mosquitoes, germs, and disease had not at that time been thoroughly established. It was usually thought that unpleasant odours alone were sufficient to cause disease, the very word "malaria" means "bad air", and the Europeans in India had long believed that if the air round them was pure it minimised the chances of catching diseases. Europeans had in fact been carrying out preventive measures against disease for some time in India, though without being sure why their methods were effective. As early as the 1800s Viscount Valentia noted that "The British, who, from official or commercial concerns, are

[4] Russell, p. 106.

[5] Foreign Pol. Con., 12 Feb. 1807, nos 4 & 20.

[6] Foreign Con., 24 March 1853, no. 46.

attached to the great cities of India, have generally fixed on a spot at a little distance, where they have constructed modern residences, free from the stench and confinement of Asiatic narrow streets,"[7] and by the 1840s, when a number of books had been published specifically for the European in India, the British were being told to avoid building near damp, marshy grounds and away from "the most objectionable though common sites of town or city dwellings, the vicinities of meat or vegetable bazaars – burial grounds – dirty stagnant ponds – public drains and crowded native hamlets."[8] It was not explained why these sites were to be avoided apart from vague talk about dangerous effluvia.

There is no dispute that the old part of Lucknow did undoubtedly provide a breeding ground for disease. As British officers in charge of the Lucknow hospitals began to submit reports on Indian patients, a horrifying picture was built up of endemic diseases like syphilis (which affected half the patients seen), smallpox, and leprosy – which was common. In August 1842 a thousand Indians died in a single day during an epidemic of an unidentified disease,[9] and a cholera epidemic in the winter of 1848–9 killed thousands, including 700 Indians, in a day.[10] Without comparative statistics from other similarly sized towns one cannot say that Lucknow was unusually unhealthy. But the result was that the more the British became aware of the risks inherent in overcrowded and unsanitary conditions the more did they seek to alter these conditions where they had the jurisdiction, and the more did their fear increase of the native city, which was "filthy, ill-drained and ill-ventilated" and, as with Lucknow, outside their control.

From criticisms on filth to criticisms on moral grounds was but a short step for many Victorians, and the following passage from the *Calcutta Review* of 1845, speaking of those places where the British

[7] Valentia, i, p. 73.

[8] Grant, H. & Colebrooke, E., *Anglo-Hindoostaner Hand Book* (Calcutta 1850), i, p. 430.

[9] India Pol. Con., 6 Jan. 1844, no. 105.

[10] India Pol. & Foreign Con., 8 Feb. 1850, no. 150.

did have a measure of control, makes a direct correlation between the two. There was, it was stated, "a very striking reduction of the average mortality. Year after year has seen a progressive improvement, for year after year has seen jungles cleared away, and marshes drained and thick walled, well-raised houses erected, whilst simultaneously with these important changes, sobriety and moderation have steadily advanced, and rapid strides have been made in the progress of medical science."[11]

This report paints a rosy picture of improvements, which were by no means universal, but its most interesting item is the juxtaposition of sobriety and moderation with more practical measures. It is undeniable that together with the new consciousness about public health in India also came a new surge of Christian morality, hastened by the British Government's policy of allowing missionaries in India more freedom after 1813. "Ruffianism had gone out of fashion," wrote a commentator in 1844. "People drank less, gambled less, swore less and talked less obscenity,"[12] and for the rest of the nineteenth century cleanliness went more or less hand in hand with godliness.

But even before this upsurge of Christian morality European commentators on India had begun to adopt didactic overtones when describing the vastly differing lives of the Indian rulers and their subjects, as this passage shows: "The streets all this way were narrow and dirty, and crowded with bazaars and poor people presenting upon the whole, an air of wretchedness that much disappointed the expectations I had formed of the splendour of this celebrated capital [Lucknow]. It was evident that this splendour was confined to the palace, while misery pervaded the streets: the true image of despotism",[13] and "on passing and repassing through the streets, I observed the same wretchedness as before. There must be much that is 'rotten in the state' whose chief city, the residence of the sov-

[11] *Calcutta Review* (Calcutta 1845) Jan.–June, p. 78.

[12] *Calcutta Review* (Calcutta 1844) Jan.–June, p. 319.

[13] Twining, p. 308.

ereign presents such an appearance."[14] Another important passage in the same vein written from Lucknow in 1798 says:

> Amidst all this blaze of wealth and magnificence, thousands of poor wretches are seen on the road to all appearance in real want. There is not, perhaps, in the whole compass of human affairs a more striking display of the inequality of conditions, than this scene affords. Extravagant wealth is amassed in the hands of one man, and is confined to the narrow circle of his favourites; and this superfluous store is grinded from the faces of the indigent, who are wallowing in all the filth of penury and wretchedness . . .[15]

Later the author, after visiting Asaf-ud-daula's menagerie, said "the food employed in this manner [i.e. to feed the animals] would remove want from the city, if not from the kingdom of Oude: but the art of government is less understood, or more perverted, by the Indians, than any other science, meanly as we may regard their attainments in them all." These sentiments were to be repeated many times before 1856 and the more the extravagance (or splendour as some saw it) of the nawabs increased and was manifested in the buildings and gardens of Lucknow, so did the volume of complaints increase when commentators saw no visible improvement in the lot of the inhabitants of the city. There was a growing feeling that people in positions of authority (the nawabs, in this case) should not pursue their selfish pleasure at the expense of their subjects, and measures that could ameliorate the lot of the poor began to be discussed, including the annexation of the province.

An important article on Awadh appeared in the *Asiatic Journal* for 1834[16] which received even wider circulation when it was reprinted almost word for word in Emma Roberts' book *Scenes and Characteristics of Hindostan* three years later. The article starts:

> The fate of the kingdom of Oude seems now verging to a crisis, and, in all probability, a short period will decide whether it is to continue under

[14] Twining, p. 313.

[15] Tennant, ii, p. 409.

[16] *The Asiatic Journal*, New Series (London 1834), vol. 15, pp. 214–25.

> the mismanagement of its present rulers, or be placed entirely under the control, of the British Government. At the present period, Lucknow affords an almost perfect realization of the *beau ideal* of the court of an Asiatic despot, though the power over life and limb has been somewhat abridged by the presence of the British Resident . . . in a state in which the people have no voice, in respect of the amount of kind of taxation, or as to the disposal of the revenue raised, every sort of improvement must depend upon the ruling power. Everywhere we saw proofs of the frivolity of the amusements of the sovereign, and of the lavish expense at which they are gratified; nowhere could we perceive any public work in progress for the benefit of the community. What *might* not be done in this kingdom.

The writer also noted "a more than ordinary degree of dirt, filth, and squalid poverty, which are placed in juxtaposition with its [Lucknow's] grandest features: the lanes leading from the principal avenues are ancle-deep in mud, and many of the hovels, which afford an insufficient shelter to a swarming population, are the most wretched habitations the imagination can conceive." Privately too, officials in Lucknow shared the same opinion. In 1840 the Acting Resident James Caulfeild attended the anniversary of Nawab Muhammad Ali Shah's coronation and reflected in a letter to the Political Secretary to the Government in Calcutta on the "sumptuous regalia of the Palace, when contrasted with the systematic and unrelenting oppression that is fast devastating the country, [which] can only elicit a sigh, that the splendour of the Court should be maintained at such a sacrifice, when it might be increased two fold and the country restored to opulence and tranquillity by a moderate interference on the part of the British Government."[17] Though these extracts well illustrate both the severe condemnation by the British of the nawabs and their proposals for righting the wrongs they saw by annexation or at least "interference", one should ask how long-standing and deep-seated were the humanitarian and liberal ideas abroad at the time in Britain as well as in India – where William Ben-

[17] India Pol. Con., 22 June 1840, no. 54.

tinck was busy promoting a deeper concern for the welfare of Indians. The idea that public works should benefit the community rather than exhibit the splendour of the ruler was, after all, comparatively new. Contemporary with the criticism of the nawabs' extravagance is an apposite exchange which took place in 1807 when Gore Ouseley, one-time aide-de-camp to Saadat Ali Khan, was being questioned at Westminster on building in Lucknow:

> "State what improvements he [Saadat Ali Khan] began about Lucknow at that time."
>
> "I cannot state positively, it was about 1799 he began those improvements; from the time I commenced an intimacy with him, he commenced improvements, which became extensive in building palaces, and inclosing parks about his own palaces and mosques."
>
> "Did not his zeal in improving his situation and the splendour of his palaces excite the wonder and astonishment of the natives of Lucknow?"
>
> "I cannot answer that question, because Asoph ul Dowlah's palaces were more lavish than his."[18]

Improvements at this time, then, were taken to mean the building of palaces and the making of parks around such palaces and mosques, not the widening or cleaning of streets in the old city or the provision of open spaces to be used by the inhabitants of Lucknow, or indeed any of the reforms which were being slowly introduced in Britain during the first half of the nineteenth century. In Lucknow the efforts of the nawabs, such as they were, were meant to placate or impress British opinion in the shape of the British Resident at the Court and the East India Company in Calcutta. These were foredoomed to failure because the nawabs were frequently overtaken by changes in British ideas. What had been considered laudable by one generation was condemned by the next as "proofs of the frivolity of the amusements of the sovereign," and the zeal of the British reformers could not accommodate the slower accep-

[18] *Asiatic Annual Register* (London 1807), p. 176.

tance of foreign ideas by the nawabs, or worse still, the rejection or perversion of such ideas.

There was little doubt in British minds that the nawabs could and should learn from those Europeans who visited Lucknow, and surprise was expressed that they had not benefitted more:

> Both the present [Nasir-ud-din Haider] and former rulers of Oude have manifested a strong partiality for European fashions and European manufactures, but their love of novelty has not been productive of any national improvement; they have thought of nothing beyond some idle gratification or indulgence, and their minds have not expanded, or their views become more enlightened, by constant intercourse with the people who possess so much knowledge, both moral and political. A great number of foreigners have for many years been attached to the court of the king of Oude; a large proportion unquestionably might be styled mere adventurers, ignorant of every art excepting that which teaches them to profit by the follies and weakness of mankind, but there were others of a superior order, from whom many lessons of the highest practical utility might have been acquired.[19]

So not only were the nawabs expected to sort the wheat from the chaff of those Europeans in their capital (both the outright adventurers and the political adventurers of the East India Company), but they were also expected to keep *au fait* with the considerable changes in British attitudes during the first half of the nineteenth century. No wonder that the response of the last three nawabs was to withdraw into the more familiar world of Muslim culture, for it

[19] But oddly, Nasir-ud-din Haider was accused by one English traveller of not appearing to be ostentatious enough in his buildings. Major Archer, who had been present at Ghazi-ud-din Haider's coronation in 1819 and who returned to Lucknow briefly between December 1827 and April 1828, describes the Mobaruk Manzil, which was in the Moti Mahal complex, as a "building quite in Hindoostani style, with low rooms and small doors. The taste of natives and Europeans is at extremes: there was nothing princely in the house, no splendour or magnificence about it to warrant the appellative it possesses: the 'happy abode' was fitting for anyone of moderate rank attached to the court." Archer, i, p. 26.

must have seemed to them that any action would bring British criticism from one quarter or another.

Visitors to Lucknow, no matter how brief their stay or how crowded their itinerary (even to the extent that they confused two entirely different palace complexes), had no hesitation at all in criticising the architecture and recording their instant impressions of the city, often in scurrilous terms: "unutterable degradation",[20] "all very degenerate",[21] "a grotesque grace",[22] "ridiculous absurdities",[23] and "execrable taste"[24] are only a few of the expressions used to describe the city.

The first attack was on the "impurity" of the European-style buildings, which some critics assumed had been erected entirely without European assistance (an example of criticism without historical perspective). Fergusson, the doyen of Indian architecture, has this to say of Lucknow: "It is, in fact, amazing to observe to what an extent this dynasty [the nawabi rulers] filled its capitals with gorgeous buildings during the one short century of its existence, but all – or with the fewest possible exceptions – in the worst possible taste."[25] After describing the tombs, mosques, and imambaras of the city, which he names as "the debased Saracenic style", Fergusson goes on to note the grotesqueness of Qaisarbagh and the Begum Kothi in Hazratganj which

> like all the other specimens of Oriental Italian Architecture, offends painfully, though less than most others, from the misapplication of the details of the Classical Orders. Of course no native of India can well understand either the origin or motive of the various parts of our Orders – why the entablature should be divided in architrave, frieze, and cornice –

[20] Parks, p. 353.

[21] Gordon, G.F., *In the Himalayas and on the Indian Plains* (London 1884), p. 118

[22] Perry, Sir Thomas, *Birds Eye View of India* (London 1855), p. 163.

[23] Keene, p. 49.

[24] Von Orlich, ii, p. 103.

[25] Fergusson, J. *History of Indian and Eastern Architecture* (London 1910), p. 324. Hereafter Fergusson.

> why the shafts should be a certain number of diameters in height, and so on . . . in India, besides this ignorance of the grammar of the art, the natives cannot help feeling that the projection of the cornices is too small if meant to produce a shadow, and too deep to be of easy construction in plaster in a climate subject to monsoons. They feel that brick pillars ought to be thicker than the Italian Orders generally are, and that wooden architraves are the worst possible mode of construction in a climate where wood decays so rapidly, even if spared by the white ants. The consequence is, that between his ignorance of the principles of Classic Art on the one hand, and his knowledge of what is suited to his wants and his climate on the other, he makes a sad jumble of the Orders. But fashion supplies the Indian with those incentives to copying which we derive from association and deduction and, in the vain attempt to imitate his superiors he has abandoned his own beautiful art to produce the strange jumble of vulgarity and bad taste we find at Lucknow and elsewhere.[26]

This long and typical extract expresses perfectly what so many visitors to Lucknow felt – a sense of outrage mingled with a patronising amusement towards those unfortunates who had not received an education in classical architecture. It was the narrowness of vision and lack of understanding of the forces which shaped Lucknow's buildings that prevented most critics from enjoying or appreciating some of the most unique architecture in the subcontinent, and contributed in no small measure to the great post-Mutiny destruction of the city. P.C. Mookherji, the far-sighted and original supporter of nawabi architecture, wrote in 1883 that "to criticize Lucknow architecture by the rules of Palladian Art, shows the partial and defective knowledge of the critic. It betrays narrow mindedness,"[27] and this is exactly what one finds in so many of the city's architectural critics, past and present. Even as recently as 1955 John Terry in *The Charm of Indo-Islamic Architecture* is noting "the full horror of the impact of stucco and European Baroque" in the Qaisarbagh Palace and "the wild incompetence of the work" here, al-

[26] Fergusson, pp. 327–8.
[27] Mookherji, p. 209.

though he does admit that "the whole has at least the vigour of bad manners which is more than can be said for the dreary plaster wastes of New Delhi."[28]

Why is it that only those European-style buildings of Lucknow came in for such abuse, for the critics are silent about the mass of private housing in the city and usually flattering about nawabi structures which were free from European influence, in particular the Rumi Darwaza, the Great Imambara and the buildings in the Macchi Bhavan complex? The answer seems to be that only when architectural elements began to appear in the Lucknow buildings that Europeans could recognise were they able to criticise the buildings with any conviction. It is much easier for a European to condemn a structure because its Corinthian columns are too attenuated, its cornices too shallow or too deep, or its statues inappropriate, than for the same European to criticise a Hindu or Muslim building. European-style buildings at once struck a response in the European mind and were criticised as though they had been erected in Europe instead of India, when they should have been seen as one more manifestation of the Indian vision and skill of assimilation.

One should also ask that if nawabi architecture was such a travesty of everything that was good in Europe, as critics claimed, who was to blame? None of the nawabs ever travelled outside India, therefore *all* the information they received came, as one saw earlier, from Europeans themselves or from European books and pictures, and the nawabs had no way of knowing whether that information was correct or not.

Thirdly, never at any time did European critics ever make the comparison between the nawabs' love of exotic European styles and the Western mania for exotic Eastern styles. To the nawabs, lifelong residents in India, the fascination exerted by the Baroque, the Palladian, and the Regency modes had the same appeal that chinoiserie and Indian Gothic exerted over the West. Had critics been able to make this correlation then they might well have been

[28] Terry, John, *The Charm of Indo-Islamic Architecture* (London 1955), p. 60.

more lenient towards nawabi architecture, for the essence of a fashion like chinoiserie is that one interprets, one does not copy slavishly. Nash's Indian Gothic Brighton Pavilion bears no more resemblance to an Indian building than does Westminster Abbey. It is not meant to, it is meant to arouse in the spectator an impression of something strange and wonderful. Until one starts to see Lucknow as an Indian interpretation of the mysterious West one will never appreciate it fully, and to criticise it for not being a "faithful" representation seems as foolish as criticising Xanadu for not being like Birmingham.

As European knowledge about India increased in the early nineteenth century, so attacks began to be mounted on Lucknow by comparing it unfavourably with the great Mughal cities of Agra and Delhi, which were rightly considered to exemplify the best Muslim building in India. Consider this post-1857 description of the Qaisarbagh: "The buildings round the square are all in stucco, and in execrable taste – a jumble of architecture, Italian, Moorish, Venetian – gilt domes, battlements, arcades, female figures and fishes: such a contrast to the chaste pink stone work of Agra, Delhi and Mathura."[29] This comparison is unfair for the builders at Delhi and Agra had easy access to superior materials with which to work, namely sandstone and marble, unlike their Lucknow counterparts who had to improvise in brick and stucco the effects achieved in stone elsewhere. The art of stucco-work over lakhori brick reached the high standard that it did in Lucknow and became a valid art form in its own right rather than as a mere imitation of a stone-built city.

Further criticism along these lines prompted by increasing familiarity with Indian buildings was that Lucknow presented a false image to the visitor and was in fact something of a sham with its false domes and stucco whitewashed to imitate marble. A description of 1915 which starts by praising the city from a distance continues: "A nearer view of these buildings destroys all the illusion. The 'lamp of truth' burnt but dimly for the architects of Lucknow. You find, on

[29] Cuthnell, Edith, *My Garden in the City of Gardens* (London 1905), p. 182.

examination, that the white colour of the buildings, which presented in the sunlight the effect of the purest marble, is simply whitewash. The material of the buildings themselves is stuccoed brick, and your taste is shocked by the discovery that the gilded domes, of perfect shape and apparently massive construction are mere shells of wood, in many places rotten."[30]

The Victorian eye had become attuned to solid structures and buildings that stood squarely, not pretending to be anything other than what they were, and theatrical effects were not appreciated. The epithet "Vauxhallish" was frequently applied to Lucknow to convey an atmosphere of sham and illusion.[31]

The vituperation heaped upon the statues in the city is a good example of such misguided criticism, especially as it has been possible to trace their origin solely to Claude Martin's building of Constantia, a fact of which most visitors were unaware. The following passage is very typical of that unpleasant blend of heavy sarcasm and dislike which was a common reaction among visitors:

> A mania prevails at Lucknow for placing marble or plaster statues, as large as life, at every turn and corner, without the slightest regard to the choice of figures, which seems to be left to the discretion of the sculptor. He copies the most antiquated French models, [i.e. based on Martin's designs] the originals of which have been out of date for many a long year, and manufactures, for a very reasonable price, shepherds and shepherdesses, British soldiers, Neptunes, or it may be Farnese pugilists, or dogs, lions, and sundry other beasts. Among them all I espied busts

[30] Beg, M.A., *The Guide to Lucknow* (Lucknow 1915), p. 7.

[31] "Vauxhall" was the pleasure gardens set up on the south bank of the Thames during the eighteenth century. It was at first a very fashionable resort, frequented by notables like William Hogarth and Dr Johnson, but by the beginning of the nineteenth century it had deteriorated and was demolished. There were many pavilions and glass-houses set among trees and flower beds and theatrical shows were given. A request was made to the Government of India in 1806 from a Mr Swaine who wanted to establish "a Vauxhall at a Garden House in Intally" (northern India), showing that the term was well established enough at that date not to need further explanation. Public Con. Index, 30 Jan. 1806, no number given.

> of Jean-Jacques Rousseau, D'Alembert, and Napoleon, standing on the ground amid the fauns and the monsters of Indian mythology, all gathered together in the most perfect harmony to defend a flower-bed. What marvellously enhances the brilliant effect of these works of art, is a discovery which certainly is worthy of notice in Europe, viz. the custom of painting the hair, eyes and feet (whether bare or shod) with a thick coating of lamp-black. The Venus de Medici appears to wonderful advantage in this improved edition.[32]

After describing the city's buildings and statues in derogatory tones visitors often moved on to abuse the people considered responsible for these affronts, as in the passage which begins: "one of the fancies of the King consists in having all the houses of the city painted white, or in colours, and covered with scenes of Indian life. It is not his object to encourage works of art, but to produce something gay and glaring to strike the eye, and make the spectator laugh."[33] This particular writer seemed to have had trouble keeping a straight face during his visit to Lucknow because in a later passage he describes the Husainabad Imambara as looking "more like the show room of a glass warehouse, than the sepulchre of a king . . . the sight of these ridiculous absurdities so amused me that I could scarcely preserve my gravity."[34]

Not surprisingly when Leopold von Orlich, the writer of the two passages quoted above, met Amjad Ali Shah he found that "his [the nawab's] mode of life and the bias of his inclinations were painfully impressed upon his languid countenance . . . effeminate, weak and without character, the King loves neither the dangers and fatigues of the chase, nor the privations of a military life, he fancies he has a taste for building, and, at present, he is possessed with the mania of having all the houses in the city coloured or painted."[35] Indeed it would have been strange if von Orlich had *not* found the nawab weak and without character for surely, the European argument

[32] Hoffmeister, p. 259.

[33] Von Orlich, p. 95.

[34] Ibid., p. 103.

[35] Ibid., p. 108.

went, only a weak and debased ruler could produce such degenerate architecture as that found in Lucknow. This odd idea that the moral or immoral traits of the nawabs must be reflected in their architecture occupied a large place in European writing on the city both before and after 1857. Naturally there is a difference in post-1857 writings because now authors were able to say with perfect justification how wicked and degenerate the nawabs had been, so bad in fact that the province of Awadh had had to be annexed by the British Government for its own good.

But pre-1857 writers too were not slow to draw direct links between the buildings they saw and the awfulness, as they believed, of the Lucknow court. Sir Henry Lawrence writes, "Yet, brilliant and picturesque as Lucknow is, still there is a puerility and want of stability about it, characteristic enough of its monarchs."[36] After 1857 architectural criticism knew no bounds, and this passage typifies the British confusion between morality and building. "A profligate Court, sunk deep in vice and debauchery, had collected around it thousands whose sole business was to minister to its degrading pleasures. Many of the most striking buildings in the city belonged to men who had risen by their own infamy to be favourites with the Kings,"[37] wrote Martin Gubbins in the post-Mutiny rash of books which appeared in Britain from 1858 onwards.

But the most damaging criticism came from Dr Alois Anton Führer who was at one time Curator of the Provincial Museum in Lucknow, and as such a man who commanded considerable respect in matters of art and culture. It is not yet clear how much demolition of nawabi building took place during his period of office, but one fears that a considerable number might have vanished on his recommendations. Führer wrote:

> But nowhere can we see more markedly the influence of a depraved oriental court and its politics upon art and architecture than in Lucknow. Whilst some of the tombs, masjids, and portals, erected by Asaf

[36] *Calcutta Review* (1855), July–Dec., p. 380.
[37] Gubbins, p. 61.

> Ud Daulah and Ghazi ud din Haider, though detestable in detail, are still grand in outline, and have a strong smack of the old solemn sepulchres of a better age . . . the more modern buildings of Nasir ud din Haider and Wajid Ali Shah are the most debased examples of architecture to be found in India. These buildings whose style was avowedly and openly copied from debased European models, are unfit to be spoken of in the same chapter as the earlier buildings. All the mongrel vulgarities which were applied in Vauxhall, Rosherville and the Surrey Gardens, took refuge in the Kaiser Bagh and Chatar Manzil when expelled from thence, as, for instance, Corinthian pilasters under Muslim domes, false venetian blinds, imitation marbles, pea-green mermaids sprawling over a blue sky above a yellow entablature etc.[38]

Nearly eighty years after 1857 guidebooks were still being produced in which tourists could read this description of the Qaisarbagh: "Judged from an architectural view-point the result is a gigantic failure; it could hardly be otherwise considering the indolent and flabby nature of its parent Wajid Ali Shah,"[39] and to this day no objective analysis of the architecture of Lucknow has been made.

Why was it necessary for the British to convince themselves and their audience at home that Lucknow's buildings were so decadent? I suggest the chief reason was that to infer otherwise would imply that the nawabs had an appreciation of the finer arts, and this in turn would lead people to question whether the stories of vulgar, degenerate, and coarse rulers were entirely accurate. Could a man who had understood and appreciated the intricate rules of Palladian architecture really be a gross and insensitive ruler? Conversely could the man responsible for the Qaisarbagh, which broke all the rules of conventional architecture, be a fit person to rule the province? If this sounds a far-fetched argument, consider the description of Ghazi-ud-din Haider which appeared in the *India Gazette*

[38] Führer, Dr A., *The Archaeological Survey of India: The Monumental Antiquities and Inscriptions in the North West Provinces and Oudh* (Allahabad 1891), p. 267.

[39] Hilton, p. 70.

in 1823: "The patronage which his majesty has of late extended to music, as well as other branches of the fine arts, demonstrates the liberality of his heart and the refinement of his taste";[40] and this sentence of 1816 – "the successive sovereigns and the government of Oude are repeatedly presented to us in many respectable points of view. [This was a minority opinion.] If the adoption of European arts and improvements is a merit, then they appear to possess it."[41] The architecture of Lucknow had of necessity to be seen as decadent and debased in order to fit in with nineteenth-century British notions of the nawabs, for to imply that it was otherwise would raise too many uncomfortable questions.

One of the logical results of seeing "the adoption of European arts and improvements"as a merit means that the Indian fine arts are necessarily denigrated and considered but a poor second to European culture. There is a striking neglect of the artistic life of Lucknow enjoyed by its Indian citizens, and no mention at all by Europeans of the rich poetical heritage of the city. The only hint given that Europeans were not totally insensitive to Lucknow's culture comes during Asaf-ud-daula's time, when men like Antoine-Louis Polier and Richard Johnson, Assistant Resident, commissioned and collected works by Lucknow artists, poets, and musicians. The following passage which throws a rare insight on Asaf-ud-daula shows that at this period Europeans had not adopted that scornful attitude which so damaged cultural appreciation later in the nineteenth century:

> His Excellency's collection of Indian pictures is considerable, and preserved in large port-folios. From the common daubings of the present country painters no adequate conception can be formed of these. Most of them are antique productions, and though the figures are generally small, yet is the drawing often correct, and the colouring admirable. In many, a story is completely told, with clearness and precision instantly discernible, the characters accurately defined, and the passions naturally

[40] *The Asiatic Journal*, July–Dec. (London 1823), vol. 16, p. 504.
[41] *The Asiatic Journal*, June–Dec. (London 1816), vol. 2, p. 602.

> exhibited, and strongly marked . . . although widely different in manner from European matters, neither taste nor elegance are wanting to these compositions; and in the article of neat and delicate finishing, they are inimitable.[42]

This liberal and tolerant view was all too rare, and by the end of the eighteenth century there was no discernible interest by Europeans in Lucknow in the Indian fine arts. Patrons like Claude Martin, Antoine-Louis Polier and Richard Johnson had died or returned to Europe, and after Asaf-ud-daula's death the nawabs were judged on their appreciation of the fine arts of Europe, not India. So successful was the propaganda against Wajid Ali Shah that only recently has his character been reassessed and his considerable achievements and patronage in the field of music, dance and poetry given their proper place in the artistic heritage of Lucknow.[43]

[42] *Asiatic Annual Register* (London 1800), pp. 100–1.

[43] See for example Raza, and the film by Satyajit Ray, *The Chess Players* (1978).

Bibliography

Records and Manuscripts

The following abbreviations have been used:

Bengal For. Con.	Bengal Foreign Consultations
Bengal Pol. Con.	Bengal Political Consultations
Bengal Pub. Con.	Bengal Public Consultations
B.M.	British Museum
For. Pol. Con.	Foreign Political Consultations
I.O.L.	India Office Library and Records

Amir-ud-daulah Public Library, Lucknow

Imam Baksh Bedar, "Tarikh-i-Saadat". Persian manuscript in rhyming couplets, *c.* 1805.

British Museum

Cases of Ozias Humphry & James Paull (including the inventory of F.M. Arnott). Add 13, 532.

Copies of letters and papers sent by John Bristow, Resident at the Court of the Nawab Wazir of Oudh. Add 29, 120 and 29, 130.

Description of the Political Condition of the Native States. London 1852 I.S. 207/5.

Humphry, Ozias, Three Sketch-Books. Add 15,959, 15,962, 15,965.

Letters from Claude Martin (Warren Hastings' Papers), Sept. 1785–15 March 1786. Add 29,169.

Letters from Lucknow Residents, Sept. 1799–3 May 1805. Add 13,530.

Nawab's Household Accounts, Oude Accounts, etc. 1777–83 (Warren Hastings Papers). Add 29,093.

Parliamentary Papers Index relating to the East Indies (1801–1907), London 1909. LXIV 757.

Shore, Sir John, Correspondence relative to Oude 1796–1798. Add 13,522.

Chicago, University of

Fisher, Michael, "The Imperial Court and the Province". Unpublished Ph.D. thesis, 1978.

India Office Library

Bengal Foreign Consultations 1781–1815.
Bengal Inventories 1780–1801.
Bengal Political Consultations 1775–1857.
Bengal Public Consultations 1780–1811.
Bengal Secret and Foreign Consultations 1773–1779.
Home Miscellaneous Series, nos 195/1, 220/1, 345/1.
Humphry, Ozias, Diary 5 Feb.–19 June 1786 (photostat of manuscript from Yale University). Photo. Eur. 43.
Lawrence, Sir Henry, Private Papers 1830–57. Mss. Eur. F. 85.
Lawrence, Honoria, Private Papers 1830–57. Mss. Eur. F. 85.
Massie, W.H., Eastern Sketches. Mss. Eur. B. 74.
Orme, Robert, Private Papers 1767–1803. Mss. Eur. C. 297.
Shore, the Hon. Frederick, Private Papers 1814–1837. Mss. Eur. E. 307.
Smith, Robert, Sketch-Book No. 312/1–29.
Strachey, Richard, Letters from Lucknow 1815–17. Mss. Eur. D. 514.

Mahmudabad Library, Uttar Pradesh

Correspondence between the India Board and the Court of Directors of the East India Company. Calcutta n.d.

Royal Academy Library, London

Ozias Humphry Collection 1789. Manuscript Letters.

National Archives, New Delhi

The City [Lucknow] surveyed in 1862/3 and 1865/7. Map.
Foreign Consultations and Foreign Political Consultations, 1775–87, 1790–1803, 1806–59. Manuscript.
Home Public Index and Consultations, 1774–84, 1786–90, 1805, 1813, 1822–3, 1850–1, 1853, 1856. Manuscript.

The Oudh Papers, 1808–15, 1849–56

Paton, Capt. J., "British Government and the Kingdom of Oudh 1764–1835". Manuscript.
Press List, 1775–9.
Secret Index, 1772–82, 1788–9, 1797–1800, 1812–13. Manuscript.
Secret and Military Consultations, 1775–90. Manuscript.
Secret and Political Consultations, 1787. Manuscript.

State Library and Museum, Lucknow

Photograph Albums, 4 vols. Nos A2 36A & 36B, 37A & 378, 89 & 90, Photographs from 1858, *c.* 1920.

Primary Sources: Books and Journals

Anon., *Sketches of India, or Observations Descriptive of the Scenery etc. of Bengal.* London 1816.
Anon., *The Oude Catechism, or Answers to Questions Concerning Oude, its History and its Wrongs.* London 1857.
Archer, Major, *Tours in Upper India.* London 1833.
Ashmore, Mrs, *A Narrative of a Three Month's March in India and a Residence in the Dooab.* London 1841.
Asiatic Annual Register, London 1799–1811. 13 vols.
Asiatic Journal, London 1816–45. (Three series).
Asiatick Researches, London 1801. 4 vols.
Asiaticus, *The East Indian Chronologist.* Calcutta 1801.
Bengal Calender and Register, Calcutta 1790 and 1792.
Blane, William, *An Account of the Hunting Excursions of Asoph ul Doulah, Vizier of the Mogul Empire and Nabob of Oude.* London 1788.
Blondel, François, *Cours d'architecture enseigne dans l' Academie Royale d'Architecture.* Paris 1698 2 vols.
Buck, Nathaniel and Samuel, *Buck's Antiquities: or Venerable Remains of Above Four Hundred Castles, Monasteries, Palaces, etc. in England and Wales. With Near a Hundred views of Cities and Chief Towns.* London 1774. 3 vols.
Builders Magazine. London 1774.
Calcutta Annual Register and Directory. Calcutta 1814–57.
Calcutta Review. Calcutta 1846–1912.
Caunter, Hobart, *Oriental Annual.* London 1834–40.

Copper-Plate Magazine, or Monthly Cabinet of Picturesque Prints consisting of Sublime and Interesting Views in Great Britain and Ireland. London 1792–1802. 5 vols.

Correspondence between the India Board and the Court of Directors of the East India Company, Calcutta n.d.

Deane, Anne, *A Tour through the Upper Provinces of Hindostan (between 1804 and 1814)*. London 1823.

Dodgson, D.S., *General Views and Special Points of Interest in the City of Lucknow*. London 1860.

East Indian Kalendar or Asiatic Register for the Year 1791. Calcutta 1791.

Eden, Emily, *Up the Country*. London 1866. 2 vols.

Englishman, The. Calcutta Newspaper 1855.

European Magazine. London 1790.

Fane, H.E., *Five Years in India*. London 1842.

Forrest, Lt. Col., *A Picturesque Tour along the Ganges and Jumna*. London 1824.

Forster, George, *A Journey from Bengal to England*. London 1798.

Gentil, J.B.J. *Memoires sur l'Indoustan*. Paris 1822

Grant, Colesworthy, *Rural Life in Bengal*. London 1849.

Grant, Colesworthy, *An Anglo-Indian Domestic Sketch*. London 1849.

Grant, H., and E. Colebrooke, The *Anglo-Hindoostanee Hand-Book*. Calcutta 1850.

Grose, J.H., *A Voyage to the East Indies*. London 1772.

Gubbins, M.R., *An Account of the Mutinies in Oudh*. London 1858.

Hamilton, Walter, *The East-India Gazetteer Containing Descriptions of Hindostan*. London 1828.

d'Hancarville, *Antiquites Etrusques, Grecques et Romaines*, Paris 1785.

Heber, Bishop Reginald, *Narrative of a Journey through the Upper Provinces of India from Calcutta to Bombay 1824–1825*. London 1828. 2 vols.

Hodges, William, *Travels in India During the Years 1780, 81, 82, 83*. London 1793.

Hoffmeister, Dr W., *Travels in Ceylon and Continental India*. Edinburgh 1848.

Ireland, John, *From Wall Street to Cashmere*. New York 1859.

Johnson, Daniel, *Sketches of Field Sports as Followed by the Natives of India*. London 1822.

Johnson, George. *The Stranger in India or Three Years in Calcutta*. London 1843. 2 vols.

Khan, Seid Gholam Hossein, *Seir-i-Mutaqherin*. Calcutta. 3 vols.

Knighton, William, *Private Life of an Eastern King*. London 1855.

The Lucknow Almanack (Taqwin Baitan Sultanate). Lucknow 1849.

Lumsden, Thomas, *A Journey from Merut in India to London During the Years 1819 and 1820*. London 1822.

Mackay, Rev. J.A., *From London to Lucknow*, London 1860. 2 vols.

Mackenzie, Helen, *Six Years in India*. London 1857.

Macintosh, William, *Remarks on a Tour through Europe, Asia and Africa*. Dublin 1786. 2 vols.

Martin, Claude, Claude Martin's Will, privately printed pamphlet at La Martinière. Lucknow n.d.

Martin, Montgomery. *The Despatches, Minutes and Correspondence of the Marquess of Wellesley*. London 1836, 6 vols.

Mecham C.H., and G. Couper, *Sketches and Incidents of the Siege of Lucknow*. London 1858.

Modave, Comte de, *Voyage en Inde du Comte de Modave 1773–1776*, Texte établi et annoté par Jean Deloche, École Française d'Extrême-Orient. Paris 1971.

Moore, W.J., *Health in the Tropics or Sanitary Art Applied to Europeans in India*. London 1862.

Mundy, Captain, *Pen and Pencil Sketches, Being the Journal of a Tour in India*. London 1832. 2 vols.

A New and Complete Dictionary of Arts and Sciences (Comprehending all the Branches of Useful Knowledge, with Accurate Descriptions as well of the Various Machines, Instruments, Tools, Figures and Schemes Necessary for Illustrating Them). London 1754.

Nugent, Lady Maria, *A Journal from the Year 1811 till the Year 1815*. London 1839. 2 vols.

Orlich, Captain Leopold, *Travels in India*. Translated by H. Evans Lloyd. London 1845. 2 vols.

Parks, Fanny, *Wanderings of a Pilgrim in Search of the Picturesque*. London 1828.

Pasley, C.W., *Outline of a Course of Practical Architecture*. Chatham 1826. 3 vols.

Perry, Sir Erskine, *A Bird's Eye View of India*. London 1855.

Pester, J., *War and Sport in India 1802–1806*. London. n.d.

Polehampton, Rev. Henry, *A Memoir, Letters and Diary*. London 1858.

Price, Captain Joseph, *Some Observations on a Late Publication Entitled 'Travels in Europe, Asia and Africa' on the Real Author of That New . . . Asiatic Atalantis His Character and Abilities Are Fully Made Known to the Public*. London 1783.

Private Journals of the Marquess of Hastings, ed. by the Marchioness of Bute. London 1828. 2 vols.

Repton, Humphry, *Sketches and Hints on Landscape Gardening Collected from Designs and Observations Now in the Possession of the Different Noblemen and Gentlemen, for Whose Use They Were Originally Made. The Whole Tending to Establish Fixed Principles in the Art of Laying Out Ground*. London 1794.

Roberts, Emma, *Scenes and Characteristics of Hindostan*. London 1837. 2 vols.

Russell, W.H., *My Indian Mutiny Diary*. London 1860.

Russell, W.H., *My Diary in India in the Year 1858–9*. New edition. London n.d.

Ruutz Rees, L.E., *A Personal Narrative of the Siege of Lucknow*. London 1858.

Salt, Henry, *Twenty-four Views in St. Helena, etc*. London 1809.

Saltuikov, Prince, *Letters sur L'Inde*. Paris 1849.

Schonberg, Baron Eric von, *Travels in India and Kashmir*. London 1853.

Shah, Nawab Wajid Ali, *Reply to the Charges Against the King of Oude*. Calcutta n.d. (but post- 1856).

Sharar, Maulana, *Guzashta Laknau*. Lucknow n.d.

Shore, the Hon. F.J., *Notes on Indian Affairs*. London 1857.

Sleeman, Sir William, *A Journey Through the Kingdom of Oude*. London 1858. 2 vols.

Sprenger, Aloys, *A Catalogue of the Arabic, Persian and Hindistany Manuscripts of the Libraries of the King of Oudh*. Calcutta 1854.

Spry, Henry, *Modern India*. 1837. 2 vols.

Stocqueler, J.H., *The Handbook of India – A Guide to the Stranger and the Traveller and a Companion to the Resident*. London 1844.

Tayler, William, *Sketches Illustrating the Manners and Customs of Indians and Anglo-Indians*. 1842.

Teignmouth, Lord, *A Memoir of the Life and Correspondence of John, Lord Teignmouth*. London 1843. 2 vols.

Tennent, Rev. William, *Indian Recreations*. London 1804. 2 vols.

Thornton, E., *A Gazetteer of the Territories Under the Government of the East India Company and of the Native States on the Continent of India*. London 1857.

Tieffenthaler, Joseph, *Description Historique et Geographique de l'Inde*. Berlin 1786–8. 3 vols.

Twining, Thomas, *Travels in India a Hundred Years Ago*. London 1893.

Valentia, Viscount George, *Voyages and Travels to India, Ceylon, the Red Sea, Abbyssinia and Egypt in the years 1802–1806*. London 1809. 3 vols.

Vitruvius Britannicus or the British Architect. 1731. 4 vols.

White, Captain W., *The Prince of Oudh or the Claim of Nawaab Ekbal-ood-Dowlah Bahadur to the Throne of Oude*. London 1838.

Williamson, Captain Thomas, *The East India Vade Mecum or Complete Guide to Gentlemen, Intended for the Civil, Military or Naval Service of the Honourable East India Company*. London 1810. 2 vols.

Williamson, Captain Thomas, *The European in India – From a Collection of Drawings by C. Doyley*. London 1813.

Wilson, Col. T.F., *The Defence of Lucknow: A Diary*, London 1858.

Secondary Sources: Books and Journals

Ahmad, Safi, *Two Kings of Awadh: Muhammad Ali Shah and Amjad Ali Shah (1837–1847)*. Aligarh 1971.

Aitchison, C.U., *A Collection of Treaties, Engagement and Sanads*. Calcutta 1909. Vol. 8.

Anderson, A.T., *A Short History of Lucknow*. Allahabad 1913.

Andrews, W.E., *Major-General Claude Martin*. Lucknow 1942.

Anon., *Lucknow, the Garden of India*. Lucknow 1928.

Archer, M., "Company Architects and Their Influence", *R.I.B.A. Journal*. August 1963.

Archer, M., *Indian and British Portraiture 1770–1825*. London 1979.

Awasthi, M.D., *The Lucknow Guide*. Lucknow 1925.

Bearce, George, *British Attitudes towards India 1784–1858*. London 1961.

Bengal: Past and Present, Journal of the Calcutta Historical Society. Calcutta 1907 onwards.

Betjeman, John, *Ghastly Good Taste*. London 1933.
Bhatnagar, G.D., *Awadh Under Wajid Ali Shah*, Banares n.d.
Calendar of Persian Correspondence. Calcutta 1911 onwards.
Cambridge History of India. Cambridge 1922 onwards.
Case, M., *South Asian History 1750–1950: A Guide to Periodicals, Dissertations and Newspapers*. Princeton 1968.
Compton, H., *A Particular Account of the Military Adventurers of Hindustan from 1784 to 1803*. London 1892.
Cringle, Tom, *Jottings of an Invalid in Search of Health*. Bombay 1865.
Darogah, Haji Abbas Ali, *The Lucknow Album*. Calcutta 1874.
Dewar, Douglas, *Bygone Days in India*. London 1922.
Diskalker, D.B., "Foundation of an Observatory at Lucknow", *Journal of the United Provinces Historical Society*, 9–10. Allahabad 1936–7.
Elliot, H.M., and J. Dowson, *The History of India as Told by Its Own Historians*. London 1867–77. 8 vols.
Fayrer, Sir Joseph, *Recollections of My Life*. London 1900.
Fisher, Michael, "The Imperial Court and the Province", thesis. University of Chicago 1978.
Fitzgerald, Desmond, "Nostalgia for the Days of the Raj", *Apollo Magazine*. London 1970.
Foster, William, *The English Factories in India 1618–1869*. Oxford 1912.
Führer, Dr A., *The Archaeological Survey of India: The Monumental Antiquities and Inscriptions in the North West Provinces and Oudh. Allahabad 1891, Gazetteer of the Province of Oude*. Allahabad 1877. Vol. 2.
Gordon, C.F., *In the Himalayas and on the Indian Plains*. London 1884.
Grieg, S.C., *The Letters of Warren Hastings to His Wife*. London 1905.
Haider, Kamal ud din, *Tawarikh-i-Awadh*. Lucknow 1879. 2 vols.
Hardie M., and M. Clayton, "Thomas Daniell and William Daniell", *Walker's Quarterly*, Nos 35–6. London 1932.
Harris, John, *A Country House Index*. London 1971.
Hay, Sidney, *Historic Lucknow*. Lucknow 1939.
Hill, S.C., *Claude Martin*. Calcutta 1901.
Hilton, E.H., *Guide to Lucknow and the Residency*. Lucknow 1934.
Hoey, William, *Tafuzzil Ghafi'lin* (History of Asaf-ud-daula). Allahabad 1885.
Hoey, William, *Tarikh-i-Farahbaksh*. Allahabad 1888.
Hussey, Christopher, *English Country Houses*. London 1958. 3 vols.

Index to the Foreign and Political Department Records 1756–1780. Delhi 1957.

Innes, J.J. Macleod, *Lucknow and Oudh in the Mutiny*. London 1896.

Irwin, H.C., *The Garden of India*. London 1880.

Keene, H.G., *A Handbook for Visitors to Allahabad, Cawnpore and Lucknow*. Calcutta 1899.

Khan, Yusuf, *Ajaibat-i-Farang*. Lucknow 1873.

Kidson, Murray and Thompson, *A History of English Architecture*. London 1965.

Lowenthal D., and H.C. Prince, "English Landscape Tastes", *Geographical Review*, vol. 55, no. 2, April 1965.

Lucknow and the War of Independence, essays by various writers. Lucknow 1957.

Marshall, P.J., "Economic and Political Expansion – The Case of Oudh", *Modern Asian Studies*, vol. 9, no. 4 (1975).

Mason, Philip, *A Matter of Honour*. London 1974.

Maude F.C., and J.W. Sherer, *Memories of the Mutiny*. London 1894. 2 vols.

Minutes of the Managing Committee from August 1883–31 March 1888, The North Western Provinces and Oudh Provincial Museum, Lucknow. Allahabad 1889,

Mookherji, P.C., *Pictorial Lucknow*. Lucknow 1883.

Moore, Rev. T., *Guide to the Residency*. Lucknow 1885.

Memoirs of William Hickey, London 1919–25. 4 vols.

Mukerjee R., and B. Singh, *Social Profiles of a Metropolis Lucknow 1954–1956*. Bombay 1961.

Municipal Committee for Public Convenience, *A Brief History of Lucknow*. Lucknow 1862.

Murray, John, *A Handbook for Travellers in India and Pakistan*. London 1962.

Narain, Mahesh, "Lucknow – A Study in Historical Geography", *Agra University Journal of Research* (10), January 1961.

Newell, H.R., *Gazetteer of Lucknow and Oudh*. Lucknow 1922.

Newell, H.R., *Lucknow, the Capital of Oudh*. Bombay n.d.

Nilsson, Sten, *European Architecture in India 1750–1850*. London 1968.

Nizam, Aladin Mahmud Mulla, *Bani Dars Nizami*, Ferangi Mahal. Lucknow n.d.

Oxford History of India. Oxford 1958.

Pemble, John, *The Raj, the Indian Mutiny and the Kingdom of Oudh 1801–1859*. London 1979.

Rapoport, Amos, *House, Form and Culture*.

Raza, Sikander (ed.), *Wajid Ali Shah and Monuments of Avadh*. Lucknow 1974.

Roy, Professor Theo, "Claude Martin – A Kindly Condottiere", *Bengal Past and Present*, vol. xcv, pt 1, no. 180.

Russell, Ralph, *Three Mughal Poets – Mir, Sauda, Mir Hasan*, London 1969.

Seton-Kerr, W.S., *Selections from Calcutta Gazettes 1789–1797*. Calcutta 1865. 2 vols.

Sandes, E.W.C., *The Military Engineer in India*. Chatham 1933.

Sharar, A.H., *Lucknow – The Last Phase of an Oriental Culture*. London 1975.

Spear, Percy, *The Nabobs – A Study of the Social Life of the English in Eighteenth Century India*. London 1932.

Srivastava, A.L., *The First Two Nawabs of Oudh*. Lucknow 1933.

Srivastava, A.L., *Shuja-ud-daula*. Calcutta. 1939–45.

Terry, John, *The Charm of Indo-Islamic Architecture*. London 1955.

Varady, R.G., "The Diary of a Road: A Sequential Narrative of the Origins of the Lucknow–Kanpur Road (1825–1856)", *The Indian Economic and Social History Review*, vol. xv, no. 2.

Wainwright, M.D., and N. Matthews, *A Guide to Western Manuscripts and Documents in the British Isles Relating to South and South East Asia*. London 1965.

Williamson, Dr G.C., and Lady Victoria Manners, *Zoffani*. London 1920.

Index